Business is Business
As It Pleases God®

The SECRETS to Being About Our Father's Business

Dr. Y. Bur

AVAILABLE TITLES

ASITPLEASESGOD.COM

Business is Business
As It Pleases God®

The **SECRETS** to Being About Our Father's Business.

Copyright © 2024 by R.O.A.R. Publishing Group. All rights reserved.

Visit www.DrYBur.com or www.AsItPleasesGod.com for more information. No part of this publication may be reproduced, stored in a retrieval system, or transmitted in any way by any means, electronic, mechanical, photocopy, recording, or otherwise, without the prior permission of the author except as provided by USA copyright law. All rights reserved.

R.O.A.R. Publishing Group
581 N. Park Ave. Ste. #725
Apopka, FL 32704
ROAR-58-2316
762-758-2316
www.RoarPublishingGroup.com

Send Questions or Comments to:
CustomerService@RoarPublishingGroup.com

Published in the United States of America
ISBN: 978-1-948936-78-1
$22.88

AS IT PLEASES GOD® MOVEMENT

ASITPLEASESGOD.COM

Send All *Business is Business: AIPG* Testimonies, Donations, or Orders to:

Dr. Y. Bur
R.O.A.R. Publishing Group
581 N. Park Ave. Ste. #725
Apopka, FL 32704
ROAR-58-2316
762-758-2316

Dr.YBur@gmail.com

Visit Us At:

AsItPleasesGodMovement

AsItPleasesGod

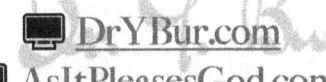 DrYBur.com

AsItPleasesGod.com

Please Donate

Please DONATE to this *Missionable Movement of God* as a GIVE-BACK to the Kingdom. Thanks for your support. Many Blessings.

AIPG Donation Link

Scan to Pay

ASITPLEASESGOD.COM

TABLE OF CONTENTS

Introduction 11
Chapter One 17
  Platforming Leverage 17
    Higher Purpose 22
    Prescriptional Purpose 26
    Are you ready to do business? 27
Chapter Two 31
  The Secret Covenant 31
    Kingdom Financials 34
    Business Consultant 39
Chapter Three 43
  Being About Your Father's Business 43
    Creative Financing 44
    Something Else 45
    Why Plan? 52
    Developing a Planning Mindset 54
      Action Planning 55
      Visionary Planning 56
      Roadmap Planning 56
      Strategic Planning 57
      Balanced Scoreboard Planning 57
      Productivity Planning 58
      Management Planning 58
      Mind Map Planning 59
      Innovation Planning 59

Business-Resolving Planning 60
Resolutionary Business Planning 60
Steadfast Planning 60
Resolute Planning 61
Persistent Planning 61
Growth Planning 62
Mental Creative Performance Building 62
Credibility Planning 62
Unfaltering Planning 63
Collaborative Planning 63
Communicable Planning 63
Reflective Documenting 64
Productivity and Performance Planning 65
The Pen-to-Paper Planning 65
The 'Get it Done' Planning 66
Retention Planning 66
Purposeful Planning 66
Product Planning 67
Relational Intelligence Planning 68
Technical Planning 68
Marketability Planning 68
Trajectorial Planning 69
Reciprocal Planning 69
Incorporatory Planning 69
Safe Haven Implementational Planning 70
Revenue Planning 70
Brandable Planning 70
Territorial Planning 71

    Comparative Planning 71
Chapter Four 73
  Credit Portfolio 73
    What is a Credit Card? 77
    Why do we need Credit Cards? 78
    What do I need to get a credit card? 78
    What is the Purpose of Having Credit? 81
    The Power of Credit In The Eye of God 86
      Spiritual Juice 89
      Kingdom Levels 92
      Kingdom Brownie Points 94
      Kingdom Mentality 97
Chapter Five 99
  Proactive Family Portfolio 99
    In The KNOW 103
    Divine Potential 106
    Overcoming The Gold-Digging Mentality 112
    The Stronghold Taboos 114
    The Voice of God 116
Chapter Six 119
  Passionate Brainstorming 119
    Mind mapping 125
Chapter Seven 135
  Kingdom Alignment 135
    The woman at the Well 141
    Scouting Miracles 142
    Spiritual Table Manners 144
    Budgeting Saints 149

Saving Money	152
Chapter Eight	**155**
Bridging the Gap	155
AIPG Give Back Bridge	163
Chapter Nine	**169**
Business is Business	169
The Mental Glitch	175
The Emotional Glitch	176
The Physical Glitch	178
The Spiritual Glitch	183
The Financial Glitch	185
Chapter Ten	**189**
Leveraging Business	189
Baited HOOK!	200
Chapter Eleven	**211**
Proactive Management	211
Chapter Twelve	**219**
The Spiritual Negev	219
Diamonds in the Rough	225
Four Corners	228
Business Credit	233
Writing A Business Plan	241

INTRODUCTION

Have you ever struggled with identifying your strengths and weaknesses? Do you find it difficult to admit your mistakes? Is it challenging for you to build good relationships with people? Does it make you uncomfortable when someone corrects you? Do you often feel like you are not receiving fair treatment? Have you ever felt like you are not good enough? Do you think that most people do not really understand you? Do you believe that there is more to your life than what meets the eye? Are you considering starting your own business and making a change in your life?

Well, look no further; *Business is Business: As It Pleases God* is designed to build the confidence you need in your pockets first, all the way to the Four Corners of your MINDSET, developing the MOVEMENT of Prophecy. From the Ancient of Days until now, this book is like no other, giving you the Divine Information needed from God's Divine Perspective, along with the processes of the HOW-TO in being about your Father's Business!

According to your Predestined Blueprint, this time-appointed information is designed to BUILD and BRIDGE your known or unknown gaps, Mentally, Physically, Emotionally, Spiritually, and Financially with Purposeful Intent and no shame attached. All of which will give you the authority of *The Secret Covenant* to say: "Why did you seek Me? Did you not know that I must be about My Father's business?" Luke 2:49. This verse is spoken by Jesus when he was twelve years old, when his parents found him in the Temple, astounding the Teachers of the LAW with his wisdom and understanding. When his mother Mary asked him why he had caused them so much worry, Jesus replied with this statement, emphasizing that he had a DIVINE MISSION to fulfill. In the Eye of God, this is what *Business is Business* is predicated on.

When dealing with our *Spiritual Negev* or *Platforming Leverage*, we must focus on what we can do, doing our due diligence, preparing, and implementing until we can flow, *As It Pleases God*. Why? Our Passionate Purpose is already hidden within our *Something Else*. If we fail to understand what it is or is not, we can miss out on what and who is designed to BLESS us, opting to settle for the cravings, traumas, or conflicts of the human psyche.

For our Spiritual Assignment from the Heavenly of Heavens, it is time to put this desire for problematic conflict to the side, embracing the initiative to build an internal and external roadmap, bridging the gap from where we are to where we are going. By not being conditioned and trained to overcome in this manner, we will find ourselves dealing with, settling for, and enduring whatever with whomever, costing us Mentally, Physically, Emotionally, Spiritually, or Financially in the end. More importantly, it ruins our creditworthiness and self-worth, even if we are conditioned to put up a smokescreen.

Without forging ahead with God at the forefront and changing the trajectory of our lives, we often find ourselves between a rock and a hard place, seeking, searching, and wanting better. But, at the same time, we DO NOT take the initiative to do better. Nor do we take the time to improve ourselves from the inside out, *As It Pleases God*.

Meanwhile, we use our money for leverage or as our go-to, as it pleases us instead of pleasing our Heavenly Father, the CREATOR of it all. Why do we behave in such a manner? Simply put, the first reason is that we DO NOT know how to become better, wiser, and stronger, *As It Pleases Him*, pretending as if we do. Secondly, we are afraid, or our ego will not allow us to ask, seek, or receive help. Thirdly, we are engulfed in playing pretend, assuming masks, and making up stuff as we go from the outside in or on the fly with little or no business savvy. Fourthly, our money looks funny, our credit may be a little unkempt, or we are keeping up with the Joneses.

With *Kingdom Financials*, when capitalizing on another person's pain to become selfishly profitable, we can set an internal trap for ourselves, especially when having the same opportunity to offer a helping hand or encouragement. *As It Pleases God*, the primal capitalizing process is to build LEVERAGE according to our Predestined Blueprint to avoid any regret, shame, or jaded quality attached to our *Credit Portfolios*.

According to the Heavenly of Heavens, there is GREATNESS within everyone, the good, bad, or indifferent. The only variance is whether or not we know it while remaining humble, obedient, and respectful, building a positive vibrational level of kindness and peace. More importantly, we do not come straight out the gate exhibiting the thoughts, beliefs, character, passion, or creativity of Greatness. It is developed, trained, tested, and tweaked, building a *Proactive Family Portfolio*, even with a not-so-great family background.

God has placed us in a specific genealogical or parental profile to train us to become better, stronger, and wiser, aiding in bringing forth our Predestined Blueprint. If we miss the vital lessons in Earthen Vessel, we will unawaringly put holes in the bottom of our cisterns, leaking without realizing the loss until we become dried out or empty. For this reason, we need the Holy Trinity to provide the necessary Spiritual Seals to preserve us until we are properly presented at the appropriate time.

As a *Diamond in the Rough* with the *Brainstorming Power* to top the charts, it means that we all have something to work with. We often do not know it, yet we are still required to chip away the debris. What is the purpose of chipping away at what we do not understand? It prevents us from walking around with a chip on our shoulders as if the world owes us something. When, in all actuality, we owe it to the world to become our highest and best self in Earthen Vessel with a PLAN in hand, giving us the right to STAND, or better yet, to POSITION ourselves properly.

Building a Business Plan, Plan of Action, or *Kingdom Alignment* with God in mind, *As It Pleases Him*, builds visionary, deliverable, quantified, contentable, and articulationable quality, exposing the LIGHT we carry from within. For this reason, *Business is Business: As It Pleases God*, which gives the illumination needed, with provisional resources to finance the vision we have DOCUMENTED.

If you desire to understand the LIGHT you carry, *Bridging the Gap* between where you are and where you are going, it is often hidden within your *Something Else*. Whether you understand it or not, your Predestined Blueprint has Divine Provisions embedded in your Gifts, Calling, Talents, and Creativity. For this reason, you must understand and set GOALS to unleash what is already there. You can attempt to do this yourself without Heavenly Instructions. Then again, you can join us on this Spiritual Journey, exposing the truth, tools, expertise, and leverage needed to get you into the Spiritual Know, *As It Pleases God*.

The Ancient of Days says the loudest voice you will hear will be the one from within; therefore, if you desire to have people, places, and things change in your favor, you must provide favorable conditions. So, it behooves you to make your efforts count! Why? The *Glitching Outcry* or the curiosity of the mind does not sleep. If you decide to sleep on yourself, you may have difficulty awakening at the right moment, missing your Spiritual Cue, contributing to your Divine Blessings and charactorial traits jumping the track, or blocking your sharing capacity.

In *Proactive Management*, a tree cannot eat its own fruit. If we do, we will become a Tree of Death bound by insecurities without realizing its stronghold, causing us to try to beat the system, outdo others, or secretly or openly pilfer from them. Only to find ourselves consumed with lies, deceit, and pompousness, eventually turning on ourselves, blaming others for doing likewise, or playing mind games to pick or choose the fruits we appear to lack or what we are insecure about. For example, if we are hateful, we choose people who are nice and flip out when they are not. Or, if we do not love ourselves, we choose controlled or conditional love by leveraging power, money, status, or sex as a form of enticement.

According to the Heavenly of Heavens, our fruits are designed to share and benefit others without hoarding, judging, or becoming spoilably toxic. In becoming a Tree of Life, the unconsumed fruits are designed to fall to the ground as a SEED, decaying to become soilable fertilizer as a sacrifice to reproduce, recycle, and reuse for the next batch. By developing this Divine Mindset, all things will change in our favor, even when it does not appear to do so with the naked eye. More importantly, once we add God into our equational efforts, our Tree of Life has natural tannin (bitter taste) protecting us from predators, users, or abusers. How does this apply to us? In real life, our natural tannin is our Spiritual Discerning faculties hidden within the conscience, instincts, and senses. In this book, we will share how it all works together for our good.

To expand your capacity, *As It Pleases God*, you are naturally designed to share your Gifts, Calling, Talents, and Creativity, producing more benefits, provisions, and resources for the overflow of your *Spiritual Negev*. Here is what you will learn in this book, but not limited to such:

- ☐ You will acquire knowledge on how to BUILD systems instead of learning how to beat the system.
- ☐ You will learn how to positively or proactively RESPOND, reversing the trajectory of those speaking doom and gloom, negativity, or blasphemy over you.
- ☐ You will master how to BREAK the kryptonic grip holding your finances captive, releasing your Divine Provisions.
- ☐ You will understand how to PINPOINT your Gifts, Calling, Talents, or Creativity and how to develop soundproof ideas without underestimating your God-Given Potentiality.
- ☐ You will learn how to BRIDGE where you are, connecting it to where you are going, maximizing your time, energy, know-how, and business ventures.
- ☐ You will gain REVELATION on how to write a Plan of Action, Business Plan, and Mind Map your Spiritual Journey, while

- listening, learning, and documenting for your entrepreneurial ventures.
- ☐ You will APPRECIATE the reasons for picking up the pace, Mentally, Physically, Emotionally, Spiritually, and Financially, instead of dragging your feet.
- ☐ You will understand the IMPORTANCE of awakening from your slumber with gratefulness and thanksgiving.
- ☐ You will BECOME more likely to stray from lollygagging to preparing, learning, and strategizing to choose the right opportunities, according to your Divine Blueprint.
- ☐ You will LEARN the value of investing and leveraging your finances through building and maintaining your credit and budgeting instead of overspending.
- ☐ You will RECEIVE INSTRUCTIONS on becoming busy, effectively creating win-wins with a positive mindset, incorporating strategic and proper planning.

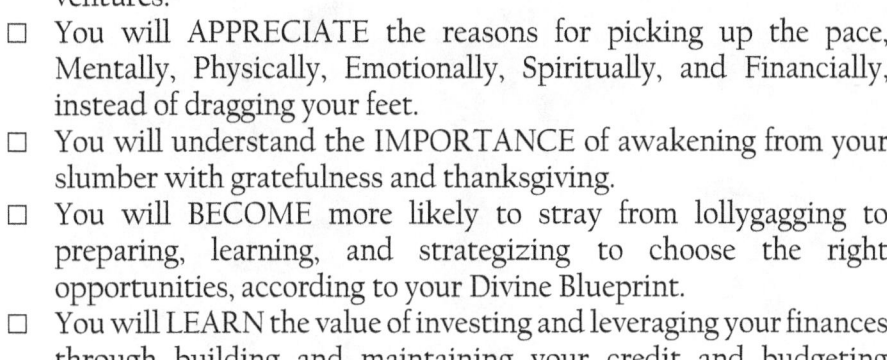

In creating a lifestyle of Supernatural Opportunities or obtaining your full potential, *As It Pleases God*, it is imperative to intentionally position yourself as close to the Spiritual Mark as possible, ensuring you do not miss the Move of God. To nest, mentor, build, or rebuild dreams and entrepreneurial opportunities from the ground up, *As It Pleases Him*, you would definitely want to be *In The Kingdom Know*, operating with Divine Principles, Wisdom, and Understanding according to your Divine Blueprint.

In this book, *Business to Business: As It Pleases God*, the Spiritual Seal that binds it is as follows: "*Seek first the kingdom of God and His righteousness, and all these things shall be added to you.*" Matthew 6:33. Now, if you are ready to call forth your THING or *Spiritual Negev*, let us use these Divine Precepts of the underground Cisterns of Greatness, putting an accurate perspective on what you already possess in Earthen Vessel.

www.DrYBur.com

Chapter One

Platforming Leverage

According to the Ancient of Days, there are many levels, bevels, and devils in life. The moment we fail to understand the level we are on, the angle at which it joins us to our *Something Else*, or the enemy lying within, we inadvertently lose our credibility in or out of the Kingdom. Once we operate as a loss in such a manner, we will find ourselves overcompensating in another area, attempting to prove ourselves worthy to cover up our secret insecurities. For this reason, it is imperative when *Platforming Leverage* to involve God, our Heavenly Father, in the equation of all things. If not, we will force our perceptions, insecurities, and biases upon others to discredit them instead of accrediting, putting our Predestined Blueprint at risk.

How can we put our Predestined Blueprint at risk, especially when we are all created differently? Based upon the seeds sown in or out of season, they will bear fruit in due time, regardless of our differences, uniqueness, or predestination. Unbeknown to most, our seeds have their own Spiritual Debit and Credit System, building us up or breaking us down to the core. What does this mean in layman's terms? What we feed our psyche determines our output, positively or negatively.

For example, if we feed ourselves raging and combative thoughts, our reactions to others will reflect likewise, causing us to lash out the moment we feel offended when we do not get what we want or it contradicts what we believe. All of which distorts our internal leverage, eventually affecting our money, possessions, and wealth in some way, especially when we have the same opportunity to use the Fruits of the Spirit, Christlike Character, and positivity as a seed.

Business is Business: As It Pleases God is crucial in the Spiritual Platform needed to obtain, endure, and maintain the GREATNESS encapsulated in our Divine Design. What makes this so crucial?

Our Divine System is predicated on CREDIT and DEBIT transactions Mentally, Physically, Emotionally, Spiritually, and Financially, linking us to the worldly system in which we currently live. Listen, if we limit our credit and debit transactions to just our finances, we will create internal and external imbalances, causing us to fall short or misunderstand areas we should work on to become better, stronger, and wiser.

In this book, *Business is Business: As It Pleases God* will help 'It' make sense. What do we need to make sense of? Whatever our 'It' is or is not. We all have different wants, needs, desires, or know-how, requiring us to put something in to take something out, similar to planting a seed for harvest. What is not said is that we must weigh the options of the seeds we desire to plant for an anticipated harvest. What is the purpose of weighing the options on seeds sown in or out of season? They tend to rock us into balance (wake-up call) or out of it (downfall) when we least expect it.

According to the Heavenly of Heavens, if we have not grafted God, our Heavenly Father, into our equational efforts, we may have difficulty understanding what we are going through, why, and what we should do or should not do. We can pretend as if it does not matter, but it does! As the Ancient of Days is upon us, we must put a Kingdom Perspective on articulating how God's Mind works from the silent yet profound VOICE within us.

When *Platforming the Leverage* of God, *As It Pleases Him*, it increases our humility, helping us to refrain from putting on a show or indulging in selfish hustles, to put in the work from the inside out. What can this do for us, especially if we have it going on? Weighing ourselves and taking an accurate stand for the Kingdom of God helps develop our instincts, character, and fruits, with profitable seeds multiplying, bringing forth much fruit. *"By this My Father is glorified, that you bear much fruit; so you will be My disciples."* John 15:8.

In Earthen Vessels, we are a Tree of Life, giving life to *Something Else*. Whatever branch of our *Something Else* is or is not depends upon us and the decisions we make or choose not to make. For this reason, we must branch or leverage ourselves with the Holy Trinity (Father, Son, and Holy Spirit).

What is the purpose of leveraging ourselves in such a manner with a Branch Mentality? The Branch Mentality, *As It Pleases God*, contains Spiritual Principles, keeping us rooted and grounded in the Will of God, causing all things to work together for our good. John 15:1-2 says, *"I am the true vine, and My Father is the vinedresser. Every branch in Me that does not bear fruit He takes away; and every branch that bears fruit He prunes, that it may bear more fruit."* When dressed in the Holy Trinity, our life will naturally balance itself out, giving us leverage to embark upon our Divine Blueprint.

Do we need God for our Divine Blueprint to work? Of course, He created all things; He knows what is best for us. Plus, it invokes a *Spirit to Spirit* Relationship or Communication with Him. Even if we fail to worship, praise, pray, forgive, repent, or acknowledge Him, He is always working in the background in our favor. Yet, for our Divine Blueprint, we must involve Him because He has the instructions given to no one outside of us. Really? Yes, really! Please allow me to align accordingly, "*You are already clean because of the word which I have spoken to you. Abide in Me, and I in you. As the branch cannot bear fruit of itself, unless it abides in the vine, neither can you, unless you abide in Me. I am the vine, you are the branches. He who abides in Me, and I in him, bears much fruit; for without Me you can do nothing.*" John 15:3-5.

Suppose we do our own thing without God anywhere in the equation? We have free will to include or exclude Him, but we risk NOT having the whole portion of our Divine Blueprint, dwindling it down to only a taste or dollop, creating pangs of hunger, thirst, longings, and smoke screens. Is this Biblical? I would have it no other way, "*If anyone does not abide in Me, he is cast out as a branch and is withered; and they gather them and throw them into the fire, and they are burned.*"

Disobedience redirects the smoke of life to blow in our faces, burning our eyes and getting the stench of smoke in our clothes and hair, causing us to look like what we are going through. Then again, it may cause others to see, pretending as if they do not. It all depends upon the seed sown and the rotten fruits produced in and out of season.

On the other hand, when we are obedient to the Will of God, the smoke of life may have the same effect, but we will NOT look like what we are going through, what we have been through, or our current underlying condition. Why? It is due to our Spiritual Covering; therefore, we should place all things under the Blood of Jesus, allowing the Holy Spirit to do what He is designed to do.

Is Spiritual Covering fair, or is it outright favoritism? When dealing with obedience versus disobedience, they are both seeds, and we must decide which one we are planting. Unbeknown to most, we determine what is right, fair, just, and favorable by our actions, thoughts, beliefs, biases, cultures, or mentalities, giving us a fair or unfair advantage. Simply put, regardless of how life appears to the naked eye, if we desire righteousness to gravitate toward us, do what is right; if we desire fairness, be fair; if we want justice, be just; if we want favor, give favor! Once again, they are all seeds, and if we want Divine Leverage, it behooves us to use them *As It Pleases God.* According to scripture, this is why I choose obedience while using the Fruits of the Spirit and Christlike Character, "*If you abide in Me, and My words abide in you, you will ask what you desire, and it shall be done for you. By this My Father is glorified, that you bear much fruit; so you will be My disciples."* John 15:7-8.

What does *Platforming Leverage* have to do with our finances or credit? With a Kingdom Mindset, our finances are leveraged provisions. All of these are predicated on our mindsets, thoughts, beliefs, habits, and actions, positively or negatively, determining our happiness and joy, or the lack thereof.

What does happiness or joy have to do with our provisions? According to our Divine Blueprint, God works better in our *Spirit to Spirit* Relationship than when we are Spiritually Blind, Deaf, and Mute, operating with a stiff neck, dullness, and in misery. Simply put, when we are not operating in happiness and joy, unhappiness and misery are awaiting their turn to shine brightly, zapping our peace and eventually showing up in our finances. Really? Yes, really! Please allow me to align to keep us from formally lying to ourselves: *"Destruction and misery are in their ways; and the way of peace they have not known. There is no fear of God before their eyes."* Romans 3:16-18. We always hear the cliché, 'Misery loves company,' and now we know why!

As we move on, if we desire joy to expound from within, we have specific Spiritual Criteria to adhere to. If not, we can turn on ourselves, extending our frustrations outwardly with barreling pretenses covering up who we are. How is this possible when we all have issues? We will confuse happiness with joy and joy with happiness. What is the difference? Happiness is an outward manifestation predicated on the tangibles of life that can be bought, traded, exchanged, cultivated, or manipulated. Joy is from within and derived from the Spiritual, Mental, and Emotional Intangibles that money cannot buy, which aid in keeping our internal sanity and peace. In knowing this, and for the record, 'Joy loves company too!'

No one or nothing can block life out! As long as the sun rises in the east and sets in the west, it will keep coming back, doing what it is designed to do. As long as this happens, the Vicissitudes and Cycles are needed to nurture and mature us for our Heaven on Earth Experiences in Earthen Vessels. For this reason, in *Business to Business*, we must awaken from our slumber, Spiritually Tilling our own grounds, *As It Pleases God*.

When TILLING from a Spiritual Perspective or being about your Father's Business, you must become strategic in obtaining a new lease on life, being *In Purpose On Purpose*, and embracing *The Win-Win of Divine Greatness* the way God intended from the BEGINNING. *"And whatever you do, do it heartily, as to the Lord and not to men, knowing that from the Lord you will receive the reward of the inheritance; for you serve the Lord Christ."* Colossians 3:23-24.

Why must we understand business from His Divine Perspective or be about His Business? Just because you understand something does not make it right in the Eye of God! Nor does not understanding something or someone make it wrong. Plus, it also does not justify exhibiting rotten fruits, or an excuse to traumatize others with corrupt character. Above all, you need the Wisdom of God to guide, provide, and anoint to ensure you do not miss the answers you have been seeking or are destined to obtain.

How can one miss what they seek, especially if they are a fervent prayer and Believer? Most often, God will not send it in a package to your liking, which forces you to use your Spiritual Discernment or add Him into your equational efforts. Without properly discerning, *As It Pleases Him*, you can unawaringly entertain Angels in disguise, even if they look like you or you are familiar with them. Really? Yes, really!

When it comes to being about our Father's Business, no one knows who God is using unless He reveals it to them through the Holy Spirit; therefore, it is always best to exhibit RESPECT at all times. One act of DISRESPECT to the wrong person at the wrong time can set in motion a Spiritual Decree offering Divine Grace or Credit. Then again, it can also reap a heap of coals on our heads, similar to the Sodom and Gomorrah Experience in Genesis 19:1-28. Which category one would fall in depends on one's Spiritual Relationship and character.

What does our character have to do with being about our Father's Business, As It Pleases Him? Although He does not expect perfection from us, He does have certain charactorial expectations whether we are doing business with Him or not. *"Therefore, as the elect of God, holy and beloved, put on tender mercies, kindness, humility, meekness, longsuffering; bearing with one another, and forgiving one another, if anyone has a complaint against another; even as Christ forgave you, so you also must do. But above all these things put on love, which is the bond of perfection. And let the peace of God rule in your hearts, to which also you were called in one body; and be thankful. Let the word of Christ dwell in you richly in all wisdom, teaching and admonishing one another in psalms and hymns and spiritual songs, singing with grace in your hearts to the Lord. And whatever you do in word or deed, do all in the name of the Lord Jesus, giving thanks to God the Father through Him."* Colossians 3:12-17.

For the record, once again, for your *Higher Purpose*, you do not need to be perfect for your Divine Blueprint to avail itself; however, you must become WILLING and RESPECTFUL. If you are ready, follow my lead as we go deeper.

HIGHER PURPOSE

We are all called to a *Higher Purpose* in life, and we are all DESTINED for a Specific Purpose. If we do not know or understand what it is, we can become aloof to the pressing issues that are before us, regardless of whether we realize it or not. But more importantly, if we miss the Spiritual Elements associated with what we have been born to do or become, we will feel a secret or open void from within.

When understanding your Talents, Gifts, or Calling, you cannot afford NOT to have this book in your Repertoire of Greatness. Why do we need *Business to Business: As It Pleases God* on our bookshelves? When being about your Father's Business, you must become INTENTIONAL about pursuing your Purpose with your Predestined Blueprint in hand. Here are a few things you will need in being about your Father's Business, *As It Pleases Him*, but not limited to such:

- ☐ You will need to learn how to maximize your integrity in your approach.
- ☐ You will need to learn how to apply Spiritual Principles regardless of how you may or may not feel.
- ☐ You will need to learn how to follow your Conscience, Inner Guide, or the Voice from Within and understand the red flags.
- ☐ You will need to learn how to understand yourself from the inside out while being true to yourself without becoming a victim.
- ☐ You will need to learn the value of having a positive mindset.
- ☐ You will need to learn the valuable people skills necessary to communicate effectively.
- ☐ You will need to learn the value engulfed in controlling your emotions, thoughts, and attitude.
- ☐ You will need to learn the lessons hidden in obedience.
- ☐ You will need to develop your Spiritual Senses.
- ☐ You will need to learn how to tame your ego.
- ☐ You will need to learn how to put your selfishness on the back burner to do what is right in the Eye of God.
- ☐ You will need to learn the Law of Reciprocity.

With or without this checklist or regardless of what you need to learn, you CANNOT afford to be out of PURPOSE. Then again, for your *Higher Purpose*, you must become a work-in-progress, *As It Pleases God*. "*Therefore, my beloved brethren, be steadfast, immovable, always abounding in the work of the Lord, knowing that your labor is not in vain in the Lord.*" - 1 Corinthians 15:58.

What is the big deal about Higher Purpose? There are many purposes under the sun, but not limited to such:

- ☐ We have a lower-created purpose.
- ☐ We have a mediocrity-created purpose.
- ☐ We have a loser-created purpose.
- ☐ We have a winning-created purpose.
- ☐ We have a self-created purpose.
- ☐ We have a people-created purpose.
- ☐ We have a love-created purpose.
- ☐ We have a hate-created purpose.
- ☐ We have a word-created purpose.
- ☐ We have a fabricated purpose.
- ☐ We have a stress-created purpose.
- ☐ We have an emotion-created purpose.
- ☐ We have a desperation-created purpose.
- ☐ We have an anger-created purpose.
- ☐ We have a trauma-created purpose.
- ☐ We have a bias-created purpose.
- ☐ We have a condition-created purpose.
- ☐ We have a self-created purpose.
- ☐ We have a God-Created Purpose.

Regardless of where you are right now, you can switch from average purpose to Divine Purpose by changing your mindset and reconciling with the Blood of Jesus. Is this Biblical? I would have it no other way: "*For it pleased the Father that in Him all the fullness should dwell, and by Him to reconcile all things to Himself, by Him, whether things on earth or things in heaven, having made peace through the blood of His cross. And you, who once were alienated and enemies in your mind by wicked works, yet now He has reconciled in the body of His flesh through death, to present you holy, and blameless, and above reproach in His sight— if indeed you continue in the faith, grounded and steadfast, and are not moved away from the hope of the gospel which you heard, which was preached to every creature under heaven, of which I, Paul, became a minister.*" Colossians 1:19-23.

What if we are clueless about Divine Purpose? Our business is indeed wrapped up in our God-given Talents, Gifts, Callings, Passions, or the things we may enjoy doing. "*Let your light so shine before men, that they may see your good works and glorify your Father in heaven.*" Matthew 5:16. Although we may enjoy doing a lot of things, there is something God has placed in our hearts by design that brings peace to our souls like nothing else on the face of this earth. And it is our responsibility to find, use, and share it without tooting our own horns!

Before we begin, let us clarify one fact: This is not Bible study; this is business development, *As It Pleases God*, assisting in being about our Father's Business. However, getting to that burning desire inside of us is indeed Spiritual. So, we need to RESPECT the intent. Now that this understanding has been established, the Divine Blueprint or Purpose must be sought after, applied, and protected.

Why must we go through all the motions for our Divine Blueprint or Purpose? First, we have the free will to remain average, dealing with mediocrity, secret insecurities, and an ungoverned psyche. Secondly, as a part of human nature, we genuinely appreciate what we work for a little more, rather than having it fall in our laps. Thirdly, we are able to use our Spiritual Tools and Skills to their maximum capacity or their highest and best use.

In *Business is Business: As It Pleases God*, we are not dealing with the fly-by-night shake-and-bake, pyramid-selling dream. We are talking about your Empire from Within and being about your Father's Business. I am not saying this to knock anyone's business or hustle. I am saying this so that you can build a business of your own with YOUR NAME on it, coming into a Divine Covenant with the CREATOR of your Predestined Blueprint. Why do we need a Divine Covenant to do so? If you want to download detailed instructions, *As It Pleases Him*, a Spiritual Covenant is required for a Higher Purpose as such.

Then again, if one desires to vibrate on a lower level, one has the free will to follow suit. Thus, when doing so, one cannot complain, whine, or have a temper tantrum. When choosing our hard...we must face the repercussions as well, especially when opting for doing business our way instead of being about our Father's business or adding Him into our equational efforts.

Regardless of the amount of abilities we possess, we are held accountable for how we invest them, use them, master them, share them, expand them, and activate the Law of Reciprocity. The bottom line is that we must become INTENTIONAL with them. If we hoard or bury our

Gifts, Talents, or Callings, we will lose them by Divine Default, or they will lie dormant. If one has not noticed, this is why we find ourselves trying to make our children live the dreams we have missed, depriving them of their own. This behavior will indeed create an endless cycle of dream-killing until someone boldly steps up to the plate with enough courage. Yes, they need enough stamina to step out in faith and live their hearts' desires despite the naysayers or the expectations of others.

Here in the world in which we live, everyone is afraid to live their dreams. We have become conditioned to the 9 to 5 dead-end jobs, hoping one day we will finally be able to live our dreams. But the bills keep coming in, and we feel as if there is no possible way we can live the desires of our hearts without having to work, pay bills, provide for our families, put food on the table, or maintain our lifestyles. So, guess what? We are in a chokehold, or we become yoked by life's distractions. As a result, our dreams get put on hold. Our Talents, Gifts, or Callings have to wait because we do not know what to do, who can help us with our longings, how to fill in the gaps, or how to strategize our way out.

In the *Higher Purpose*, we must understand whether or not it is a God-given talent, hobby, habit, or just a phase. Why must we know the difference? About 70% of start-up businesses fail because they go into business simply because of a good sales pitch, money, or to show off. In my opinion, those are indeed the wrong reasons to go into business, *As It Pleases God*.

Nonetheless, I am not here trying to sell a business or convince you about yours. According to my Predestined Blueprinted Purpose, I am only here being about my Father's Business. Meanwhile, bringing forth an understanding of how *Business is Business* works in the real world, compared to how to do Kingdom Business, *As It Pleases Him*.

Although our cultures have trained us to lie to ourselves, saying we can become anything we set our minds to become. However, I do not totally agree with this propaganda. What is the reason for disagreeing? Everything is not for everyone because we all have unique Blueprints and reasons for being. From what we are discussing right now, there are certain things in life that we need to stay in our lane, especially when Spiritual Gifts are involved!

Here is the deal: Outside of Divine Purpose, we are adaptable based on our survival instincts and genetic makeup. We can learn or be trained on almost anything, but we may not fit in properly. In so many words, we will stick out like a sore thumb. For example, this is like a Harley-Davidson

Rider on a moped. It would not take a rocket scientist to notice something is out of character for that rider. I have much respect for a Harley Davidson Rider, and I have nothing against a Moped Rider, but they present a different passion for each rider. Well, this is the same concept! I believe in helping build the dreams of others, but I also want others to be honest with themselves as well. The first rule to being about our Father's Business is, 'Be true to thyself!' Why? In authenticity lies the ANTIDOTE or the Prescriptional Purpose for whatever we need, whenever we need it, however, wherever, and with whomever. On this note, here is a Secret to being in PURPOSE on Purpose with Spiritual Intentionality.

PRESCRIPTIONAL PURPOSE

When moving forward in the Spirit of Excellence and being about our Father's Business, life will be lifing because that is what it is designed to do. Whether they are Vicissitudes, Cycles, or Seasons, they will do two things:

- ☐ Our lives will become a little easier.
- ☐ Our lives will become more complex.

For the *Prescriptional Purpose*, these items will make us BITTER or BETTER. What is the purpose of knowing this information when doing business, especially when we have it going on? Rich, poor, or somewhere in between, money does not fall at our feet. I have not yet found a tree on which it grows; therefore, we have to work for it. Of course, life is not about money, but without it, life becomes challenging and miniscule.

Regardless of where we are in life or the obstacles we are facing, the moment we become hungry or thirsty enough, our inner drives will make us, help us overcome, teach us, or break us. Despite our outcomes, there will also be an OPPORTUNITY hidden within our obstacles or setbacks, invoking some form of growth with an attachable lesson. Suppose we decline, repress, or lack the understanding of it. In this case, it brings a known or unknown VOID, resulting in some form of sickness or disease, Mentally, Physically, Emotionally, Spiritually, or Financially.

When we have a sickness, we go to the doctor for a prescription. Whenever we have a problem with our cars, we go to a mechanic. Whenever we are born poor, to whom do we go? Do we go to the bank? How can we possibly go to the bank when we are not well invested, especially if we do not have assets? Listen, being poor, broke, or financially unstable is a liability to the bank. In this case, we are stuck, right? Wrong! In my opinion, the best-known prescription for poverty, being broke, or financially unstable, is to change the way you THINK and GIVE your way out of it.

If you have been poor all of your life, how is it possible to give what you do not have? The first step is to change your MINDSET. *"And do not be conformed to this world, but be transformed by the renewing of your mind, that you may prove what is that good and acceptable and perfect will of God."* Romans 12:2.

It is possible to give your way out of poverty, especially when you become CREATIVE. Here is the Spiritual Seal: *"Give, and it will be given to you: good measure, pressed down, shaken together, and running over will be put into your bosom. For with the same measure that you use, it will be measured back to you."* Luke 6:38. With a Positive Mental Attitude, coupled with Creativity, you will be amazed at what you can do if you remove the limitations from your mind.

I have often heard this colloquialism, 'Caring is sharing.' And it is true! If one would ever dare to break the poverty mentality, one must open one's hand first. If we cannot open our hands to give, we then restrict our minds as well. It is indeed possible to have money in the bank, while our mentality causes us to squander or hoard any and everything we have.

Listen, everyone has something to give. It may not be money, but you do have love, you have time, you have hope, and most of all, God will always give you a TALENT. One thing I will always promise you is that when you are down to nothing, God will always leave SOMETHING behind. Although you may have to look for it, it will always be there, especially when being about your Father's Business, *As It Pleases Him.*

ᐯARE YOU READY TO DO BUSINESS?
Have you trained yourself to become business savvy? Have you updated your people skills? Have you put in the work to develop a business mindset?

Starting a business can be a thrilling and rewarding experience, but it also comes with challenges, especially if you do not know your Divine Purpose, *As It Pleases God.* Why would we face challenges? You may become bored quickly or jump from one thing to the next. Therefore, you must be honest and evaluate your business readiness before taking the plunge. With or without a business consultant, here are some indicators that you may be ready to start a business, but not limited to such:

- ☐ You have a clear business idea. A successful business starts with a clear idea of your goal. If you have a unique business idea you are passionate about, it could be a sign that you are ready to start a business.

- ☐ You have a solid business plan. A business plan is a roadmap for your business. It outlines your goals, strategies, and financial projections. If you have a solid business plan in place, it shows that you have thought through the key aspects of your business.

- ☐ You have the financial resources. Starting a business requires capital, and it is imperative to have the financial resources tocover your startup costs and sustain your business until it becomes profitable.

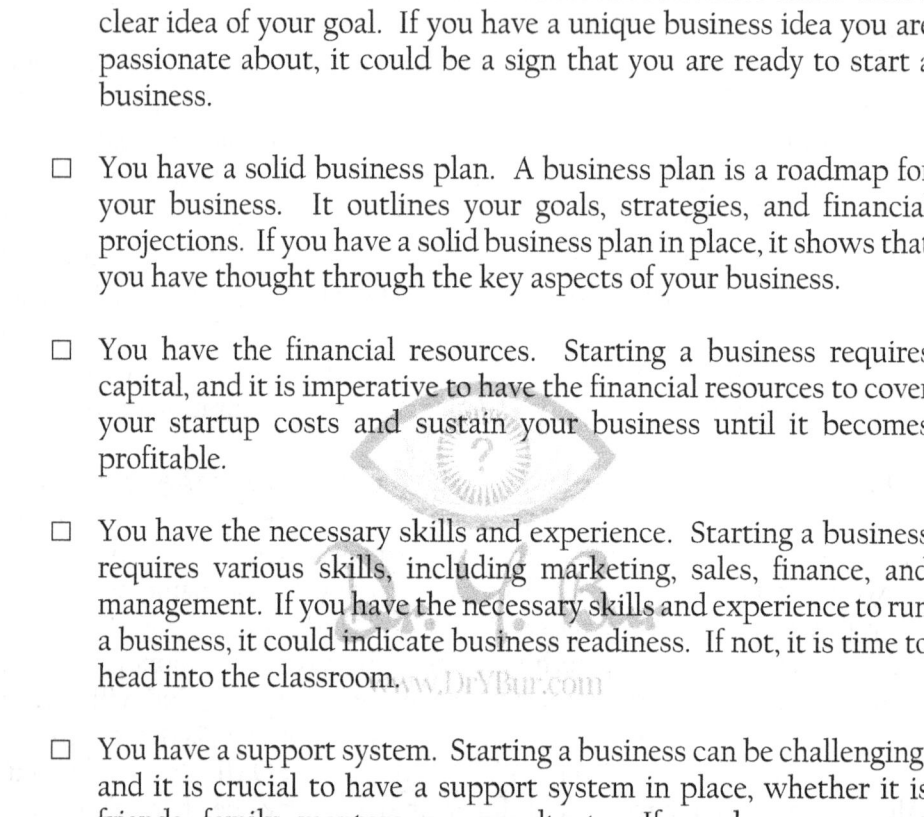

- ☐ You have the necessary skills and experience. Starting a business requires various skills, including marketing, sales, finance, and management. If you have the necessary skills and experience to run a business, it could indicate business readiness. If not, it is time to head into the classroom.

- ☐ You have a support system. Starting a business can be challenging, and it is crucial to have a support system in place, whether it is friends, family, mentors, or consultants. If you have a support system that believes in your business idea and is willing to help you along the way, it could be a sign that you are ready to start a business.

These are just a few indicators that you may be ready to start a business. Ultimately, starting a business requires careful consideration and planning before leaping. If you are unsure whether you are ready, consider consulting with a business coach or mentor for guidance, but make sure you read this entire book. It has vital information that most would not have from a Spiritual Perspective.

Why do we need a Spiritual Perspective when doing business? We are Spiritual Beings having a human experience. If we approach from a worldly perspective, we may miss the mark by not involving the Holy Trinity in our equational efforts. Why? Your uniqueness is your BRAND.

If we are new entrepreneurs or sustainable business owners, we all need a consulting mentor. Talking to others when building a new or existing business can be incredibly valuable. By sharing your ideas and asking for feedback, you can gain insights and perspectives you may not have considered. Additionally, speaking with potential customers or clients can help you better understand their needs and preferences, which can be critical when developing products or services and fulfilling a need or solving problems.

Networking with other entrepreneurs, investors, and industry professionals can also be beneficial as they offer advice, mentorship, and potentially even funding opportunities. Collaborating with others can also help you access new resources and skills you may not have, such as marketing expertise or technical know-how.

When building a new business, talking to others can help refine ideas, gain valuable feedback, access new resources and opportunities, and develop your people skills. More importantly, it is essential to approach these conversations with an open mind and to seek out diverse perspectives to help you make informed decisions.

The *Business is Business* CHARACTERISTICS of a conversation:
- ☐ Active Listening.
- ☐ Empathy.
- ☐ Open-Mindedness.
- ☐ Respectfulness.
- ☐ Thoughtfulness.
- ☐ Patience.
- ☐ Non-judgmental.
- ☐ Encouraging and Understanding.

The *Business is Business* strategies for ENGAGING conversations:
- ☐ Ask Open-Ended Questions.
- ☐ Avoid Making Assumptions.
- ☐ Show Genuine Interest.
- ☐ Practice Active Listening.
- ☐ Take a Pause.
- ☐ Avoid Interrupting.

The *Business is Business* CHALLENGES:

- ☐ Emotional Triggers.
- ☐ Cognitive Biases.
- ☐ Power Dynamics.
- ☐ Cultural Differences.

Working with a business consultant can be a powerful tool for success in the business world. Here are some steps to becoming more influential in business with the help of a business consultant:

- ☐ Define your goals. Before you start working with a business consultant, clearly understanding what you want to achieve is essential. Whether it is increasing revenue, expanding your market share, or improving your company's culture, be specific about your goals so your consultant can help you develop a customized plan.

- ☐ Choose the right consultant. Look for a consultant with experience in your industry who understands your company's unique challenges and has a proven track record of success. Finding someone you feel comfortable working with and trust to provide honest feedback is also essential.

- ☐ Collaborate on a plan. Once you have chosen a consultant, work together to develop an action plan. This should include specific steps for achieving your goals, timelines for implementation, and metrics for measuring success.

- ☐ Take action. Working with a consultant is only effective if you act on their recommendations. Be willing to make changes and try new approaches, even if they initially feel uncomfortable.

- ☐ Evaluate progress. Regularly evaluate your progress and adjust your approach as needed. Your consultant can help you identify areas for improvement and provide guidance on how to stay on track.

By following these steps, you can become more powerful in business with the help of a consultant and connect to *The Secret Covenant*. Remember, the key is to be open to new ideas and willing to take action on the recommendations provided.

Chapter Two

The Secret Covenant

We think that God wants us to suffer, but this is so far from the truth. God is not broke! He is not begging us for anything! The last time I checked, He is indeed the SOURCE of everything; He is the BEGINNING and the END; therefore, we are somewhere in between.

For some odd reason, we think we are doing God a favor when the wealth of the Universe belongs to Him. *"The earth is the Lord's, and all its fullness, The world and those who dwell therein. For He has founded it upon the seas, And established it upon the waters."* Psalm 24:1-2. The Wealth hidden in the soil of the earth is His. *"For thus says the Lord, Who created the heavens, Who is God, Who formed the earth and made it, Who has established it, Who did not create it in vain, Who formed it to be inhabited: "I am the Lord, and there is no other".* Isaiah 45:18. And the Wealth within our souls is His as well. We are merely caretakers of what He has endowed us with; therefore, we must become good stewards.

In His word, He says He wants us to be fruitful and multiply; that is why he created Adam and Eve. *"And as for you, be fruitful and multiply; Bring forth abundantly in the earth And multiply in it."* Genesis 9:7. He has not changed His mind; He just wants us to be about His Business first.

Whatever we set our hands to do, it should be multiplying. What if it is not multiplying? In all simplicity, we are operating to please ourselves or others (selfishness) and NOT being about His Business, *As It Pleases Him* (selflessness). How do I know? Here is the Spiritual Seal: *"For I will look on you favorably and make you fruitful, multiply you and confirm My covenant with you."* Leviticus 26:9.

As the Secret Covenant avails, if we are inside of a Spiritual Covenant, *As It Pleases God*, we will multiply by default. On the other hand, if we are NOT multiplying, it means that we are out of covenant, things will dry up, or we will turn on ourselves without realizing it, even if we have cash flow.

God wants us to be wealthy from the inside out, not the outside in. He has our best interests at heart, and that is why He created us a little lower than Angels, and poverty is not what He had in mind. *"The blessing of the Lord makes one rich, and He adds no sorrow with it."* Proverbs 10:22.

God blesses us to be a blessing, and He also blesses us to serve a greater purpose that may or may not be known to us. *"As for every man to whom God has given riches and wealth, and given him power to eat of it, to receive his heritage and rejoice in his labor—this is the gift of God."* Ecclesiastes 5:19.

Although we may have to put in a little work for our wealth, we must not forget where we came from; we must give back to help those who are in need. It is also imperative that we follow the passion we have from within the depths of our souls. Please keep in mind that the soulish longing we have is often feared if we are not trained to use it...which could be a Gift, Calling, Passion, Talent, Skill, etc. Thus, if you do not know what it is, then it is time to get in the know!

The scripture I want you to understand about *The Secret Covenant* is: *"Thou shalt remember the Lord thy God: for it is He that giveth thee power to get wealth that He may establish His covenant which He sware unto thy fathers, as it is this day."* Deuteronomy 8:18. From this point on, it is indeed your lifeline! Always remember, without God, there would be nothing. He gave the inheritance to our Forefathers. Now it is time for you to reclaim your BIRTHRIGHT. Yes, that means you are a Heir; now it is up to you to claim it.

If you have had financial hardship for some odd reason, you must gird up your loins and speak life into your situation. Regardless of where you are on your business journey, I encourage you to pray to God, your Heavenly Father, repent, forgive, and fast on occasion. However, I also want you to speak life into yourself, as well as your situation, with scriptures and positive affirmations.

After you take your situation to God in prayer as you ought, then He gives you the POWER. He does not give your situation, your money, or your wealth the power; He gives the power to YOU! Always remember this! Also, make sure you never abuse it because abusing the God-given power of wealth will cause your wealth to backfire. Of course, you do not want to lose money, right?

Okay, getting back on track, reciting scripture grants you the power and unlocks the doors of wealth; however, we must follow the path of righteousness to keep the doors open. No, I did not say you have to be perfect; I am saying you must allow yourself to become used as a vessel or a work-in-progress to accomplish great works for a greater purpose. Whatever it may be, it is between you and your Heavenly Father. I am not saying you cannot become a millionaire outside of God, because you can genuinely be rich outside of having a relationship with Him. Yet being a happily rich, blessed millionaire is a different story.

Although some people are born into wealth or are the beneficiaries of old money, most self-made Millionaires have multiple streams of income. For this reason, you must never limit your stream to just one way of making money. If you do, you will become limited. It would be best if you mastered your first stream and then move to the next. As a word of caution, Millionaires are not wishy-washy; they do not jump from one business to the next. They master each stream of income before moving on. They do not invest in a business that is not making them money or a business that does not make sense, unless it is a hobby.

To master your first stream, let us look at it as a GIFT. What do you have to offer to the world that God is confident in using you as a Vessel to feed His sheep? I am asking this question to get your wheels turning. Although I am not asking you to reinvent the wheel, I am only asking you to do some soul-searching. I firmly believe everything you need is already within; I simply need to ask the right questions to draw it out. God uses people like us to accomplish his great works, and He does reward us greatly. Besides, there is no reason why you should not reap the rewards of your efforts of being about your Father's Business.

In or out of doing business, there are a lot of rich, middle-class, and poor people who are addicted to drugs, suicidal, psychotic, abusive, unhappy, unruly, selfish, and lonely. They may or may not have problems with money, but their internal problems are bigger than what we could ever imagine. In my opinion, if you want to become wealthy, *As It Pleases God*, it is better to get it the right way, the God-given way, the blessed way, and under the Law of Reciprocity. Why? *"Wealth gained by dishonesty will be diminished, but he who gathers by labor will increase."* Proverbs 13:11.

I have found the quickest way to reclaim one's Birthright is to enforce the Symbolic or Secret Covenant between you and God, using it for Kingdom Purposes. How do we make this make sense? In so many words, take whatever Gift, Talent, Purpose, or Calling you have and find a way to help others, opening up a stream of income. Once you open up one stream with one talent, your one talent must become two according to the Law of Reciprocity. If your one talent remains one talent or your stream becomes blocked, then you must question if you are on the right track.

Before we move on to *Kingdom Financials*, let me clear the air. Having wealth is not a sin; however, the LOVE of it is. It means if we worship money or do sinful things to hurt an innocent person, it is indeed sinful! Remember, the Law of Reciprocity is in full effect! Therefore, we must understand the difference between the Rules of the Covenant and the Laws of the Covenant!

KINGDOM FINANCIALS

When it comes to *Kingdom Financials*, we often tend to forget the true meaning of currency. According to the Heavenly of Heavens, currency is a multiplier, not a buyer, divider, or manipulator. How is this possible, mainly when we use currency to buy? Of course, we buy with currency; however, the MOTIVE is the key here, especially when using Divine Leverage, *As It Pleases God*. Blasphemy, right? Wrong. *"But the LORD said to Samuel, 'Do not look at his appearance or at his physical stature, because I have refused him. For the LORD does not see as man sees; for man looks at the outward appearance, but the LORD looks at the heart.'"* 1 Samuel 16:7.

Why do we need to know the motives of currency? As Believers, we have become so confused about how the Kingdom and worldly system operate. Listen, for the record, there is Kingdom Wealth, Success, and Stature. And then, we have worldly wealth, success, and stature. The only difference is which God we serve, our fruits or character, how many lies we tell ourselves, and how we have become biasedly deceived. Now, regardless of this fact, *"Peter opened his mouth and said: 'In truth I perceive that God shows no partiality. But in every nation whoever fears Him and works righteousness is accepted by Him.'"* Acts 10:34.

In the world in which we live today, the worldly system has taken the lead in capitalizing on Kingdom Principles. When Believers sit around debating scriptures that they often do not understand or apply, *As It Pleases God*. How is this possible, especially when worldly people are considered evil? Unfortunately, this is where we embark upon Spiritual Error due to different belief systems and biases.

We should already know God will use anything or anyone to accomplish His Divine Purpose, including the bad, evil, or indifferent. Yet, amid all, we are quick to point the finger, calling good evil and evil good when it is a matter of perception. According to scripture, it says, *"Woe to those who call evil good, and good evil; Who put darkness for light, and light for darkness; Who put bitter for sweet, and sweet for bitter! Woe to those who are wise in their own eyes, and prudent in their own sight!"* Isaiah 5:20-21.

For example, with all due respect, it is mostly the proclaimed Believers who know me personally who ganged up on me to discredit my writings, calling me all types of names, dragging me through the mud to get a negative reaction, or using me by taking my kindness for a weakness without lifting a finger to help me. Why would this happen from Believer to Believer? Our fruits and character traits reveal the type of currency being used in or out of the Kingdom. If the Holy Spirit does not reveal to someone the level of respect needed, neither will I. Why not? I know Spiritual Principles, so I grab the Spiritual Lesson needed to feed God's sheep while keeping it moving in the Spirit of Excellence.

What is the Spiritual Lesson? First, God loves us all. Secondly, we all have a little shady evil hidden underneath our triggers and traumas. And, thirdly, this is why we need repentance, mercy, grace, and forgiveness for our Spiritual Seals to work properly. More importantly, we will never know what or who He will use to establish us Mentally, Physically, Emotionally, Spiritually, and Financially, according to our Predestined Blueprint. Really? Yes, really! Here is the Spiritual Seal: *"But God has chosen the foolish things of the world to put to shame the wise, and God has chosen the weak things of the world to put to shame the things which are mighty."* Corinthians 1:27.

Now, here is the deal: If the ungodly use the Spiritual Principles we know nothing about or what we should be using, *As It Pleases God*, then who is at fault here? When we say there is no success outside of God Almighty, we need to look around to see who is picking up the ball, running with it, capitalizing, and doing real business. Then, take a second look around to see:

- ☐ Who is dropping the ball?
- ☐ Who is fighting against each other over Religion?
- ☐ Who is engaging in combat about who is more Holy or Chosen?
- ☐ Who is contending with those who hear the Voice of God?
- ☐ Who is debating about who can lose their Salvation and who cannot?
- ☐ Who is attempting to assassinate those who are in Purpose on purpose?
- ☐ Who is casting people into the Pit?
- ☐ Who is violating the free will of others without governing their own lack of self-control?
- ☐ Who is falling short with Spiritual Fruits, Christlike Character, and mean as a junkyard dog?
- ☐ Who is proclaiming to know and understand the Word of God, missing the Spiritual Principles altogether?
- ☐ Who is oblivious to Kingdom Business or being about their Father's Business?

In *Business is Business: As It Pleases God*, I am not here to point fingers, but we have to do better than this!

Small successes are just as important as big successes in dealing with *Kingdom Financials*. Why? It teaches us gratefulness, helping us to create a win-win while developing our Spiritual Fruits, Christlike Character, and People Skills amid our flaws, mishaps, and handicaps. Please allow me to align a CHARACTORIAL PRINCIPLE we often overlook: *"Give to him who asks you, and from him who wants to borrow from you do not turn away. You have heard that it was said, 'You shall love your neighbor and hate your enemy.' But I say to you, love your enemies, bless those who curse you, do good to those who hate you, and pray for those who spitefully use you and persecute you, that you may be sons of your Father in heaven; for He makes His sun rise on the evil and on the good, and sends rain on the just and on the unjust."* Matthew 6:42-45. What is the purpose of knowing this? We have been built upon a PROMISE; even if we are in denial, we do not understand it, or we can care less about it.

When doing business in multiplicity form, *As It Pleases God*, we must approach life with obedience, humility, and faith with 'The-Lord-Will-Provide' Mentality. What is the purpose of doing so? First and foremost, multiplicity also means wealth. Secondly, from the Ancient of Days until now, we all have wealth potentiality within us. And thirdly, once used appropriately, it changes the trajectory of our faith and hope by default.

Is any of this Biblical? Of course, especially when we are in a Spiritual Covenant with our Heavenly Father or in Purpose on purpose. Here is the scripture, *"Abraham called the name of the place, The-LORD-Will-Provide; as it is said to this day, 'In the Mount of the LORD it shall be provided.' Then the Angel of the LORD called to Abraham a second time out of heaven, and said: 'By Myself I have sworn, says the LORD, because you have done this thing, and have not withheld your son, your only son—blessing I will bless you, and multiplying I will multiply your descendants as the stars of the heaven and as the sand which is on the seashore; and your descendants shall possess the gate of their enemies. In your seed all the nations of the earth shall be blessed, because you have obeyed My voice.'"* Genesis 22:14-18.

Under the multiplicity of a Spiritual Forum of today's currency, it is intertwined through the use of credit and debit cards, as tangible cash is being phased out. If we are not leveraging the time in which we live, we will become left behind with a trail of dust, smoking us out by paying higher prices, deep debt, and with limited benefits. Above all, we cannot omit God, our Heavenly Father, from the equational efforts of managing our finances. What does He have to do with our finances? He is in everything!

The moment we forget 'God is in everything,' misuse and abuse Mentally, Physically, Emotionally, Spiritually, and Financially are on the horizon. Is this Biblical? I would have it no other way. "*And you shall remember the LORD your God, for it is He who gives you power to get wealth, that He may establish His covenant which He swore to your fathers, as it is this day. Then it shall be, if you by any means forget the LORD your God, and follow other gods, and serve them and worship them, I testify against you this day that you shall surely perish. As the nations which the LORD destroys before you, so you shall perish, because you would not be obedient to the voice of the LORD your God.*" Deuteronomy 8:18-20.

As Divine Grace and Mercy abound from the Heavenly of Heavens, God has granted us a line of Divine Credit and Provisions we fail to use in Earthen Vessels. How is it possible to have Divine Credit or Provisions? According to our Divine Blueprint, God gives us intangible seeds, ideas, thoughts, concepts, or whatever is needed to facilitate our Gifts, Callings, Talents, Creativity, and Purpose. Yet, in our Heaven on Earth Experiences, we have grandmas, grandpas, dads, moms, singles, entrepreneurs, students, and even children with credit cards, forgetting about who they are from the inside out. Only to define themselves by their credit score or by buying what they cannot afford to showboat. All of these are based upon a system designed to work for or against us, depending upon our MINDSETS and the seed sown in or out of season. For this reason, in this book, *Business is Business: As It Pleases God*, I will share information on how to have the best of both worlds.

For the record, we do not want to provoke God when dealing with our finances, even if we think it does not apply to our Spiritual Relationship with Him. Although our *Spirit to Spirit* Relationship with our Heavenly Father is not about money, He will use it as a Spiritual Training Tool or Rod of Correction to develop accountability in becoming a good steward of what we have. What does this mean in layman's terms? Here is what we need to know: "*As each one has received a gift, minister it to one another, as good stewards of the manifold grace of God.*" 1 Peter 4:10. If we desire to unfold the layers of Divine Grace, *As It Pleases Him*, we must use our GIFTS or BLESSINGS to help others without being selfish. Still, we need to know what they are and how to use them first, *As It Pleases Him*, not ourselves, right? Absolutely. So, let us get an understanding by taking this chapter up a notch.

With all due respect, if we are reckless with money, we will become reckless in our *Spirit to Spirit* Relations, similar to the behavior of King Saul. Really? Yes, really! Recklessness and irresponsibility cause a form of Spiritual Blindness, Deafness, Muteness, Dullness, or a Stiff Neck (Disobedience), as we appear right in our own eyes, placing limits on ourselves. For example, this is when we know there is more to what we need to do, but cannot figure it out or understand who we are from the inside out. While simultaneously coming across to the human psyche as a thirst, longing, void, or emptiness, only to find ourselves spending money, buying what we do not need as a temporary fix, or determining our worth by a label.

If you are in this place right now, all is not lost, and no one is exempt from this process. The only reason I can effectively write about this, *As It Pleases God*, is through many experiences, fiery trials, and shedding many tears.

According to the Ancient of Days, God will test us with our finances, outright poverty, or have us shoveling and smelling sheep dung like King David and Moses. Why does God go to such extremes? Firstly, this is designed in the Eye of God to see if we will bow down to any false gods. Secondly, to determine if we will sell our souls. Thirdly, to train, test, and mold us before Divinely Commissioning us to move forward in the Gifts, Calling, Talents, Purpose, Creativity, or Predestined Blueprint set forth. Fourthly, *"Moreover it is required in stewards that one be found faithful."* 1 Corinthians 4:2. For this reason, God will use the most faithful individuals above the seemingly perfect.

Faithfulness in the Eye of God determines the real MOVERS and SHAKERS for the Kingdom, who possess good fruits and character from the wolves in sheep's clothing. Yes, you know who! The fake ones who leave victims all over the place with a trail of rotten fruits and corrupt character, without attempting to do or become better, stronger, and wiser, *As It Pleases God*, but only to please themselves. Nor do they apologize or repent for their actions, reactions, thoughts, beliefs, or biases. So, when someone says they are moving for the Kingdom without being tested, trained, and commissioned, I already know what time it is without saying one word! What time is it? It is deception, distraction, fault-finding, or character assassination time!

Okay, let us get back on track with *Business is Business: As It Pleases God*. In the real world, credit cards are needed to establish credit properly, to prove ourselves as creditworthy, and to determine our ability to manage our credit outside of having a mortgage or car payment. Fortunately, credit cards are in great demand, but we must use them properly regardless of the type of demand or leverage they provide.

Of course, we have those who oppose having credit cards; however, the keyword is to manage credit, period. Regardless of where we are from, who we are, or what we have going on, in the society in which we live today, we need CREDIT, period! Without it, we become limited by default, even if we have the cash flow or we are Holy Ghost-Filled and Fire-Baptized. All jokes aside, bad credit ruins your credibility even if you are a great person, in the church or out of it, especially if you are not working on it or developing a plan of action to become better, stronger, and wiser.

Paul says, "*Therefore you must be subject, not only because of wrath but also for conscience' sake. For because of this you also pay taxes, for they are God's ministers attending continually to this very thing. Render therefore to all their due: taxes to whom taxes are due, customs to whom customs, fear to whom fear, honor to whom honor. Owe no one anything except to love one another, for he who loves another has fulfilled the law.*" Romans 13:5-8.

As It Pleases God, if we love others as we ought, we will also respectfully pay our bills to the best of our ability without trying to get over, use people, or beat the system. According to the Vicissitudes and Cycles of Life, we will all have our moments, hiccups, or issues, helping us to help ourselves. Still, we should never go into debt out of jealousy, envy, pride, greed, or to covet another, causing us to void the Fruits of the Spirit or operate in Spiritual Error, leading us into *Something Else*. What that *Something Else* is, we will discuss a little later in this book...thus, let us talk about getting a *Business Consultant* when being about our Father's Business.

BUSINESS CONSULTANT

There are several stereotypes associated with business consultants. One common stereotype is that they are overpaid and do not provide any real value to a company. Another stereotype is that they are arrogant and tend to think they know everything about a business, even if they do not have any experience in that particular industry. Additionally, some believe consultants are only interested in making money for themselves rather than helping their clients succeed. Finally, there is a stereotype that business consultants are only hired by large corporations and are not helpful for small businesses or startups. However, these stereotypes are not always accurate and should be taken with a grain of salt. Why? Good business consultants can provide valuable insights and guidance to companies of all sizes and industries. More importantly, you choose the person that fits your mold, period!

Why do we NEED a business consultant? Business consulting, mentoring, or guidance can be a precious resource for entrepreneurs and companies of all sizes or stages of development. A consultant, mentor, or guide can provide an outside perspective based on their experience and expertise, offering insights into areas such as strategy, operations, marketing, and finance. They can help identify areas for improvement, develop solutions to specific problems, and provide guidance on implementing changes effectively.

One of the key benefits of working with a consultant, mentor, or guide is that they can bring a fresh perspective to a business or an individual's mindset. Often, when you are deeply involved in the day-to-day operations of a company, it can be challenging to see the big or little picture. They can help you step back and look at your business objectively, identifying blind spots, blurred lines, hazards, and growth opportunities. In addition, when understanding that *Business is Business*, they can also help you save time and money by providing specialized expertise that you may not have in-house or that can be outsourced.

For example, a consultant, mentor, or guide can help you navigate the process more efficiently and effectively when launching a new product, service, or entering a new market. Whether you want to grow your business, improve your operations, or address a specific challenge, they can provide valuable insights, expertise, and guidance to help you achieve your goals or bounce around ideas.

What are the BENEFITS of having a business consultant, mentor, or guide? Whether a startup or an established business, they can provide the expertise you need to help your business grow and thrive. Here are some of the critical benefits of having one, but not limited to such:

- ☐ **Expertise**: They bring a wealth of knowledge and experience to the table, providing insight and advice from marketing and sales to operations and finance.

- ☐ **Objectivity**: As a neutral outsider, they can provide an objective perspective on your business, identifying areas where you may be blind to problems or opportunities.

- ☐ **Cost savings**: They can help you identify areas where you can cut costs or increase efficiency, which can help you save money in the long run.

- **Focus**: They can help you focus on your goals and priorities, develop a strategic plan, and ensure that you are making progress toward your objectives.

- **Networking**: They can help you build your network and connect you with other businesses and professionals in your industry.

In the Eye of God, finding the right consultant, mentor, or guide can provide the guidance and support you need to take your business to the next level to be about your Father's Business. Whether you need help with strategic planning, marketing, operations, social media, or finance, they can provide the expertise you need to succeed through the appropriate vetting process.

Remember, success is a subjective term and can mean different things to different people, regardless of where you are or what you are doing. In *The Secret Covenant*, here are some key things to keep in mind:

- **Determine your needs**: Before looking for a consultant, determine what you need help with. Do you need a consultant to help you with marketing, finance, or operations? Once you know what you need, you can start looking for a consultant, mentor, or guide who specializes in that area.

- **Look for experience**: When looking for a consultant, mentor, or guide, you want someone with experience in your industry who can deal with your specific challenges. In addition, make sure they have a proven track record of success and can provide references.

- **Consider cost**: Hiring a consultant, mentor, or guide can be expensive, so you need to consider the cost and whether it is worth the investment. Ensure you understand the consultant's fee structure and what you will get for your money.

- **Communication is vital**: When you hire a consultant, mentor, or guide, it is essential to establish clear lines of communication. Ensure you both understand the scope of the project, the timeline, and what you expect from each other.

- **Build a relationship**: You want to work with someone you can trust and feel comfortable with. Make sure you take the time to get to know the consultant, mentor, or guide before you make a decision.

In *The Secret Covenant*, it is imperative to choose someone who speaks your language, leading you into Divine Purpose, not away from it. What does this mean in layman's terms? *The Secret Covenant* is a POWERFUL CONCEPT that revolves around the idea of being guided by someone who speaks the same language as you and leads you toward your Divine Purpose. To be about your Father's Business, *As It Pleases Him*, you must choose a mentor, consultant, or guide who is aligned with your goals and aspirations rather than someone who takes you away from them.

In today's world, we are constantly bombarded by information and opinions from various sources. Thus, it can be challenging to sift through all the noise and find guidance that resonates with our values, standards, and beliefs, *As It Pleases God*. For this reason, this book, *Business is Business*, comes with Spiritual Guides, Principles, and Concepts to help you navigate your unique journey and pinpoint someone who speaks your language.

Chapter Three

Being About Your Father's Business

In the beginning of this chapter, with outright humility, 'We will all have a *Something Else*, we all make mistakes, and we will all fall into hard times.' Regardless of where we are, what we have been through, or where we are going, we should never give up on ourselves or remain in such a state. In light of our faithfulness, we must become a work-in-progress, Mentally, Physically, Emotionally, Spiritually, and Financially.

When working on yourself or *Being About Your Father's Business*, you must account for what you are thinking, how you treat yourself when no one is looking, your self-talk or inner chatter, your *Spirit to Spirit* Relationship with the Holy Trinity, and the allotment of provisions given. In the Eye of God, all of this means SOMETHING, only hidden underneath your *Something Else*.

What is the purpose of knowing about the meaning of *Something Else*? Everyone's *Something Else* will vary from person to person, situation to situation, culture to culture, bias to bias, mindset to mindset, trauma to trauma, and so on. Unfortunately, the *Something Else* hidden under something or someone will often hit our pockets first. So, it behooves us to know what it is or is not. Please allow me to align the importance of being *In The Know* of our *Something Else*. *"For which of you, intending to build a tower, does not sit down first and count the cost, whether he has enough to finish it—lest, after he has laid the foundation, and is not able to finish, all who see it begin to mock him, saying, 'This man began to build and was not able to finish.'* Luke 14:28-30.

According to the Heavenly of Heavens, if we desire Divine Wisdom to speak on our behalf, we must know what gives us dominion and the foundational factors needed for our Heaven on Earth Experience, *As It Pleases God*. In dealing with our *Something Else* or when doing business, we must become creative, exercising this natural power hidden within. The moment we block our creative juices, we become thirsty for recognition, leading us into Spiritual Error or Omission, and away from our Predestined

Blueprint. All of which can cause Mental, Physical, Emotional, Spiritual, and Financial blockages, we are most often unaware of.

When dealing with the creativity associated with our *Something Else*, we cannot assume. We must think and ask fact-finding questions to obtain the information regarding whatever or whomever. What makes this so important? When *Being About Your Father's Business*, creativity and clarity are needed to deal with your mental wheels, *As It Pleases Him*. Thus, you must keep your mental wheels turning in the right direction to safeguard your emotions. Then, branch out into other areas without jumping to conclusions or becoming a copycat, especially without involving God in the equation.

CREATIVE FINANCING

Why do we need creativity in doing business? Being creative helps open the mind to other areas associated with our finances, allowing us to exhaust our resources. For example, if we want to start a business, we may need creative financing. What is creative financing? Financing from another person's viewpoint. There are many ways of funding what we so desire; however, to get funded properly, we must have personal credit as leverage to build business credit. If our personal credit is not up to par, we may find ourselves limited in what we can do, say, or become in the real world. Therefore, it behooves us to pay attention to our credit, or if we need to work on it, then do so.

Do we still need to work on our creditworthiness if we have faith? Of course. Faith has requirements and influence, beginning from the human psyche and spreading outwardly. For example, with faith, we need trust; with trust, we need belief; with belief, we need hope, creating the substance in or out of our *Something Else* called things. We can call this a play on words, but in the Kingdom, words have power. So, it behooves us to find the right creative words to work on our behalf. Is this Biblical? Absolutely. *"Now faith is the substance of things hoped for, the evidence of things not seen."* Hebrews 11:1.

What are the ingredients of faith? Trust, belief, and hope are the recipe for our faith when dealing with *Something Else*. Most would assume that faith, trust, belief, and hope are the same, but they are not! They work together as ONE, having different functions. For the record, this recipe of faith works positively and negatively. In my opinion, it is always best to remain on the positive side of the spectrum, especially when the evidence will avail itself in due time.

On the other hand, with or without faith, trust, belief, and hope, we still must establish and maintain our credit. Why? First, if the enemy wants to sucker punch us, they will attack our credibility. Secondly, they will go for the jugular (our weaknesses). Thirdly, they will go for our financial capacity or what is NOT in our pockets. Fourthly, they will target our limited access, such as denied access to certain cliques of status or prominence, making us feel inferior. For this reason, it behooves us to work on our credibility with creativity, *As It Pleases God*, allowing us to think in or out of the Kingdom proactively.

What does our creative credibility have to do with anything? In or out of our *Something Else*, we will not value our creative credibility until we need it for something we want, value, or desire. For example, when doing business, if our ideas are all over the place or mangled, it will become challenging to get funded for yo-yo or moody creativity and execution. According to the Heavenly of Heavens, FOCUS is needed to develop balance within our *Something Else*.

Why do we need focus and balance when *Being About Our Father's Business*? It keeps us from jumping from one thing to the next with zero consistency. Having unresolved or underlying issues with power, money, and sex causes the mind to wander off or create images of dissatisfaction, folly, or ungratefulness.

Why must we focus when becoming creative? From the Garden of Eden, distractions are designed to impede our focus. Once our focus is fragmented, it leads to broken creativity by default unless we learn how to self-correct from the inside out, beginning with self-talk. What is the purpose of beginning with ourselves? If we do not begin with ourselves, we will focus on *Something Else* that has nothing to do with us, causing a negative spread. In my opinion, this analogy is similar to Eve partaking in the Forbidden Fruit and then giving it to Adam as a form of extended deceptive manipulation.

SOMETHING ELSE

From back then until now, God has given a side-eye to deceptive manipulation and those who do not take the time to use what they have in their hands positively. Yet, they take enough time to covet, use what is in someone else's hand without putting in the work, or draw the innocent into their mess. What is the purpose of God giving us a side-eye? When we do not use what is readily available, we tend to become ungrateful for what we already possess. Secondly, coveting another man's Gifts, Calling,

Talents, and Creativity creates bad habits, leading to other negative habits such as jealousy, envy, pride, greed, dullness, or a stiff neck. Thirdly, competitiveness causes the mind to jump the track, leading us away from our Divine Blueprint to the next quick fix or trend.

In our *Something Else*, we must invoke the PASSION for learning, practicing, executing, and self-correcting. Why must we invoke our PASSIONS? It helps to awaken and develop our brain's mindfulness and supernatural powers, connecting us to the Holy Trinity, our Predestined Blueprint, and the Big Picture. Listen, our PASSIONS have a secret connection to the body, giving us the will to live for our Heaven on Earth Experiences. Without them, we tend to want to give up on people, places, and things easily, without knowing or understanding our reasons for existing. What does this mean? We must understand ourselves, others, and both from God's Perspective.

Although understanding can become a little tedious, it is doable. How do we go about doing so? When we listen to ourselves Mentally, Physically, Emotionally, Spiritually, and Financially, we can self-analyze ourselves and our perceptions. What if we choose not to do a self-analysis? God does not force us to self-reflect; we must want it for ourselves. Why? We must consciously choose to become better, stronger, and wiser to glean from the reservoir of Greatness, according to our Predestined Blueprint.

Why is God so adamant about us making conscious and free will choices? Simply put, He did not create us as robots; we are conscious yet Spiritual Beings having a human experience. With this formal connection from the Heavenly of Heavens, it means three things in the Eye of God, but not limited to such:

- ☐ What comes out of the mouth is what is in the mind.
- ☐ What is in the mind is in the psyche (soul).
- ☐ What is in the soul is a SEED.

Why are these three factors so crucial in the Eye of God? Positively or negatively, what is in the seed creates our reality or perception in due season. If we do not self-correct, we will place our mindset on others who may think differently. For example, when conversing about specific issues, instead of someone allowing me to complete my sentence or story, they interject their thoughts, feelings, or beliefs, often taking what I am speaking about all the way to the left. After gleaning their thought patterns and mindset for trainable wisdom, I interject with, 'I did not say that,' giving them an opportunity to mentally backtrack what they heard, as opposed to what I actually said. Then I will ask, 'Can I complete the story?'

When dealing with our *Something Else*, we must master our listening and silencing skills. Why? If we fail to remain silent, fail to listen, or fail to ask the right questions effectively, we miss the valuable lessons taking place within our psyche, or we may rub people the wrong way. Not listening to understand or outright talking too much creates receptory blockages, breaking the ability to communicate with ourselves from the inside out properly.

What do receptory blockages have to do with us? The body has a voice, and speaking a language requires intuitiveness. If not appropriately activated, *As It Pleases God*, we become somewhat repulsive to ourselves and others. While at the same time, amid our blind, repulsive state of being, people do not often have the guts to tell us our people skills suck, or that we are hard to deal with.

Why would someone hide the way they feel about our character? Most often, it is for fear of offending or fueling the hidden beast, especially if we do not take the time to self-correct or become better, wiser, or stronger for ourselves. As a result of this type of self-omission, we usually become ghosted or avoided due to our projected rotten fruit or corrupt character. Really? Yes, really!

Due to the underlying trait of self-omission, more people dislike themselves than we care to imagine, while covering it up with *Something Else*, or they make the lives of others miserable. We can tiptoe around the insecurity issues all we like, but our inner insecurities do not lie. They speak loud, demanding our attention, and want the story told. Why? We are prewired to have dominionated freedom from the inside out. Without tapping into this Spiritual Reservoir, tilling our own ground, or uprooting the weeds choking our growth, the voice from within will secretly or openly cry out, asking us, 'What have you done?' or 'What are you not doing?' In my opinion, this is like the Blood of Abel speaking, provoking us to effectively query ourselves without covering up, ignoring what needs our attention, downplaying our *Something Else*, or becoming a vagabond. Here is the scripture, "*And He said, 'What have you done? The voice of your brother's blood cries out to Me from the ground.*" Genesis 4:10.

Whether we are the brother or sister turned inwardly, or it is a brother or sister from another mother, we are all ONE; so, queries are required to properly self-correct, *As It Pleases God*. What is the purpose of self-queries? Please allow me to answer this question with another: 'When the veil is lifted, then what will we see?' The Spiritual WYSIWYG (What You See

Is What You Get) is not a laughing matter in or out of the Kingdom, especially when dealing with the transformative efforts associated with Divine Liberation from the inside out.

Here is what we must know about the VEIL: "*But even to this day, when Moses is read, a veil lies on their heart. Nevertheless, when one turns to the Lord, the veil is taken away. Now the Lord is the Spirit; and where the Spirit of the Lord is, there is liberty. But we all, with unveiled face, beholding as in a mirror the glory of the Lord, are being transformed into the same image from glory to glory, just as by the Spirit of the Lord.*" 2 Corinthians 3:15-18.

What does the veil, our transformative efforts, or our *Something Else* have to do with our finances? If we do not have a passion for keeping our finances in order, we will keep getting in trouble, digging ourselves into deeper debt with God, ourselves, others, and our creditors. Therefore, it is always best to gain leverage to think on or off our feet, Mentally, Physically, Emotionally, Spiritually, and Financially through self-examination. Really? Yes, really! Here is what King David shared with us in Psalm 26:1-2, "*Vindicate me, O LORD, For I have walked in my integrity. I have also trusted in the LORD; I shall not slip. Examine me, O LORD, and prove me; Try my mind and my heart.*"

According to the Heavenly of Heavens, it is through self-examination that Kingdom Treasures, Wisdom, Understanding, and Know-How are granted. What if God really grants us wisdom without examining ourselves? I cannot discount what type of wisdom is being obtained, but I will say this: Trickles of wisdom do not equate to the FLOW of Divine Wisdom. Nor does it give us an excuse not to Spiritually Till our own grounds according to our Predestined Blueprint, Gifts, Callings, Talents, or Creativity. What does this mean? They all need development!

If we do not develop *As It Pleases God*, the world will develop us with a short circuit, missing wires, or inaccurate information, and we may not like the results. All of this leads to hyperinflated ego boosts, not doing us a bit of good, or barring us from the Spiritual Classroom of Greatness. How is this possible when God is no respecter of persons? It can easily happen if we become Spiritually Blind, Deaf, or Mute, operating in the Spirit of Error or Omission without total submission to the Will and Ways of God.

In or out of the Kingdom of God, we must become extremely teachable while listening, learning, obeying, growing, and sharing, *As It Pleases Him*, not ourselves. With Spiritual Development on any level, we must use examination as a part of the process. For example, I do not know of one school where we can obtain knowledge without taking some form of examination. So, why do we think God should not examine His product?

Or, better yet, why do we think we should not examine ourselves, *As It Pleases Him?*

According to the Heavenly of Heavens, improper examination is one of the greatest forms of deception known to mankind in Earthen Vessel. If we do not examine ourselves, we tend to complain, bicker, worry, fuss, and fight with ourselves first, then with others. All of these cause us to become secretly or openly ungrateful, disobedient, self-seeking, dull, and stiff-necked while appearing right in our own eyes. Simply put, without saying one word, these are some of the character traits I look for, especially when someone proclaims God said this and He said that.

What is the purpose of paying attention to specific character traits? First, if God said to do something, then we should do it without reservation! Secondly, if God said to give, then we should give without broadcasting it! Thirdly, if God said to examine ourselves against the Fruits of the Spirit and Christlike Character, and we do not, then what do we have here? Let us take it to scripture, *"Is it not from the mouth of the Most High That woe and well-being proceed? Why should a living man complain, A man for the punishment of his sins? Let us search out and examine our ways, And turn back to the LORD; Let us lift our hearts and hands To God in heaven."* Lamentations 3:38-41.

In *Business is Business*, our innovative ideas, thoughts, and beliefs require participation, especially if we desire freedom, *As It Pleases God*. Here is the deal: God has placed our Gifts, Callings, Talents, Creativity, and Purpose in or under our *Something Else*. The moment we pretend as if we are perfect, and our *Something Else* does not exist, we will find ourselves on the lacking side of whatever or whomever.

We are designed to learn, grow, and sow back into the Kingdom when called upon, creating a Spiritual Gravitational Pull, aligning us to our Predestined Blueprint. Suppose we are not adequately trained to do, say, and become what we are predestined to become at the appropriate time. In this case, we will find ourselves pulling for straws, overlooking our Divine Potential, or becoming overwhelmed with exhausting insecurities. All of these zap our peacefulness from the inside out.

When moving forward in the Spirit of Excellence or when facing our *Something Else*, we must remain calm. Why should we remain calm, mainly when chaos is all around us? The oil of calmness is soothing to the human psyche. More importantly, it keeps us from panicking under pressure. Listen, the moment we become panicky, we begin to see people, places, and things differently based on our perceptions, biases, or traumas, similar to having a flashback. Meanwhile, remaining calm helps us to flash forward with proactiveness, seeing people, places, and things as they are without becoming reactive. Although we may take this for granted, in the Kingdom, it is vital to usher in the Promises of God.

In staking my claim to my Divine Birthright, I used the Spiritual Principle hidden in my *Something Else* as a part of my DO-OVER and my GIVEBACK to the Kingdom, invoking the Law of Reciprocity. Even when the naysayers and critics had their foot on my neck, calling me everything but a Child of God, I did not relent to the mockery or rejection. I stood my ground, and now here we are. In doing likewise, here is what you need to know: "*If anyone speaks, let him speak as the Oracles of God. If anyone ministers, let him do it as with the ability which God supplies, that in all things God may be glorified through Jesus Christ, to whom belong the glory and the dominion forever and ever. Amen.*" 1 Peter 4:11.

More importantly, with the information I am sharing with you, I wish someone had shared this information with me when I was younger; I would have avoided many costly mistakes. As my Divine Testament, I have the experience to set the record straight for those willing to learn, grow, and sow back into the Kingdom of God.

When *Being About Your Father's Business,* regardless of what your *Something Else* is or is not, it is imperative to GIVE THANKS without becoming a hardwired grinch, making everyone miserable around you. What is the purpose of giving thanks when your *Something Else* has you in a chokehold? Gratefulness can change the trajectory of anything. Suppose you ask for the lesson or understanding about whatever or whomever. In this case, God will show you the way, especially when dealing with the privileges of having a *Spirit to Spirit* Relationship.

In receiving Divine Guidance in any area of your life, Mentally, Physically, Emotionally, Spiritually, or Financially, simply pray, repent, forgive, learn, grow, document, and sow back into the Kingdom when called upon. Here is the *Something Else* Divine Covering that is hidden in plain sight, "*Beloved, do not think it strange concerning the fiery trial which is to try you, as though some strange thing happened to you; but rejoice to the extent that you partake of Christ's sufferings, that when His glory is revealed, you may also be glad with exceeding joy. If you are reproached for the name of Christ, blessed are you, for the Spirit of glory and of God rests upon you. On their part He is blasphemed, but on your part He is glorified.*" 1 Peter 4:12-14.

Can we glorify God in our finances? Absolutely. God and I would have it no other way. Listen, the Spiritual Strategy of Joseph's financial glory remains until this day, but it is often overlooked. "*Then Joseph gave a command *to fill their sacks with grain, to restore every man's money to his sack, and to give them provisions for the journey. Thus he did for them."* Genesis 42:25. In the Eye of God, the best way to restore ourselves is to restore another who has fallen short or caused an offense. Regardless of how it is perceived or whether the receiver rejects it, it gives us KINGDOM LEVERAGE. God knows the intents or wounds of the heart, and for Joseph to internally heal, he activated a Spiritual Principle hidden within, positively restoring another, placing a Spiritual Seal on the Law of Reciprocity.

Can someone place a Spiritual Seal on the Law of Reciprocity? We do it all the time, not realizing what we are doing. Here is the Spiritual Seal: *"While the earth remains, Seedtime and harvest, Cold and heat, Winter and summer, And day and night Shall not cease."* Genesis 8:22. Why does this not say the Law of Reciprocity? This Divine Exchange System is referenced in the Bible as Seedtime and Harvest.

Our *Something Else* is predicated on the positive or negative SEEDS and DEEDS sown. How can we sow good seeds, *As It Pleases God*? First, we must use God as our soil or fertilizer because we are created in His Image. Secondly, we must water our seeds with the Blood of Jesus as our formal sacrifice for grace, mercy, and repentance, regardless of whether we fall short or stand tall. And lastly, we must cover our seeds with the Holy Spirit for protection, correction, and direction, guiding us on the use of the Fruits of the Spirit, Christlike Character, or the regrafting process of them both.

What is the purpose of this three-step seedling of our *Something Else*? Surrendering our seeds to this process enables the Cycles and Vicissitudes of Life to govern the distribution of whatever, with whomever, causing all things to work in our favor, even when it does not appear so to the naked eye. All of this grants us Kingdom Credit that needs to be Spiritually Converted and Extracted from the Heavenly of Heavens, helping us to properly manage our credit for the system we presently live in.

How do we connect the Kingdom's System and the worldly, primarily when we are taught to divide? Often, we are taught to divide instead of multiplying; however, if we do not MASTER the multiplication process, our system of division becomes thwarted. What is the difference? Division draws the line, dividing one from another and causing segregation.

Multiplying crosses the lines, placing the cross in the appropriate places to PRODUCE more after its own kind, bringing UNITY. However, in the extracting and converting process, they both work positively and negatively, so it behooves us to understand this from God's Divine Perspective.

In the *Something Else* of our positives, negatives, divisionary, and multiplicator processes or seeds, continue to follow my lead, and I will share how to *Be About Our Father's Business*.

WHY PLAN?

We must plan to achieve. In designing our AIPG Goals, we must commit to them, document them, and design a road-mapped plan. Does it work? Absolutely. When I started a roadmap for myself, I thought it was so far-fetched, but I documented the desires of my heart anyway. I did not know the how-to, yet I did know the WHAT and WHY.

After several moves, somehow, my roadmap got lost in the shuffle. Many years later, lo and behold, after finding it, I accomplished and exceeded every goal without realizing it. It was like a gravitational magnet, teaching and training me for a time such as this. For this reason, I wholeheartedly stand behind developing roadmaps, *As It Pleases God*.

What are the benefits of having a plan, developing systems, or mastering strategies? It prevents us from being all over the place with our ideas, thoughts, emotions, and creativity. It also helps to avoid becoming mired by defeat or winging it, expecting God to bless our mess. Knowing your strengths, weaknesses, skills, values, attitudes, and interests will make you better prepared for the surprises that life may bring. I know you have your business or life plan in your head, but it is much better to have it documented on paper. Having your plan written down on paper will help you stay on track more than just having it in your head, becoming a hot mess, clueless, or goalless.

The key to accomplishing what we want is to learn how to plan our lives in a backward motion from the intended goal or destination. However, some may look at anything backward as being negative or demonic. Unfortunately, this is where deception has caused a Spiritual Taboo or Yoke to ensnare our Mind, Body, and Soul, having us walk around not knowing whether we are coming or going. According to the Heavenly of Heavens, this mindset must come to a complete halt. Why? It is causing us not to plan or document projectively, *As It Pleases God*, contributing to our mental blocks, lack of focus, or outright defeat. Is this type of planning Biblical? I would have it no other way; it says, "*Remember the former things of old, For I am God, and there is no other; I am God, and there is none like Me, Declaring the end from the beginning, And from ancient times things that are not yet done, Saying, 'My counsel shall stand, And I will do all My pleasure.'* " Isaiah 46:9-10.

When we plan our lives backward, in reverse, or proactively, we can better determine the steps needed to reach our desired destination. It also helps us envision the vision, *Bridge The Gap*, or backtrack if necessary. Plus, it gives us better control of our ability to focus on what we want instead of what we do not want. When we focus on what we do not want, we become fearful and give up before getting started. Plus, we must know where we want to go or what we want to achieve in life to govern or redirect our Destiny, just in case we get off track, distracted, or lost.

What does planning have to do with our Spiritual Gifts, Callings, Talents, or Creativity? The IMPARTATION is the conveyance between God and man, awakening their dormancy. Here is what Romans 1:11-13 says, *"For I long to see you, that I may impart to you some spiritual gift, so that you may be established—that is, that I may be encouraged together with you by the mutual faith both of you and me. Now I do not want you to be unaware, brethren, that I often planned to come to you (but was hindered until now), that I might have some fruit among you also, just as among the other Gentiles."*

Once we master this planning technique, we can then plan forward, *Bridging the Gap* between where we are and where we are going, eliminating the limited mindset or belief system. How will this help us? It allows us to align ourselves accordingly, getting rid of the misalignments or making the necessary changes through our questionable queries. Here are a few questions to get a jump start on designing the rest of your life:

- ☐ If you could do anything, what would you do?
- ☐ If you could become anything, what would it be?
- ☐ If you could accomplish anything, what would you accomplish?
- ☐ What do you like to do in your spare time?
- ☐ What are your technical skills?
- ☐ What do others say you are really good at?
- ☐ What interests you the most?
- ☐ What are your hobbies?
- ☐ What are your marketable qualities?
- ☐ Do you have time to run a successful business?

Answer those questions honestly, and you will be well on your way to setting and achieving the desires of your heart. What is the purpose of querying in the planning process? If you are considering constructing, building, or enhancing, make sure you lay the proper groundwork to ensure it becomes an ASSET and not a LIABILITY. Not only this, but be very cautious about investing in something or someone that will cost you Mentally, Physically, Emotionally, Spiritually, or Financially more than you are willing to pay. How would we know? We must look for the RED FLAGS.

Developing a Planning Mindset

When *Being About Our Father's Business*, to unlock our full potential and achieve success, we must make planning a top priority, *As It Pleases Him*. By proactively anticipating challenges and opportunities, we can significantly increase our chances of success. With *Business is Business*, focusing our resources on adequate strategies and maintaining a clear sense of direction and purpose, we can stay on track toward achieving our goals.

When we commit ourselves to careful planning and remain steadfast in our pursuit of success, we position ourselves to reach new heights and unveil our Divine Blueprint.

Finding the benefits of anything or with anyone takes work, even if we downplay our roles and responsibilities of where we are, where we are going, and how to get there. Writing a business plan is essential when starting a new business or seeking an investment for an existing one. However, in this process, you must PLAN for the business to avoid having it become an overwhelming feat or an infamous foe.

Why do we need to plan when *Being About Our Father's Business*? A well-written business plan can help you to clarify your business idea, identify potential challenges, and set realistic goals, especially when you incorporate your PASSION. Although we will go into our business plan in more detail in Chapter 12, for the time being, when developing a *Planning Mindset*, here are some of the key benefits of writing a business plan you will often hear or read:

- ☐ Clarify your business idea. Writing a business plan forces you to think through your business idea in detail. This can help you to identify potential challenges and opportunities and develop a clear strategy for success.

- ☐ Secure funding. If you are seeking funding for your business, a well-written business plan can help you secure investment from banks, investors, or other sources.

- ☐ Set realistic goals. A business plan can help you set realistic goals for your business and develop a clear plan for achieving them. This can help you stay focused and motivated as you build a successful business.

- ☐ Identify potential challenges. Writing a business plan can help you to identify potential challenges and develop strategies for addressing them. This can help you avoid common pitfalls and ensure your business is well-positioned for success.

Overall, a well-written business plan can be a valuable tool for any entrepreneur or business owner. It can help you to clarify your business ideas, secure funding, set realistic goals, and identify potential challenges. However, it may not incorporate the PASSION needed to blaze with GREATNESS. For this reason, we will put our spin on planning your business, incorporating your life around your business, or the benefits of minding your business.

What are the benefits of writing a Business Plan? The most profound downfall of today is not planning, forgetting to plan, passing the buck on planning, or omitting it altogether. With *Business is Business: As It Pleases God*, we dare you to think and plan differently. We will not just tell you HOW to do it; we will break down the WHY, giving you a better understanding of the importance of planning your way to the TOP.

When *Being About Your Father's Business*, what you truly desire in life will not come to you by luck; it will come by SKILL, using what you already possess. Why would this happen in such a manner? It builds VALUE and GRATITUDE, weeding out superficial insecurities and lies.

In designing the ideal business plan, we will begin with various ways of PLANNING, getting the ball rolling on your documentation abilities while developing your understanding of the importance of doing so.

Action Planning

Action Planning helps clarify your business ideas, thoughts, and beliefs while identifying potential obstacles, detours, and competitors. With anything in life, you are required to exhibit action, period! Without it, the Cycle of Life places you in a chokehold full of drama, chaos, and confusion. If you take the time to establish a plan of action, it will help you think on your feet or become proactively diligent without falling apart under pressure.

More importantly, it helps us understand our WHAT and WHY. If you know, understand, and document these two, everything else will flow to you. When you place a DEMAND on your WHAT and WHY, it assists in your uniqueness and authenticity.

Usually, my first two questions are, 'What are you doing?' And, 'Why are you doing it?' If they fumble in this area, exhibit arrogance, or attempt to brainwash me like I am boo-boo the fool, I know they are not ready for me! Why? I wholeheartedly believe in ACTION...more so in MENTAL ACTION. Getting your wheels inexcusably turning mentally in the right direction is imperative before taking action physically.

Visionary Planning

Visionary Planning provides a documented roadmap for achieving your goals, passion, or vision. By far, this keeps you from jumping from one thing to the next or being all over the place, depending on who you are with.

A documented roadmap helps us develop consistency in our thoughts, actions, beliefs, behaviors, and desires. I often hear people talk about being on a journey, and when I ask for the roadmap or documentation, they have nothing to show me.

How is it possible to engage in a journey without a roadmap? Although possible, it leads to aloofness, getting lost, or wandering around in a cycle of déjà vu. For this reason, you must put pen to paper, documenting your ideas, thoughts, beliefs, feelings, desires, and so on. Spiritually, this is to ensure you do not forget about the map you planned for yourself or your business when the issues of life arise.

Roadmap Planning

Roadmap Planning is designed to identify your target audience and market from the infant to adult stages, determining your potentiality or the lack thereof. Although designing a roadmap or mind map is similar, your reasoning is slightly different. If you design the roadmap for the tangible journey of your business, you can create a mind map for the intangibles of what is in your head.

In the beginning, dividing the two will keep you from becoming overwhelmed, and once you merge them, you have a better understanding and respect for where you are going, why you are going, and how you will get there.

Strategic Planning

Strategic Planning encourages you to understand your competition and brainstorm your way to the top without hopping over dollars to pick up a nickel. When you set aside time to document strategies only, you will find your mind kicking into high gear, bombarding you with ideas that you must sort through. You can do this session alone or with others, but it is wise to do it yourself, pushing the limit of your mental capacity.

For example, if someone is trying to decide on the name of their business, I advise them to come up with a list of 100 names and document them. At first, they thought this was impossible, but after consoling and telling them to write whatever came to mind, good, bad, or indifferent, they relaxed. More importantly, they realized it was easier than they thought.

For the record, I have not had a list returned to me that does not have the ideal or unique name of their business. The mind operates better with a challenge. Why would the mind operate in such a manner? It is not obligated to yield its content if you do not push or place a demand on it.

What is the purpose of placing a demand? In my opinion, the mind is similar to a locked door...if you do not use a key or do not have one to open it, entry is denied unless you break the door down. Besides, it is not like you are breaking into your mind because it belongs to you...It is more like breaking down the barriers blocking your access to the information you want.

Balanced Scoreboard Planning

Balanced Scoreboard Planning enables you to identify and analyze potential risks, what you can bring to the table, or what needs to be removed. Creating a check and balance system for yourself and your business keeps you on the leading edge of GREATNESS. When you target the positive, eliminate the negative, and create a win-win out of them both, you are well on your way to the ultimate bliss.

Why is Balanced Scoreboard Planning important? It helps you develop and maintain your niche, even when the naysayers come along to discredit your vision. When doing the work and doing your best, you will have less time playing cleanup or worrying about what others think. Listen, when doing what you do in the Spirit of Excellence, it does not make you perfect, but makes you pliably usable for the good. Giving people, places, and things your best shot with good intentions profoundly impacts those who are afraid to take a shot at becoming better, stronger, and wiser.

Productivity Planning

Productivity Planning helps you identify your unique selling proposition, pinpointing your niche to enable you to stand out or shine brightly. You cannot sit around twiddling your thumbs, especially when you must become better daily, not out of insecurity but out of responsibility.

Of course, we all must begin somewhere; however, I look for the track record of PROGRESS, whereas most look for perfection. The work-in-progress mentality is more POWERFUL than the so-called perfect mentality. Why is the work-in-progress mentality more powerful? Unfortunately, there is no such thing as a perfect mentality.

On average, we use less than 10% of our mental capacity, even if we are degreed up, lawyered up, powered up, played up, or laid up. Only a few people have exceeded the 10% capacity. How so? By expanding their ability to build their lives and others according to their Predestined Blueprint and *Being About Their Father's Business*.

Getting to this point concerning our mental capacity is not about how much we know. In the Eye of God, it is knowing how to use and maximize what you do know for the greater good. For this reason, it is imperative to know when to power down, download and upload information, or recharge without blurring the lines. What does this mean? To exceed the norm, you must plan for it, use it, multiply it, and help others with it, harming no one.

Once harm, superiority, or degradation is involved, you will receive less by default or become depleted. Yet, you still have the option to receive more if you have a positive change of heart for righteousness and repentance. Amid Productivity Planning, you already have what it takes; however, you must learn how to use and maximize it according to your Predestined Blueprint. So, pull out your little journal, and let's get busy.

Management Planning

Management Planning helps you pinpoint potential sources of funding or capital. Management, as such, will assist in establishing value within yourself and your business. Often enough, many people run businesses without believing in the business or establishing value, leading to stunted growth.

What is the reason for becoming stunted? Some people luck up on a business, some may have taken someone's idea, some are obsessed with the illusion of owning their own business, and some may have the capital to invest in something profitable for the money. Who knows the reason, but if it is NOT your Blueprinted Purpose or a part of your reason for being, you will lose interest with time. Therefore, managing your documents helps develop a passion for what you are doing, or it will indicate a low-burning flame before getting into debt for a business your heart is not into, just to say you own a business.

Mind Map Planning

Mind Map Planning allows you to develop a marketing strategy surrounding the documented information. When you think documentation is unimportant, you create a disservice to yourself and others. Why is this such a disservice? It creates a symbolic unsolved puzzle or riddle from within, which often leads to seeking the opinions of others, plugging and playing, becoming a copycat, or degrading others to make yourself feel better.

Whereas, if you take a few minutes a day to mind map or journal your thoughts, business ideas, problems, projected solutions, and so on, you will find the answers being sought; they will find you! To do so, you must align yourself accordingly or want it for yourself, allowing others to inspire or trigger the best in or out of you. A little hand-eye coordination and putting pen to paper will do the trick.

Innovation Planning

Innovation Planning gives breathing room to develop a sales strategy, understanding the product or service, its benefits, and how to close or ask for the sale, presumably, with believability and credible people skills. Whether you are selling a product or service, people buy you, your vision, your concept, or how you make them feel. For this reason, you owe it to yourself to innovatively plan for this, leading the field in this area.

More importantly, just because you own a business does not mean you do not affect it. Your positive involvement is crucial to the success of your business. What if the business is succeeding without you? My question would be, 'How much better would the business become with your proactive and positive involvement?'

Making money in a business is good, but changing or positively impacting lives is always BETTER. Bringing money, change, and impact together for the betterment of all involved will make your business a GIANT POWERHOUSE. If you do not possess this right now, it is time to get busy documenting and innovatively planning.

Business-Resolving Planning

Problem-Solving or Business-Resolving Planning helps you develop or mind map an operations strategy to know and understand your product. While simultaneously allowing the questions you ask to align with the benefits offered to reverse engineer the sale. Everyone has something to work on or at; therefore, placing yourself in an unrealistic bubble is not wise. For this reason, it behooves you to engage in or develop skills in problem-solving or business-resolving, gaining the proactive agility needed to think on your feet.

Why is this so important? If you do not exercise this ability, the thinking process can become murky when placed under pressure, tenaciously challenged, when you are thrown out to the wolves, or if you find yourself between a rock and a hard place. This scenario is similar to being lost in the jungle; if you prepare, you will survive because you have prepared mentally with your survival instincts at full alert.

If you DO NOT prepare, you will 'get got' from the inside out by how you think or perceive your state of being, causing you to give up easily and lose the will to survive.

Resolutionary Business Planning

Resolutionary Business Planning helps you to govern or identify your staffing and human resources needs. When planning the needs of your business, you must consider the end result. Understanding your end game, goal, or resolution helps you fill the gaps between the start and finish lines.

After pinpointing the WHAT and WHY, I always ask, 'What is the end resolve or resolution?' Why this question? It reveals MOTIVE. Once you know the motive, it is easier to backtrack or fill the gaps with positivity to create a win-win for yourself and others. If you leave this out, you will think and feel like you are winning but losing all the way to the bank; as money finds holes in your pocket, you become a victim of theft, sleeping with the enemy, or dealing with the inability to trust anyone.

Steadfast Planning

Steadfast Planning allows you to identify or assess your training needs for the betterment of yourself, your employees, and your business. In or out of doing business, you must always remain on a continuous learning path, even if you feel you have reached your capacity. There is always more to learn, and you cannot limit yourself, your employees, or your business to mediocrity.

Steadfast Planning and documentation will assist in breaking the monotony of our self-induced psychosis or complacency. No one or nothing is exempt from this process. In the same way that dust will always find its way into your house without you seeing the specks falling, your mental cobwebs are the same. Therefore, it is imperative to whip out the dust buster daily to get your mental wheels turning in the proper and positive direction.

Resolute Planning

Resolute Planning opens your mind to setting realistic goals and objectives without fail. The unyielding desire for better incorporates gratefulness with a knowing and understanding of better as an increasable force of stature, wisdom, and sharing for the greater good of all mankind. In this type of planning, you must focus on GRATEFULNESS and the GREATER GOOD.

If you are planning based on selfish thoughts, ambitions, or desires, you can thwart your inner growth or the growth of your business. Dysfunctional growth is not ideal; however, you can plan your way into positive functionality through Resolute Planning. For example, everyone is trying to sell a system, and some make millions doing so. But the truth is, they are selling a system they bought, claiming they developed it on their own.

Although they have money in their pocket, there is also a looming thought in their minds of being a loser because they did not put in the work to obtain, sustain, and maintain the system. Lost value, as such, causes us to overcompensate with varying negative habits or become very hard on people who appear beneath us due to our secret insecurities.

In actuality, all you need to do is become a part of the systemic planning and execution process to build workable and worthy value, developing a positive and productive mindset without trying to get over or attempting to beat the system with deceptive measures.

Persistent Planning

Persistent Planning provides the documentation needed to keep track of your progress or the lack thereof. If you do not know where you are or where you stand, it becomes difficult to know where you are going and how you will get there. For example, when you get into your car, you have a destination in mind, even if you make pitstops along the way.

The same applies to your business plan; document it and fill in the gaps along the way until you get there. Everyone's there, or landmarks will be different due to our unique Blueprinted Purpose. Thus, if you document your personal or business journey, *"Write the vision and make it plain on tablets, that he may run who reads it."* Habakkuk 2:2.

Growth Planning

Growth Planning can help you identify areas for improvement and growth. Remember, there is no perfect business. Everyone has something to work on or work at, so it behooves us to develop a work-in-progress mentality in our documentary efforts. More importantly, this is how your good becomes better, your better becomes your best, and your best becomes GREAT.

Mental Creative Performance Building

Mental Creative Performance Building can help you better communicate or paint a picturesque view of your vision to your partners, investors, team, customers, or suppliers. If you cannot paint it in your mind's eye, selling it with believability and solidarity will become problematic.

Why would our vision become problematic, especially when having it going on, needing no one or nothing? Regardless of your known or unknown wants, needs, or desires of vision solidarity, you were created as a relational being to build around others, planting good seeds instead of eating them by yourself.

When properly planting good seeds into others, you must develop your Mind-Eye Coordination to maximize your highest and greatest potential, regardless of whether you roll solo or roll bolo. Then again, this is how fast talkers, slow talkers, or manipulators get over on someone whose Mind-Eye Coordination is keeled.

Now, if you think you are already good at what you do, I challenge you to improve. If you follow my instructions, you will find that you have only scraped the surface of your Divine Potentiality, guaranteed!

Credibility Planning

Credibility Planning is a well-documented action plan that builds credibility with your partners, investors, team, customers, or suppliers. If you do not put pen to paper, your credibility is lost the moment you open your mouth. Why would credibility become an issue? Pulling for straws is not a business mindset, whereas aligning them is.

Our business model does not need to be perfect; however, documenting provides a symbolic connection to your visions, passions, thoughts, or beliefs. It does not matter if we write, scribble, or connect the dots with one word at a time; you must do this for yourself. There is POWER and CONNECTION in documenting.

Unfaltering Planning

Unfaltering Planning assists in making informed decisions to avoid costly or repetitive mistakes with little or no growth. Planning in such a manner helps you expand your capacity to receive when you are dedicated to becoming better, stronger, and wiser for your sake.

Why not for the company's sake? The company starts with you; if you become better, stronger, and wiser, it flows into the company. However, if the company improves without you, it is only a matter of time before control is lost, Mentally, Physically, Emotionally, and Spiritually. For this reason, you must remain involved. If your company succeeds without you, it is possible that someone else has interjected their vision into yours, carrying the weight you have omitted to carry.

Unfortunately, this leads to most business owners getting got or feeling insecure about their lack of involvement or contribution. For the record, if it is your business, get involved with the planning and documentation process. And whatever they know, you should become familiar with, even if you feel inadequate, think it is beneath you, or it is below your pay grade. GET INVOLVED!

What is the purpose of getting involved, especially when already making money? Most businesses go out of business because the owner is not involved, they lack the skill of sustenance while involved, or they delegate because they do not know the process or what to do to keep the business afloat without sinking. If you allow someone else to run your business into the ground while you sit back, twiddling your thumbs, you cannot blame anyone, period.

Collaborational Planning

Collaborational Planning helps you to stay focused on your goals, remain motivated, organized, and accountable, building a foundation based on team efforts. Planning in such a manner eradicates selfish efforts by incorporating others into our vision. For example, a business cannot survive without customers, employees, vendors, and so on; therefore, you must plan with them in mind.

Communicable Planning

Communicable Planning helps to build a strong foundation for your business, brand, reputation, team, and culture. When you effectively communicate with yourself, your vision, your team, and your customer, you place yourself on the leading edge to receive informative updates, suggestions, advice, and so on. People are more likely to help those who document and take notes than those who do not.

Why would they help a notetaker rather than someone who is not taking notes? They feel more important, heard, and valued when you take the time to document and reflect. Going in one ear and out the other is not the ideal impression you should establish in a striving and successful business, primarily when having to backtrack on something that should have been documented. Regardless of the insignificant information, you can learn something from everyone.

As a prerequisite of wisdom, you must keep an open mindset to create a win-win out of everything, even if it appears negative, unproductive, and unfruitful—grab the lesson and keep it moving in the Spirit of Excellence. You never know if the information will become your next greatest idea, platform, or leverage.

Besides, some things I write about are taken from my documented notes from 20-30 years ago that were irrelevant back then. Still, I documented them anyway out of obedience, not realizing it was the platform needed for a time such as this. For this reason, I come LOADED with WISDOM; you would never know it until I open my mouth. What is the purpose of withholding information? I do not withhold information; it is all documented, yet obediently timely in the release.

Plus, when dealing with wisdom, Divine Wisdom to be exact, humility is required. Doing so lets you know when to transfer the information and when to sit back to watch, listen, learn, and plan to hit the objective or subjective target. I am held accountable for my hit or missed targets, so I do not use the transfer of information aimlessly or for show, and neither should you.

Reflective Documenting

Reflective Documenting and Planning provides a better understanding of your customer and supplier base. When revisiting the foundation of your company keeps you from becoming rudimentary. You and your business must continue to grow positively and relevantly. What does this mean? For example, we have a company that has been around for 50 years, and they are still using a typewriter for invoices, a rotary phone to make phone calls and take orders, they do not have internet, and they handwrite receipts and checks.

Do you think this is a relevant company? For some, maybe, but for others, it is an inconvenience and a mental setback for those accustomed to ordering online, using the internet, receiving direct deposits, paying with credit cards, and not having to wait for a handwritten receipt. It behooves you to stay current and on a continued learning path in your personal and professional lives because one affects the other, primarily when operating in a contemporary deficiency when doing business.

Productivity and Performance Planning

Productivity and Performance Planning help you develop confidence in yourself, your partnership network, and your business savvy. With this being said, you are designed to produce and perform positively or negatively; therefore, you must decide which elevational process will occur on paper.

Why on paper? It becomes a personable, binding agreement with you. Then again, without an agreement, a symbolic connection is lost between you and your business. For this reason, you will find companies doing a little bit of this and that, bouncing all over the place. Whereas you will find others sticking to their vision; if something or someone does not fit into it, they reject it, period.

The most successful companies have a business plan, accepting nothing less, even if they started without one. Why did they begin without one and now require one? Is this not a double standard? They learn the value of having one, growing with one, and how important it is to follow a mission, especially when everyone's goal is to be the boss from the bottom to the top. Then again, those at the top will do anything to avoid going from the top to the bottom.

Although it may not appear to be a big deal now, try operating without a plan of action and watch how your business takes on a whole different form, positively or negatively. It may be a good thing if it is positive, but if it is negative, it could mean a downfall. Once again, PLAN. It does not need to be perfect or long, but you must begin documenting, getting the pen-to-paper methodology working on your behalf.

The Pen-to-Paper Planning

The Pen-to-Paper Planning Methodology provides a roadmap to building a solid online, personal, and social presence or referral network. You can tiptoe around this methodology, but it has been around since the BEGINNING of time.

What if we cannot write? Find someone who can write for you. You should never use this as an excuse not to document your thoughts, beliefs, desires, vision, or whatever. Even if you have been trained not to document what is in your head, it serves no purpose if it NEVER gets out, applied, or used effectively. Come on, document it, and let's get the ball rolling on building the desires of your heart.

The 'Get it Done' Planning

The 'Get it Done' Planning helps you develop an appealing customer loyalty program based on what you do, what you have done, and what you are currently doing, keeping them in the know. When you involve your employees and customers in a plan of transparency, you will find them willingly following your journey, obliging themselves to be a part of the process, or learning from you.

On the other hand, beware when you find a company hiding information, atrocities, and so on. Listen, loyal employees and customers will not leave when you are open and honest about your hiccups. Only the disloyal ones will abandon you, talk about you, or drag you through the mud. We are all subjected to err on occasion. However, documenting what you planned regarding what happened, what you are doing about it, and how you will get it done...it will make your comeback epic.

Retention Planning

Retention Planning allows you to create a customer service program based on your customers' needs, wants, and desires, or on what is trending, relevant, or from customer feedback. Your people skills are of the utmost importance when doing business, bridging the gap between where you are and where you are going. In this process, you do not want to get into the mindset of burning bridges; you must allow the bridge to burn itself.

Kindness, respect, and humility will take you where hatefulness, disrespect, and pompousness cannot keep you. For this reason, when retaining business, you should allow kindness to lead, even when unkindness is presented in unfavorable conditions.

Purposeful Planning

Purposeful Planning helps establish our product development and quality control programs. When you establish the WHY of your product or service, you can moderate it better. For example, an unlicensed business sells barbecue as their side hustle to make extra money on weekends to avoid inspection or digress from the commitment to doing business correctly. They are more apt to sell you rotten or spoiled dinners than someone who has a legitimate business, is bank-financed, and sells their unique branded recipes and sauces with professional logos, documentation, licenses, and trademarks.

Most look for quantity or the illusion of doing business, whereas I look for the quality of doing business. Unfortunately, there is a big difference. Although I may dress down when I am out and about, I look for quality, period.

Why would I dress down, especially if I am seeking quality? First, people usually look at outward appearances to determine whether you should receive quality products or services, or the lack thereof. Although you can pretend this is not happening, it is! Secondly, I need experience, judgment, and stories; therefore, I must play my role to get the information. Thirdly, my demeanor and movements are of quality, and the moment I open my mouth, my spoken words speak for themselves. Fourthly, my humility keeps Divine Wisdom flowing on my behalf as well as yours. Lastly, I do what I do for a reason, operating in my Blueprinted Purpose with no shame attached; so, I do not worry about the opinion of another, especially if they are clueless about their reason for being.

Product Planning

Product Planning assists in setting up conducive inventory and supply chain management systems and moving products from the shelf to the customer. This process keeps us from having empty shelves, being out of stock, or being overly stocked. By connecting with your product or services correctly, you can better cater to your customers' wants, needs, or desires without making them wait or running the risk of them taking their business elsewhere.

Unfortunately, loyal customers get tired of waiting for what is available right now with another company or brand, unless an initial understanding is formally established, similar to having customized products. Available products should be available to our customers or on the shelf; if not, an Estimated Time of Arrival (ETA) should be provided. Frankly, there is too much technology not to have this service available to our valuable customers. In my opinion, if self-checkout is now available, then inventory checks should be as well. Some businesses are on point, and some take this for granted as the BIG BOYS snatch their business, and rightfully so.

Why are they right in snatching business from the little man? When sitting around complaining and not relevantly upgrading, a self-induced chokehold or coma is created as customers suffer from their inadequacies, unwillingness to grow, or lack of customer service.

Should a paying customer suffer? Or, better yet, does a customer have the right to choose at their convenience? Please understand that *Business is Business*, whether you are the big or little man; thus, you must plan what you bring to the table.

In addition, we must advance with technology or get left behind with a trail of dust. Frankly, a complaint about robots or AI technology should never come into play if we have not taken the time to roboticize our hands, put pen to paper, and use what we already have in our hands.

Relational Intelligence Planning

Relational Intelligence Planning gives us a roadmap to build a solid logistics system or e-commerce platform. A roadmap in business is similar to doing a mind map, bridging our segmented thoughts together to create a whole. Even if you delegate some of the pieces, you must remain in the loop of relational intelligence. You do not want to become dumbfounded when someone takes your plan, going in the opposite direction of your heartfelt intentions, causing you to lose touch with it or develop cobwebs.

Technical Planning

Technical Planning helps you stay up-to-date with your mobile app, website, blog, marketing content, and search engine optimization. Although it can become overwhelming to keep up with the latest apps, gadgets, or whatever, you must remain in the know. In business, you may delegate this task to another; however, you must have a hands-on approach to understanding what is happening. If not, you may find yourself 'getting got' by the street-savvy techs.

Even if you think you do not have time, you do! If you take 1 hour a day to get a technical understanding, five days a week. Each month, you will have 20 hours invested; after a year, you will have 240 hours in Technical Planning. With this small investment, it will change the trajectory of your life; I am living proof! You just need to get started with a dedication to learn, grow, and document; you will thank me later.

Marketability Planning

Marketability Planning allows you to incorporate Pay-Per-Click (PPC) advertising, affiliate marketing, influencer marketing, public relations, and event marketing programs. Once again, you may outsource this planning process; however, you must get your feet wet in this area.

Although you may pay someone to do this for you, you do not want to limit your mental capacity or ability to glean information in this area. Why? You can better articulate your wants, needs, and desires, or whether you are being set up for the okey-doke. Unfortunately, some people bank on those who are unaware or unskilled in this area to get over; however, with a well-documented plan, you can understand what you are looking at and why.

Trajectorial Planning

Trajectorial Planning can help build a strong trade show presence, sponsorships, and community outreach programs. This is a great way to branch out into other areas and ways of doing business. As a rule of thumb, you are not limited to one way of doing business; there are many different ways of expanding your territory, and it is your responsibility to seek, document, and pursue, filtering what does or does not work for you, your company, or your vision.

Your Gifts, Calling, Talents, or Creativity are a personal Trajectory of Greatness, and you must create some form of movement to get your wheels turning in the right direction or to enable the training process to occur, exposing the diamond in the rough, turning it into a purposeful missile.

Reciprocal Planning

Reciprocal Planning allows you to incorporate charitable programs, share your products, engage in social responsibility services, and undergird visionary sustainability plans based on the Law of Reciprocity. When doing business in this manner, you must share, period. In your personal or professional life, you are blessed to be a blessing; therefore, you must set aside a portion to give to the underprivileged without hoarding, becoming stingy, pompous, judgmental, or ungrateful.

Incorporatory Planning

Incorporatory Planning provides a platform for employee engagement, leadership, and succession programs, building your business identity to incorporate others. When you build bonds with others, you are better able to create a safety net, leaving no one untouched by motivation, encouragement, and positivity. Even if a bad apple attempts to spoil the bunch, people will never forget how you made them feel or how you have impacted their lives for the better. For this reason, you must set the atmosphere positively, allowing the negative to weed itself out naturally.

Safe Haven Implementation Planning

Safe Haven Implementation Planning helps you assess risk, crisis, and security measures. In addition, it helps you understand and implement data privacy and legal compliance programs. When you and your employees feel safe, everyone can naturally relax, produce, and share. Some may take this for granted, but when someone is uptight, their productivity naturally decreases, as opposed to a relaxed person getting a natural environmental energy boost.

More importantly, you must plan for this to happen; if not, it will not work on its own. Why will this not work on its own? You have not set a standardized pace for it. What you plan for and document, you will attract personally, professionally, privately, and financially. On the other hand, if you are the culprit of negativity or toxicity, FIX IT!

Revenue Planning

Revenue Planning enables you to build the structure for your accounting, finance, tax, and insurance needs around your tangible income structure. Unfortunately, this is the biggest area most businesses fall short, especially when intermingling business finances with personal ones.

Initially, most businesses may use personal finances to support the business. Still, when it can sustain itself, you must pay yourself a salary using a separate account without dipping and dapping into the business finances. For this reason, you must map out an action plan to incorporate assets, liabilities, gains, and losses. You must know the difference; if not, an IRS Audit can become a hot mess for you and your company.

Brandable Planning

Brandable Planning helps you develop your consistent theme, market research, competitive analysis, product testing program, and product launch programs. When branding yourself or your company, it behooves you to document what you envision. Although you can verbally articulate it, it is also better to document it. The vibrational efforts of your spoken words may vary when written; therefore, you must master the ability to paint viable pictures of your thoughts, expectations, desires, and vision, creating ALIGNMENT.

For example, more information will flow when you speak in alignment with your Divine Blueprint. Then again, once you write it, even more will flow; therefore, you capture everything, leaving no stone unturned. For this reason, Brandable Planning is essential in your successful effort to become and remain your highest and best self.

Territorial Planning

Territorial Planning provides a documented path for product or service improvement, customer retention, or acquisition programs. Growth is extremely important when building a viable business; thus, you must plan for expansionable growth.

    For example, one business owner is okay with selling dinners out of their kitchen window. And then, we have another one, developing a plan to expand their first location to a second one, with a documented blueprint for franchising their brand. What is the difference between the two? Mindset and Planning.

Comparative Planning

Comparative Planning helps you to become strategic in your overall business strategy, paving the way to continued success. It does not matter where you are right now; get a plan together and document it, one step at a time. I was clueless when I began my journey, and now here we are. So, do not stop—keep going! If I did not have the written documentation of where I started, to compare to where I am now...I would have given up. For this reason, I do not pull any punches regarding the documentation process; I want to see it DOCUMENTED, period!

CHAPTER FOUR

Credit Portfolio

We have all types of Credit Gurus who are good at what they do. As a matter of fact, I am so grateful for them, their contributions, and their many works. However, a quick fix without understanding God's Divine Perspective can be devastating when misapplied, misappropriated, or misused. This chapter, *Credit Portfolio*, is designed to empower us with a Divine Mastery approach, breaking the internal and external limits we often do not know we possess.

In the Eye of God, when building a *Credit Portfolio* to be about His Business, it comes with multiple layers that we must understand, *As It Pleases Him*. Although this Divine Concept is nothing new, it is just forgotten Spiritual Information coming home to roost for a time such as this. Thus, we must learn the essential layers of credit along with the Spiritual Layers, bridging the two together in faith, knowledge, and understanding.

God does not want us to believe in miracles when we have not been proactively trained, when it is within our power to do so. Blasphemy, right? Wrong. If He has already given us something, we do not need a miracle to possess it. We need instructions, understanding, and know-how to possess what is already there. On the other hand, we need miracles for what is not already. Once we understand the difference, we will be better able to build a *Credit Portfolio* of Divine Mastery.

How can we misapply, misappropriate, or misuse our credit, especially with an excellent credit score? According to the Heavenly of Heavens, we must leverage a different approach to credit to ensure we possess the BALANCE needed to go to the next level, Mentally, Physically, Emotionally, Spiritually, and Financially. When our credit stops at us, without leveraging it toward our Predestined Blueprint, we can indeed operate in Spiritual Error without knowing it.

What do we need to know about credit, *As It Pleases God*? We need to know the *What, When, Where, How, Why*, and with *Whom* of what lies beneath the hidden or open issues and our overlooked charactorial habits. Why must we know the details? First, we must know what to cover with the Blood of Jesus. Secondly, we must master the ability to add the Holy Trinity to our equational efforts. Lastly, we must know what to forgive, repent, or whether we require both. All in all, in the Eye of God, it is imperative to know the underlying MOTIVES, from worldly to Spiritual and Spiritual to worldly.

What if we have excellent credit and understand how to leverage it accordingly? To God be the glory; I am so proud of the astuteness presented! However, for those desiring to be about their Father's Business, according to their Predestined Blueprint, a foundation, *As It Pleases Him*, must be established.

Why do we need a foundation as such, especially if we have free will? To open the floodgates of our Gifts, Callings, Talents, Creativity, or Genius Capabilities, we must tap into their Creator. If not, we will settle for a portion of our full potential. In my opinion, this is similar to Moses seeing the Promised Land from a distance but not being able to enter.

What caused Moses to be barred from entering? In Numbers 20:8-12, it is due to disobedience and unbelief, which are two of the prominent characteristics we are still dealing with today, causing our money to look funny, capitalizing where we have not sown, or pretending to be something we are not.

For the record, if you are fine where you are, I have no qualms at all. If you know there is more to you than what meets the eye, it is time to get God involved. Why do you need to involve God, especially when you have a degree doing what you love to do? God created your Divine Blueprint, knowing the beginning from the end. He knows precisely what you need to do, where you need to tweak, where you need to go, how to position yourself, and what walls need to be erected or torn down. Now, if you decide to include Him or not, it does not change your Divine Blueprint or what He knows about you. When you are ready, you will surrender. If not, He will wait. Remember, He is Eternal, and you are trapped in time, so you do the math!

Our unreadiness does not move God; it is all compiled training and experience getting us ready amid qualmishness. Why does He allow us to have our way? God will not violate our free will; He allows the Vicissitudes and Cycles of Life to do what they are designed to do based upon the Spiritual Law of Seedtime and Harvest. What does this have to do with us, primarily when *Business is Business*? God gives us time to consider our ways, hitting us straight in our pockets, Mentally, Physically, Emotionally, Spiritually, and Financially. Am I pulling for straws here? I do not play around with the salvation of anyone, especially those who do not know or understand Spiritual Principles.

Here is what we need to know when underlying selfishness is in the camp, *"Then the word of the LORD came by Haggai the prophet, saying, 'Is it time for you yourselves to dwell in your paneled houses, and this temple to lie in ruins?' Now therefore, thus says the LORD of hosts: 'Consider your ways!' 'You have sown much, and bring in little; You eat, but do not have enough; You drink, but you are not filled with drink; You clothe yourselves, but no one is warm; And he who earns wages, Earns wages to put into a bag with holes."* Haggai 1:3-6. Listen, He Blesses us to be a Blessing. I cannot tell you where your giveback should be; this is between you and your Heavenly Father, but I will say, 'Consider your ways.'

With or without a *Credit Portfolio*, God is steadfast and unmovable, knowing everything and considering our fruits, character, and motives. Why is He watching these things when we are doing the good works of the Lord? Doing good in public and misbehaving behind closed doors, Mentally, Physically, Emotionally, Spiritually, or Financially, will not get it, especially in the Eye of God and when being about our Father's Business. Why? We are here through His Divine Grace and Mercy by the Blood of the Lamb in Earthen Vessel, which should account for something.

In this chapter, *Credit Portfolio*, God desires for us to do a few things, but not limited to such:

- ☐ Place Him first in all areas of our lives.
- ☐ Use the Fruits of the Spirit.
- ☐ Exhibit Christlike Character.
- ☐ Cover ourselves with the Blood of Jesus.
- ☐ Repent consistently.
- ☐ Forgive quickly.
- ☐ Allow the Holy Spirit to guide us.

What is the purpose of doing all these things, especially when we are only doing business? We often find ourselves wanting more from God without giving anything back to the Kingdom.

For example, God allowed us to graduate on a wing and a prayer. Yet, we refuse to help another person freely, charge to help them out of a situation that was once binding us, or talk about them like a junkyard dog, knowing it could have been us.

How can ungratefulness cause us to forget, not to give back to the CISTERN of Divine Grace, or offer mercy to someone who needs it? Listen, if we offer help and it is rejected, we still receive Heavenly Brownie Points as if we completed the task of giving back.

On the other hand, if we choose selfishness, judgmentalism, or disobedience over acts of kindness or righteousness, we can unawaringly ruin our Bloodline, hitting our loved ones or us right in the pocket once again. Of course, we cannot save everyone, but we know when the Spirit of God leads us to do or say something, and we choose not to.

Please allow me to align: *"Thus says the LORD of hosts: 'Consider your ways! Go up to the mountains and bring wood and build the temple, that I may take pleasure in it and be glorified,' says the LORD. You looked for much, but indeed it came to little; and when you brought it home, I blew it away. Why? says the LORD of hosts. Because of My house that is in ruins, while every one of you runs to his own house. Therefore the heavens above you withhold the dew, and the earth withholds its fruit. For I called for a drought on the land and the mountains, on the grain and the new wine and the oil, on whatever the ground brings forth, on men and livestock, and on all the labor of your hands."* Haggai 1:7-11.

How does *Business is Business: As It Pleases God* apply to the labor of our hands? If we do not learn how to use what is in our hands, it will be withheld due to the lack of use, creating known or unknown limitations based upon the Spiritual Law of Use. Is this Biblical? Absolutely. The Spiritual Law of Use is hidden within the Parable of Talents in Matthew 25:14-30.

The 'Use it or lose it' cliché has been around since the Beginning of time, but the misunderstanding or mismanagement of this Divine Principle has become kryptonite for some. Why would it become kryptonite, especially when we had nothing to do with the Adam and Eve Experience? From back then until now, this is how the enemy deceives us.

Our Genetic Code cannot unknow itself unless it is manipulated or changed by a HIGHER LAW. In all simplicity, what is engrafted in our DNA already has its instructions, whether we are about our Father's Business or not. Nevertheless, here is the applicable Spiritual Decree we overlook: *"Then the LORD God said, 'Behold, the man has become like one of Us, to know good and evil. And now, lest he put out his hand and take also of the tree of life, and* eat, and live forever'—therefore the LORD God sent him out of the garden of Eden to till the ground from which he was taken." Genesis 3:22-23.

According to the Tree of Life (Blueprinted Purpose), if we do nothing, we will get nothing. Or, if we do something, in due time, we will get something, positively or negatively. So, it behooves us to incorporate the Holy Trinity in our efforts, knowing when to activate this Spiritual Law, when to fall back, and why. For this reason, let us switch gears for a minute to get an understanding of the tilling system of credit.

WHAT IS A CREDIT CARD?

A credit card is a tiny piece of plastic of compressed cash that easily fits into your wallet to make purchases. With such purchasing power from a credit system of choice, our expenditures cannot exceed a specific limit unless the credit card issuer grants unlimited spending. In so many words, based on a consumer's creditworthiness, they can borrow money from a bank or a financial institution at the drop of a dime. After doing so, the consumer can make payments to the merchants with interest, or they can pay off the balance to avoid paying interest based on the established payment terms.

To obtain a credit card with specific terms of one's liking, the consumer must complete an application establishing a conducive agreement between the credit card supplier and the customer. Once approved based on one's credit score (FICO SCORE), the credit card supplier provides the consumer with a conveyance method via credit card, with encoded security information in the form of a magnetic strip (generally located on the back of the credit card).

We want to highlight seven prominent credit card organizations in our repertoire, most of which operate in many countries worldwide. They are American Express, Citi, Diners Club, Discover, JCB, MasterCard, and VISA. Now, MasterCard, VISA, AMEX, and Discover are the most popular in the United States of America. With our unique *Business is Business* program, and when being about our Father's Business, we will also suggest these four branded cards, with a few other needed accounts, when doing business. Still, I will provide the links later.

WHY DO WE NEED CREDIT CARDS?

One would often ask, 'Why do I need credit cards? What is the purpose of having a major credit card? Can I control my spending on my own without applying for a major credit card?' First and foremost, you do not need a credit card. Possessing a credit or bank card is a privilege, and you do not have to do anything you choose not to do. If you do not look at it this way, you will tend to abuse them or lose value in them, thwarting the hidden leverage they possess. Besides, possessing a credit card is one of the quickest ways to establish credit without having a co-signer for any type of loan. Moreover, some establishments in the United States are no longer accepting cash or C.O.D. (Charge on Delivery), especially with online purchases.

Secondly, the purpose of having a credit card is to manage and leverage credit according to the society in which we live. If you think you can have what you desire without credit, you are sadly mistaken. Without credit, you will pay more for everything in the United States of America. Frankly, it will COST you not to establish credit. Why? You need credit to find a nice place to live; if not, you are forced to live with others or in a not-so-nice place, or get things in other people's names. In *Business is Business: As It Pleases God*, this same principle applies to cars, furniture, appliances, businesses, and whatever costing more than what we actually have in our pockets.

Thirdly, if you feel in control by paying more, have at it! With all due respect, being in control of our finances is done by applying wisdom. If you do not trust yourself with your finances or cannot manage your credit card debt, knowing when to spend and not to, and paying your bills on time, it is more fear than self-control. For the record, I am not here to point the finger; I am speaking from experience. Therefore, I do not want anyone to experience the setbacks associated with not knowing how to *Leverage Credit* properly, especially when being about our Father's Business.

WHAT DO I NEED TO GET A CREDIT CARD?

What you need will vary from company to company; however, you must be ready to provide your name, address, social security number, place of employment, and income, even if you have good, average, or bad credit.

However, with bad credit, you will need to provide the same information, but they may require upfront fees, which will appear on your billing statement. For this reason, before applying for any credit card, you must know your credit score before accruing an inquiry. For the record, if your credit is a little or very shaky, it is always best to apply with reputable credit card companies such as Capital One or Discover for a credit jumpstart, especially if you have been declined for unsecured ones.

Regardless of your stance, you must start somewhere...to see if you are preapproved with NO IMPACT on your credit score. Your credit score may be impacted if approved and accept the card. Click the link to get started with Capital One Credit or Discover. I am not here to twist your arm into doing anything, but if you want to start rebuilding, here is how I got restarted. If it worked for me, this process could work for you.

Once again, having a credit card is a luxury; even if you do not use cash, you have forgotten what it looks like, or you use your credit card for sanitary reasons, the demand is inevitable. The need to purchase goods or *Leverage Credit* is not going anywhere. If you do not believe me, employers now do background and credit checks when applying for menial to elite jobs.

Listen, the way society is headed, a credit score will determine our lives, and if we do not begin to master this way of living now, we are going to become left behind. *Business is Business: As It Pleases God* will provide tips and secrets about managing, leveraging, or repairing your credit and improving your credit score. However, the goal is to learn how to do it yourself.

What is the purpose of engaging in our own credit DIY? It helps to build value in having good credit by understanding its power instead of overusing or abusing it. In my opinion, engaging in the Spiritual Tilling of your credit gives you more of a reason to use it correctly.

Although every credit card company would consider itself the best, I will make suggestions based on my personal experiences for this book, *Business is Business: As It Pleases God*. Yet, it would be best if you decided for yourself as the consumer. Nonetheless, your credit history will determine where you fall on the approval scale, but you will have the information to decide what is for you and what is not.

Establishing Credit may seem daunting, but a good strategy helps. It is okay if it takes a little time to build a unique strategy for yourself, your family, or your business. Once you are equipped with the correct information and reasons why, being about your Father's Business will not be a difficult task as it becomes a lifestyle, *As It Pleases Him*. Why do we need to know this information? Please allow me to counteract this question with another: 'Are you looking for low-interest credit cards with bad credit?' Well, it is not going to happen.

When dealing with bad credit, expect high-interest rates. Simply put, High Risk, High Interest! With shaky credit, the goal is to secure a credit card, period. Then, pay the balance off monthly to avoid the high-interest charges until you build your credit portfolio.

On the other hand, with good credit, you have the pick of the litter for 0% interest for 6 to 12 months and so on, with Chase, Citi, Discover, Wells Fargo, Capital One, Bank of America, and American Express. They offer various cards, including some with unique introductory offers. However, we should not overlook what our local Credit Unions offer, such as McCoy Federal Credit Union, Navy Federal Credit Union, Alliant Credit Union, USAA Bank, and many more. Now, when the 0% interest initial period expires, you are subject to an APR (Annual Percentage Rate), which can be high or low, depending on your credit score.

How do we get started with establishing credibility? For those who are on a cash-only basis, it may work for you temporarily, but to establish credit, you must begin with the basic essential items, such as:

- ☐ You need a checking and savings account in your name. Do not overdraw your account or bounce checks. Although mistakes happen, make sure it is rectified immediately and properly documented as a mistake, not a habit.

- ☐ You need to provide a trail of credible resources, such as lights, water, cable, phone, or gas, in your name. Not having anything in your name creates an 'At Risk' customer, even if you are not. If you have a roommate, something should be in your name. If you are married, it should have both names.

Establishing yourself in such a manner helps to create a roadmap of credibility and responsibility without raising red flags. What do red flags have to do with anything? A red flag will vary from person to person and situation to situation; however, here is a question: 'Why should credit be in your name if the basic essentials of living life are not in your name?' What is the purpose of this question? Please allow me to counteract this question with another: 'What are you trying to buy if nothing is in your name?'

Suppose you dislike placing your name on something or owning anything; in this case, it is only natural to think your credit limit is free money, causing you to splurge on things you do not need. With this red flag, once your credit has been reestablished, the tendency to abuse credit is exceptionally high unless you restructure your credit strategies, patterns, or mindset.

If you do not qualify for a Visa, Mastercard, AMEX, or Discover card, you can open a gas card account with BP, ExxonMobil, Chevron, Shell, or department stores. Remember, hard inquiries will lower your credit score when doing so, so tread cautiously. In my opinion, with risky credit, you should only apply for cards with NO IMPACT on your credit score when applying. Once again, your credit score may be impacted if approved and accept the card.

If you do not qualify for anything unsecured with anyone, continue working on your credit in other ways, such as with a secured credit card, and pay your household and cell phone bills on time. If you need a prepaid card as a last resort, use BlueBird.com to avoid all the unnecessary fees. Listed below are the *Credit Portfolio* tips, but not limited to such:

- ☐ Keep monthly charges manageable within your budget.
- ☐ Buy what you can afford to pay for.
- ☐ Do not overspend.
- ☐ Please do not overdo it by getting too many credit cards, especially of the same type. Get what you need from the major players such as Visa, Mastercard, AMEX, or a Discover card for personal or business use, especially if you have good credit! With bad credit, build with one card at a time, with one year of credibility before applying for another.
- ☐ Pay the amount in full each month or keep balances below 10% of credit usage.
- ☐ Pay your bills on time.

By adhering to the guidelines above, you will eventually establish your credibility. And with time, you will qualify for an extended line of credit.

What is the Purpose of Having Credit?

Based on my educated experiences, I will share my reviews and suggestions; however, the ultimate decision is yours. Yet, if you follow my lead, I will make your credit journey easier and more sustainable, bringing you in Purpose on purpose to be about your Father's Business with the *Credit Leverage* needed to finance your Blueprinted Purpose.

In *Business is Business*, the anticipated benefits are predicated on finding what works for you. At the same time, narrowing down what fits into your lifestyle will create a win-win situation. If unsatisfied, your experiences may follow suit due to your expectations. For example, but not limited to such, if you have a credit card offering hotel stays, such as a [Hilton Honors AMEX](), and you like to shop on Amazon, this card may not be the one for you. It is better to choose [Amazon AMEX]() instead. If you like to fly, choose the [Delta SkyMiles AMEX]() or the [Free Spirit Travel]() Mastercard. If you choose your credit card around what you love to do, your passion, or your hobbies, you will find the purpose in using the credit card toward what you are already spending money on anyway. So, you may as well get something out of spending wisely to facilitate what you love or your lifestyle.

An extended line of credit is designed to help build our credit rating and portfolio, while serving as a layer of protection for emergencies. Most would consider having a credit card unfavorable, but it can only become harmful if we misuse, abuse, or refuse to pay the bill. Listen, a credit card's purpose is to extend a line of credit based on our established creditworthiness. You have the option of, but not limited to such:

- ☐ Use your credit wisely and stay free of debt.
- ☐ Abusing the card or mismanaging your credit creates a pool of debt.

Listen, you cannot overlook the benefits of having credit cards, establishing credit, or maintaining a good credit score. Whether your credit is good, bad, or indifferent, you must focus on managing or leveraging it based on realistic expectations and income. In addition, based on the type of card you have, secured cards, unsecured cards, prepaid cards, or whatever, you must know and understand what you have, the credit limit, and restrictions. If not, you will subject yourself to additional fees while missing out on cash-back rewards, reward points, airline miles, free hotel stays, merchandise, gift cards, or other bonuses, which is one of the reasons to use credit cards anyway.

Why must we attempt to build and check our credit for ourselves? It allows us to strategize and leverage our credit with an understanding of what to do and why. By depending upon someone else to do it for us, we may focus on the score alone, not the principles behind it. For example, I have come across many millionaires who have a lot of money and a good credit score, bragging about their status; yet, they never learn how to build leverage with their credit or maximize the associated benefits. Nor were they able to build sustainable business credit; at the same time, they judged those who did not have good credit. From my perspective, if we have a good credit score and have not expanded our mindsets to incorporate the why and how of our finances or have not invested in our Gifts, Callings, Talents, Purpose, or Creativity, then who are we really fooling?

According to the Heavenly of Heavens, hiding our Predestined Blueprint under a bushel or in a basket is like having bad credit in the Kingdom of God. Really? Yes, really! For this reason, we must become cautious about pointing the finger at others, especially if we have not taken the time to go from employee to employer with the resources available, doing what we are designed to do. Is any of this Biblical? I would have it no other way: "*You are the light of the world. A city that is set on a hill cannot be hidden. Nor do they light a lamp and put it under a basket, but on a lampstand, and it gives light to all who are in the house. Let your light so shine before men, that they may see your good works and glorify your Father in heaven.*" Matthew 5:14-16. For our Heaven on Earth experiences, we must govern ourselves with Kingdom Credits first, *As It Pleases God*, and then earthly credit to build Divine Leverage to be about our Father's Business.

In addition, many credit card issuers allow us to stay on top of our credit scores through their monitoring services. In my opinion, this should be one of the benefits we should look for prior to applying for a credit card. If this is not a part of the benefits, I would suggest one should look elsewhere. Nevertheless, listed below is the contact information for the three credit bureaus:

Equifax
800-685-1111
https://www.equifax.com/

Experian
888-EXPERIAN (888-397-3742)
https://www.experian.com/

Trans Union
800-916-8800
https://www.transunion.com/

With the three major credit bureaus, we can obtain our credit report to see where we stand, keep up with our credit history, keep our personal information updated, and watch out for errors. We can get one free annual report online at https://www.annualcreditreport.com/ or call 877-322-

8228. However, we do not want to wait a year to look at our credit reports, especially when it comes to our Father's Business, *As It Pleases Him*.

Another good website to have is https://www.ftc.gov/credit. It allows us to develop a DIY Mindset in leveraging our credit without paying an outside service to do what we can do for ourselves, especially if we can read.

Our FICO score will range from 300-850, determining our creditworthiness. However, this score will vary between the three agencies, depending on who reports to whom and their scoring module. Listed below are the calculations:

- ☐ Poor: 300-579
- ☐ Fair: 580-669
- ☐ Good: 670-739
- ☐ Very Good: 740-799
- ☐ Excellent: 800-850

How is our credit score calculated?

- ☐ Our payment history (on-time payments) is 35% of our score.
- ☐ Debt owed is 30% of our score.
- ☐ Length of credit history is 15% of our score.
- ☐ New credit (newly opened credit card accounts or hard inquiries) is 10% of our score.
- ☐ The type of credit (mix of credit, such as car, house, and credit cards) is 10% of our score.

Most would take credit calculations for granted, but they play a vital role in our creditworthiness, regardless of how we think, feel, or believe. So, it is conducive to strategizing accordingly to achieve the desired results, saving us money in the long run. Here is what we should try to avoid:

- ☐ Late payments.
- ☐ Overuse of credit.
- ☐ Applying for too many unnecessary accounts. We need the right mix of credit card accounts.
- ☐ Accounts in collection.
- ☐ Bankruptcy.

- ☐ Do not write bad checks or owe the bank money. If a mistake has happened or we become blacklisted due to some form of theft, we can resolve it through ChexSystems.com (Consumer Reporting Agency).
- ☐ Getting a Judgment or Lien.

Whether we choose a monitoring service or do it ourselves, we must learn the ins and outs of our *Credit Portfolio*. What does this mean? We need to know what we are looking at and what it means, ensuring we are not falling for credit gibberish or becoming easy prey to excessive fees, identity theft, and creditor abuse. Most would think creditor abuse is not real, but it is. To avoid fraudulent reports to our *Credit Portfolio*, we must become acquainted with what is on our credit report and what is not, instead of outsourcing it.

What if we do not have time to monitor our credit cards? We can set up alerts by signing up for an account through Equifax, Experian, TransUnion, or our credit card accounts. Once again, most credit card companies are offering this free service, so it behooves one to take advantage of it. Plus, this free service on our account gives us information on how to build our credit with all types of valuable information.

What do we need to look for when receiving alerts? We must take heed to any suspicious activity, such as, but not limited to:

- ☐ New credit card accounts or loans.
- ☐ Inquiries.
- ☐ Negative reports or activity.
- ☐ Legal actions.
- ☐ Medical bills.
- ☐ Judgments or liens.

If our identity is stolen, here is what we must do, but not limited to such:

- ☐ File a police report.
- ☐ Contact the fraud department at Experian, Equifax, and TransUnion.
- ☐ Notify creditors of the crime.
- ☐ File a complaint with the Federal Trade Commission (FTC).

One may be covered for fraudulent use of credit or debit cards on their homeowner's or renter's insurance policy. So, please double-check the available coverage or review the policy with the agent. As with any application you fill out or the reason for its use, ensure you read the fine print and associated fees to avoid signing off on something you will regret later. For this reason, in *Business is Business: As It Pleases God*, when managing your *Proactive Family Portfolio*, or when being about your Father's Business, I will share the *What, When, Where, How, Why*, and with *Whom* of leveraging to bring you in Purpose on purpose.

The Power of Credit In The Eye of God

When we think about credit, we often think about the power of plastic, what we can buy with it, or how much our bills are, not giving a second thought about the Creator of it all. According to the Heavenly of Heavens, we have Mental Credit, Physical Credit, Emotional Credit, Spiritual Credit, and Financial Credit, to name a few.

If one does not think this is real, then what about Divine Grace, Mercy, and Repentance? Not to mention the Blood of Jesus, it is the most proactive form of CREDIT known to man; if not, we would not exist in our folly without making animal sacrifices. Nor would we have the Holy Spirit at our beck and call...a Spiritual Credit our Forefathers did not have access to, but fought for us to have. Then, what do we do for the Spiritual Privilege of this magnitude? We do not use it, abuse it, become selfish, or overspend without paying the price to glean the benefits. Or, we weaponize worldly credit to oppress, use, and abuse others, with God nowhere in the equational efforts.

Let us talk for a moment on behalf of the Ancient of Days. "*Thus says the LORD: 'Where is the certificate of your mother's divorce, Whom I have put away? Or which of My creditors is it to whom I have sold you? For your iniquities you have sold yourselves, And for your transgressions your mother has been put away. Why, when I came, was there no man? Why, when I called, was there none to answer? Is My hand shortened at all that it cannot redeem? Or have I no power to deliver? Indeed with My rebuke I dry up the sea, I make the rivers a wilderness; Their fish stink because there is no water, And die of thirst. I clothe the heavens with blackness, And I make sackcloth their covering.' 'The Lord GOD has given Me The tongue of the learned, That I should know how to speak A word in season to him who is weary. He awakens Me morning by morning, He awakens My ear To hear as the learned. The Lord GOD has opened My ear;*

And I was not rebellious, Nor did I turn away. I gave My back to those who struck Me, And My cheeks to those who plucked out the beard; I did not hide My face from shame and spitting. For the Lord GOD will help Me; Therefore I will not be disgraced; Therefore I have set My face like a flint, And I know that I will not be ashamed." Isaiah 50:1-7.

Credit is a form of recognition, which is why we use the FICO score as a symbolic tool stating we have arrived. Now, if this is what one is looking for, then so be it. In the Kingdom, God is looking for BALANCE of the Mind, Body, Soul, and Spirit with the overflow into Divine Provisions, financing our reason for being and being about our Father's Business. In so many words, we cannot stop at our credit score; God is bigger than this! We need LEVERAGE.

For example, we work hard to get and sustain a 750 or better FICO score, only to do what? Is it only to show off material gain? Are you putting it to work for the Divine Blueprint hidden within you? Are you building a Legacy, outliving yourself? Are you showing others how to do likewise, *As It Pleases God*? Are you being about your Father's Business?

To develop influence in such a manner, we must understand that everything in life has a system or flow attached, and the workflow of doing business or your finances is no different. Do not take my word for it; let us interject scripture, *"He who is faithful in what is least is faithful also in much; and he who is unjust in what is least is unjust also in much. Therefore if you have not been faithful in the unrighteous mammon, who will commit to your trust the true riches? And if you have not been faithful in what is another man's, who will give you what is your own?"* Luke 16:10-12.

The rule of thumb here is RESPECT. When we take the time to respect ourselves and others, Mentally, Physically, Emotionally, Spiritually, and Financially, God will begin to trust us with the Treasures, Wisdom, Secrets, and Powers of the Kingdom. Until then, we are limited, and if we go to the dark side to possess what we do not have the Spiritual Authority to possess, generational curses and yokes could follow. So, beware!

In managing the profound ingredients of *Business is Business: As It Pleases God*, He will test us with worldly means first. If we cannot manage it from an earthly standpoint, we become limited with Kingdom Assets until we are adequately trained, molded, tested, and commissioned.

Listen, just because we can quote scriptures, articulate the Word of God, and attend church on Sunday, it does not mean we are adequately seasoned for Kingdom Purposes according to our Predestined Blueprint. Nor does it mean we can be about our Father's Business, *As It Pleases Him.*

Unfortunately, this is why worldly individuals appear to have more than those sold out to God Almighty. What does this mean for us as Believers? Worldly individuals have mastered Kingdom Principles to oppress those who have not taken the time to understand, learn, or use them, *As It Pleases God*. And then we wonder why they do not respect churchgoers or why we deal with so much church hurt!

The onlookers are watching to see if we will practice or live by what we preach, all hidden within our FRUITS and CHARACTER. Pay attention; the moment we get a little money or power, we tend to start acting funny, mistreating others, or swinging it high and low as if God is not watching. More importantly, the Spirit of Judgment has a way of coming upon us, causing us to associate people, places, and things with specific colors, clothes, where they live, status, or whatever, to determine their level of righteousness or the lack thereof. All of which have nothing to do with FRUITS or CHARACTER!

When we call a good person evil and an evil person good, passing judgment, we set ourselves up for a rude awakening. At the same time, the wolf in sheep's clothing is laughing at us with a straight face, boxing us into a system of control. How can this happen, especially when we are Believers trusting in God Almighty? When we have not MASTERED the ability to Spiritually See what is right before our eyes or exercise our sense of Spiritual Discernment, we will 'get got' by what we did not see coming.

The moment we find ourselves always 'getting got,' we must check our system Mentally, Physically, Emotionally, Spiritually, and Financially. Why? Playing clean-up is not Kingdomly; PROACTIVENESS is. For example, after 'getting got,' an individual asks someone for help to resolve a messy situation. Out of the kindness of this person's heart, they agreed to help. Only to have this same individual face 'getting got' again due to the lack of Spiritual Discernment while pretending to be wise.

To add insult to injury, amid receiving the much-needed help, they turn around to imply that the Spirit of Darkness binds this good person who is exhibiting the Fruits of the Spirit and Christlike Character, offering them no credit or thanks whatsoever. While simultaneously thinking the Angel of Darkness is their knight in shining armor and their ray of light, getting all the credit, thanks, and accolades while exhibiting rotten fruit and worldly character. As the good person sits back, watches, and shakes their head in dismay.

Why would the good person shake their head in dismay? They can discern what is taking place, knowing the perceived ray of light is setting them up for a takeover to capitalize on a weakness. How can the good person discern this? They watch the person possessing the Spirit of

Darkness get everyone who asks questions out of the way. How? By badmouthing or blocking them to corner the market and eliminate the fallback options for those needing help. Unfortunately, this happens when we do not prepare, do not do our homework, rush into things, omit a plan of action, leave God out of the equation while pretending as if He is in it, or outright lie on Him.

Spiritual Juice

As Believers, we must allow the Holy Spirit to guide us wholeheartedly. If we pick on people because of tangible items or their preferences, it is NOT the Holy Spirit, period. Everyone is created differently for a reason, and if we do not RESPECT their differences, especially when asking for help, it is best to seek help elsewhere. Listen to me, and listen well; the Holy Spirit deals with FRUITS, CHARACTER, and MOTIVES. According to the Heavenly of Heavens, this is a quick way to lose CREDIBILITY in the Kingdom of God.

Power, money, status, and sex will do it to us every time if we are not adequately rooted Mentally, Physically, Emotionally, Spiritually, and Financially, *As It Pleases God*. In my opinion, most of our tests will surround power, money, and sex, seeded by the lust of the eyes, the lusts of the flesh, and the pride of life. Why would God tempt us? It determines our savory or tartness and our ability to self-correct or repent. More importantly, it governs our ability to take the Fruits of the Spirit to make Spiritual Juice out of our seeds or the yielding Tree of Life from within us. Is any of this Biblical? Of course, on the third day, here is what happened: *"Then God said, 'Let the earth bring forth grass, the herb that yields seed, and the fruit tree that yields fruit according to its kind, whose seed is in itself, on the earth'; and it was so. And the earth brought forth grass, the herb that yields seed according to its kind, and the tree that yields fruit, whose seed is in itself according to its kind. And God saw that it was good."* Genesis 1:11-13.

If we consider ourselves a part of this earth, this Spiritual Principle also applies to us, and every cell of our being gives us the RIGHT to use it. On the other hand, if we do not know this Spiritual Principle or Seal, or if we are not from this earth, then we cannot enforce it. Here is the Spiritual Contingency Clause: *"You shall not revile God, nor curse a ruler of your people. You shall not delay to offer the first of your ripe produce and your juices. The firstborn of your sons you shall give to Me."* Exodus 22:28-29.

Why do we need *Spiritual Juice*? In contrast, *Spiritual Juice* is similar to a Spiritual Swig of Honey, but a more potent concoction served with

Spiritual Meat (the Word of God) and Spiritual Sauce (the Anointing). According to the Heavenly of Heavens, serving *Spiritual Juice* when being about our Father's Business ensures His sheep do not choke on our character or motives. What does this mean in layman's terms? God knows which Fruit of the Spirit is needed for His sheep's palatability without us having to play guessing roulette.

From the Ancient of Days, to avoid the guessing roulette propaganda, it is imperative to stray away from Spiritual Milk to a *Spirit to Spirit* Relationship with our Heavenly Father. In my opinion, this is similar to having a Spiritual Meaty love affair, seeking the Hand of God in all things, including doing business. Please allow me to align: *"Oh, that you were like my brother, Who nursed at my mother's breasts! If I should find you outside, I would kiss you; I would not be despised. I would lead you and bring you Into the house of my mother, She who used to instruct me. I would cause you to drink of spiced wine, Of the juice of my pomegranate. His left hand is under my head, And his right hand embraces me. I charge you, O daughters of Jerusalem, Do not stir up nor awaken love Until it pleases."* Song of Solomon 8:1-4.

Why must we engage in a *Spirit to Spirit* love affair to extract our *Spiritual Juices* from the Fruits of the Spirit? We need the Holy Trinity involved in using the Spiritual Fruits properly, *As It Pleases God*, and not as it pleases us. Once we can squeeze the *Spiritual Juices* out of the Fruits of the Spirit, the *Power of Credit*, Mentally, Physically, Emotionally, Spiritually, and Financially, makes us a POWERHOUSE in the Eye of God, putting our Christlike Character on automatic.

How can we become a Divine Powerhouse using our *Spiritual Juices*? When we become Spirit-Led, being about our Father's Business, our Spiritual Eyes, Ears, and Tongue are awakened to the Voice of God. For example, when using the Fruits of the Spirit, some may need love as opposed to peace, and vice versa. Then again, someone may need them all; who knows, besides the Holy Spirit, right? Of course.

In all reality, when being about our Father's Business, *As It Pleases Him*, we sometimes do not know what we need until the Holy Spirit reveals it. Here is the deal: We must know what the Fruits of the Spirit are and their opposite. For example, but not limited to such:

- ☐ The opposite of Love is Hate.
- ☐ The opposite of Joy is Hopelessness.
- ☐ The opposite of Peace is Chaos and Confusion.
- ☐ The opposite of Patience is Impatience or Irritability.

- ☐ The opposite of Kindness is Unkindness or Cruelness.
- ☐ The opposite of Goodness is Rottenness, Evilness, or Foulness.
- ☐ The opposite of Faithfulness is Unfaithfulness or Doubtfulness.
- ☐ The opposite of Gentleness is Abrasiveness.
- ☐ The opposite of Self-Control is Disobedience.

In addition to knowing the opposites, we need the Holy Spirit to let us know what is needed, when to hold, when to fold, or the moment we need to walk away, keeping our *Spiritual Juices* to ourselves.

Whether we are dealing with a Swig of Honey, our *Spiritual Juices*, or that Spiritual Sauce, the 'hit or miss' mentality is not Kingdom Protocol. How can we miss the mark if we are Believers? First, it happens all the time when we do not repentantly cover ourselves with the Blood of Jesus. Secondly, when we do not operate under the Spiritual Anointing of the Holy Spirit to lead, guide, and provide, we will unawaringly operate in Spiritual Error. Thirdly, if we do not master the ability to counteract negativity with positivity, we will find ourselves getting a little tart, stale, dull, or unpalatable. Lastly, when we are not being about our Father's Business, putting ourselves above Him due to the lack of humility or selfishness.

Even if we think we have it going on, especially on paper or in the mind, when operating in Spiritual Error or Omission, we will not be able to place Spiritual Seals properly, *As It Pleases God*. As a result, it affects our fruits and character. Really? Yes, really. Here is a scripture painting a viable picture: *"Set me as a seal upon your heart, As a seal upon your arm; For love is as strong as death, Jealousy as cruel as the grave; Its flames are flames of fire, A most vehement flame. Many waters cannot quench love, Nor can the floods drown it. If a man would give for love All the wealth of his house, It would be utterly despised."* Song of Solomon 8:6-7.

For example, have you ever encountered someone hitting you over the head or bullying you with the Word of God, at the same time, their attitude, demeanor, or delivery sucks with condescending arrogance or judgment? I know I have. With all due respect, if the Holy Spirit did not reveal my Spiritual Status to them, nor will I. However, it does leave room for extreme questioning or Spiritual Unsealing (becoming unglued) to occur within the human psyche. Why would this happen? Spirit knows Spirit, even if we do not know we are Spiritual Beings having a human experience!

Kingdom Levels

In the Kingdom of God, there are LEVELS, regardless of whether we understand them or not. If one is not trained appropriately or does not have home training, they will miss the mark every single time, offering disrespect where there needs to be respect. In my opinion, this is similar to disrespecting the SITTING President of the United States of America. Even if we disagree with him, RESPECT is a must as a Spiritual Decree from the Heavens Above!

For me, the lack of RESPECT lets me know there is *Something Else* operating. Frankly, aside from my experiences, it is a turnoff, mainly when they leave all types of ROTTEN FRUITS behind in the Name of God, Jesus, or the Holy Spirit. While simultaneously being convinced they are right in their own eyes or using power, money, and sex as leverage with zero knowledge about the Fruits of the Spirit, Christlike Character, or Spiritual Seals. What does the Bible say about this? Here is what I want to point out: *"Dead flies putrefy the perfumer's ointment, And cause it to give off a foul odor; So does a little folly to one respected for wisdom and honor. A wise man's heart is at his right hand, But a fool's heart at his left. Even when a fool walks along the way, He lacks wisdom, And he shows everyone that he is a fool."* Ecclesiastes 10:1-3.

Why are we considered fools, especially if we are good at managing money, lacking nothing? Unfortunately, this is not my call; I am just the Messenger! For this type of query, we must have a *Spirit to Spirit* Relationship with our Heavenly Father to DOCUMENT instructions, correction, guidance, or advice.

I will admit that God is looking for BALANCE with the use of the Fruits of the Spirit while operating with Christlike Character. Moreover, He takes special note of a repenting and forgiving heart, not perfection, especially when managing or appropriating Kingdom Business. Or when engaging in our Divine Blueprint using our Gifts, Callings, Talents, or Creativity, and being about our Father's Business. How do we make this make sense? If we use the Holy Trinity, the Fruits of the Spirit, and Christlike Character, we will be taught Kingdom Principles by default in the most beneficial Spiritual Classroom.

In reality, God-Chosen training will supersede self-chosen training any day of the week, primarily if we continue to do good and are patient with the process. Please allow me to align two Spiritual Principles:

1. *"For what credit is it if, when you are beaten for your faults, you take it patiently? But when you do good and suffer, if you take it patiently, this is commendable before God."* 1 Peter 2:20.

2. *"For you were like sheep going astray, but have now returned to the Shepherd and Overseer of your souls."* 1 Peter 2:25.

What if we are being used amid capitalizing on Spiritual Principles, the Fruits of the Spirit, or exhibiting Christlike Character? We will all face this issue; however, we cannot allow ourselves to become users. How can we avoid becoming a user? Listed below are a few ways, but not limited to such:

- ☐ Keep a positive mindset.
- ☐ Use the Fruits of the Spirit.
- ☐ Exhibit Christlike Character.
- ☐ Place God first in all things.
- ☐ Develop a *Spirit to Spirit* Relationship with your Heavenly Father.
- ☐ Cover yourself with the Blood of Jesus.
- ☐ Allow the Holy Spirit to work, whatever it is or is not, in your favor.
- ☐ Document instructions, lessons, scriptures, questions, answers, revelations, and so on as a Testament to give back to the Kingdom later, or when the timing is right.
- ☐ Become grateful for everything, regardless of how it appears to the naked eye.

Why do we need to document to avoid becoming users? It is in our nature to forget, especially the good, when something terrible happens. As Believers, even if we can remember everything, we must position ourselves to document, document, document, writing what God tells us to write.

Before moving out of the *Credit Portfolio*, please allow me to explain why we must document: *"I will stand my watch And set myself on the rampart, And watch to see what He will say to me, And what I will answer when I am corrected. Then the LORD answered me and said: 'Write the vision And make it plain on tablets, That he may run who reads it." For the vision is yet for an appointed time; But at the end it will speak, and it will not lie. Though it tarries, wait for it; Because it will surely come, It will not tarry."* Habakkuk 2:1-3.

Kingdom Brownie Points

In being about my Father's Business, if I did not take the time to document this information, *As It Pleased Him*, do you think you would be reading it right now in *Business is Business*? Well, you are no different. You are here for a reason; every experience means something, and you are designed to share what life teaches you. You never know who may need what you have to offer; therefore, it behooves you to extend your TESTIMONIAL CREDITS to another. From me to you, take your Kingdom Brownie Points without spilling them on the ground as if they have no value; besides, you earned them.

Are Kingdom Brownie Points considered works? Of course! However, the difference resides in the work for selfish or righteous reasons. In short, it is whether we are trying to prove something to a man for show, as opposed to WORKS for the Kingdom of God. Does it really make a difference in the Eye of God? Absolutely. He weighs our heart postures.

In light of my faithfulness, I want every piece of Credit or Brownie Points I can get, especially when needing something money cannot buy. Regardless of the need, I am the first to open my hand to give seeds that money cannot buy, which are commonly hidden in the Spiritual Seals from the Ancient of Days we often overlook or take for granted.

Before moving on to Spiritual Seals, let me clear the air. Those saying works do not count when serving God, *As It Pleases Him*, are spreading false propaganda. Why would they do such a thing? To get us to sit on our hands, doing nothing, squander our Blessings, turn on ourselves, or curse our own hands. Once again, God deals with MOTIVES. So, let us align this from His Divine Perspective, *"What does it profit, my brethren, if someone says he has faith but does not have works? Can faith save him? If a brother or sister is naked and destitute of daily food, and one of you says to them, 'Depart in peace, be warmed and filled,' but you do not give them the things which are needed for the body, what does it profit? Thus also faith by itself, if it does not have works, is dead. But someone will say, 'You have faith, and I have works.' Show me your faith without your works, and I will show you my faith by my works."* James 2:14-18.

We need faith, and we also need to do something about it. Faith will not work itself if we do not till the ground, giving it the Tree of Life or an opportunity to bear much-needed or good fruit. For example, a tree cannot stand without its rooting system. An ocean, river, stream, lake, or creek cannot remain without water. We cannot live without blood and oxygen flowing through the body.

After all, our faith needs life; we are the life-giver or destroyer. On this note, here are a few lifesaving Spiritual Seals needed when attempting to gain Divine Access to Heavenly Wisdom, Treasures, Secrets, and Revelations, but not limited to such:

- ☐ *"But I say to you who hear: Love your enemies, do good to those who hate you."* Luke 6:27.
- ☐ *"Bless those who curse you, and pray for those who spitefully use you."* Luke 6:28.
- ☐ *"To him who strikes you on the one cheek, offer the other also. And from him who takes away your cloak, do not withhold your tunic either."* Luke 6:29.
- ☐ *"Give to everyone who asks of you. And from him who takes away your goods do not ask them back."* Luke 6:30.
- ☐ *"And just as you want men to do to you, you also do to them likewise."* Luke 6:31.

Why is this so hard to do? It becomes challenging when we do not know the Spiritual Laws, Principles, and Concepts. In addition, it becomes more complex when we do not use the Fruits of the Spirit, Christlike Character, usher in the Blood of Jesus, or allow the Holy Spirit to guide us. Here is the reason God is calling us to a higher standard to earn our Spiritual Credits or *Brownie Points*:

- ☐ *"But if you love those who love you, what credit is that to you? For even sinners love those who love them."* Luke 6:32.
- ☐ *"And if you do good to those who do good to you, what credit is that to you? For even sinners do the same."* Luke 6:33.
- ☐ *"And if you lend to those from whom you hope to receive back, what credit is that to you? For even sinners lend to sinners to receive as much back."* Luke 6:34.

When it is all said and done, our rewards come from God. He may use people as Spiritual Vessels to get our BLESSINGS to us, so we cannot limit Him or tell Him how. Remember this, *"Love your enemies, do good, and lend, hoping for nothing in return; and your reward will be great, and you will be sons of the Most High. For He is kind to the unthankful and evil."* Luke 6:35. When doing business or being about our Father's Business, *As It Pleases Him*, here is what we must know, but not limited to such:

- ☐ Be merciful, just as your Father also is merciful.
- ☐ Judge not, and you shall not be judged.
- ☐ Condemn not, and you shall not be condemned.
- ☐ Forgive, and you will be forgiven.
- ☐ Give, and it will be given to you: good measure, pressed down, shaken together, and running over will be put into your bosom.

Why do we need to know this? Based upon this extraction from Luke 6:36-38, *"For with the same measure that you use, it will be measured back to you."* Therefore, when doing business, it is only wise to use Spiritual Principles to ensure we are not using diverse measures. What do diverse measures have to do with anything? Unbeknown to most, Proverbs 20:10-11 says, *"Diverse weights and diverse measures, They are both alike, an abomination to the LORD. Even a child is known by his deeds, Whether what he does is pure and right."* So, in weighing things out Mentally, Physically, Emotionally, Spiritually, and Financially, you must know the type of worldly credit you are using or have access to, such as:

- ☐ Debit Credit Cards.
- ☐ Standard Credit Cards, like Balance Transfer Credit Cards.
- ☐ Low-Interest Credit Cards.
- ☐ Credit Cards with Reward Programs (Airline Miles, Cash Back, Hotel Stays, Gift Cards, and Merchandise).
- ☐ Secured Credit Cards.
- ☐ Prepaid Debit or Credit Cards.
- ☐ Specialty Credit Cards.
- ☐ Business Credit Cards.
- ☐ Student Credit Cards.
- ☐ Line of Credit, Personal and Business Credit Cards.
- ☐ Non-Traditional Credit.

What is the purpose of knowing this information? You need to know where to build leverage and with whom. When we are all Kingdom and no earthly good, we create a disservice to ourselves and others. Why? If all we have is a scripture with zero skills, talents, or know-how, it is not what God had in mind for us, and it becomes challenging to be about our Father's Business without a *Credit Portfolio*. Why? It reveals the MINDSET of the individual without saying one word. Plus, walking around ill-equipped for our Predestined Blueprint is embarrassing, especially when we must PREPARE with what we already have.

Kingdom Mentality

Listen, God prepared the Children of Israel to up the ante on their skills by placing them in Egypt, allowing them to break their tent-making mentality (the mind of instability or few skills), and building on credit. In time, it allowed them to become builders with many skills, with the OPTION to break the slave mentality before taking what was owed to them when exiting Egypt.

What does a Kingdom Mentality have to do with anything, particularly when they were enslaved? First, the Children of Israel knew who they were working with. Secondly, they knew they were Chosen. What about you? Do you know what you are working with? Do you have the faith to take back what is owed to you? Do you have the tenacity to make an EXIT Mentally, Physically, Emotionally, Spiritually, and Financially from where you are to your NEXT?

As a part of being about our Father's Business, bringing individuals in Purpose on purpose with their Divine Blueprint in hand, we must grab our Egyptian Gold. What does this mean? When doing business *As It Pleases God* in our Egypt, Desert, or Promised Land Experiences, the *Power of Credit* is our Liquid Gold. Therefore, we must prepare to possess a part of what rightly belongs to us, financing our Blueprinted Journey into Greatness.

The most popular Liquid Gold UNSECURED credit cards include Chase, Citi, Capital One, American Express, Discover, Bank of America, and Wells Fargo. The SECURED credit cards are Citi, Capital One, and Discover. What is a secured credit card? In the rebuilding process, this is where you deposit money into an account, and the creditor leverages a credit limit against the amount.

Capitalizing on the *Power of Credit* is not designed to place one credit card over another; it is about choosing what is best for our Spiritual Journey. For example, having an American Express card is more highly respected than whipping out a prepaid credit card. Why? American Express has branded its motto for us not to leave home without it, building impactful leverage and security within the human psyche. Meanwhile, with a prepaid card, it has programmed us with boxed-in limits, advising us to load our card proactively before using it! Both determine our level of self-control or the lack thereof, providing a means to an end.

If one is this far along in this book, one already knows the goal is to build leverage with our Liquid Gold to finance the Vision, Promise, or Blueprint.

With this in mind, let me explain Liquid Gold for a minute. The LIQUID is considered a flowing substance, and the GOLD is considered our Divine Treasure from the Beginning, after God formed man in Genesis 2:7.

As we overlook this valuable commodity, please allow me to share the Liquid Gold, bridging the gap from back then to now. "*Now a river went out of Eden to water the garden, and from there it parted and became four riverheads. The name of the first is Pishon; it is the one which skirts the whole land of Havilah, where there is gold. And the gold of that land is good. Bdellium and the onyx stone are there. The name of the second river is Gihon; it is the one which goes around the whole land of Cush. The name of the third river is Hiddekel; it is the one which goes toward the east of Assyria. The fourth river is the Euphrates.*" Genesis 2:10-14. The liquidity of every river of GOLD is already there; it is just a matter of locating it or them. Some may have names, directions, or places; thus, it is our responsibility to determine which one or whether we are privy to tapping into all of the above.

While breathing the Breath of Life, God requires us to flow and multiply our treasures in Earthen Vessel. How do we go about doing so? We must tap into the flow of something or someone bigger than us. Listen, if we flow or multiply by zero, we will constantly get zero (nothing), while remaining in the same place with little or no growth. To be clear, I am not calling anyone a zero; I am referring to zero seeds, zero action, zero progression, zero desire, zero tilling, zero creativity, and so on.

To build a *Credit Portfolio* properly, we do not want the one-off brand credit, unless we are working on our credit to possess the Liquid Gold or rebuilding it. Is credit not credit? Yes, credit is credit, and *Business is Business*. The way we do business is not created equal, nor is it for the faint of heart. When a company brands its name and reputation among the Elites, it behooves us to follow suit and build leverage, creating Liquid Gold for the Kingdom, becoming the Tree of Life for another, and building a *Proactive Family Portfolio*.

Chapter Five

Proactive Family Portfolio

Whether we are pro-family or anti-family, whether they like or dislike us, or whether we think we deserve a better one, family is family in the same way that *Business is Business!* God chose our families for a reason, and if we ignore the reason, then who can we blame? According to the Heavenly of Heavens, our Predestined Bloodline is designed for us to learn, grow, and sow back into the Kingdom, making every generation better than the previous.

How do we become better in the Eye of God? Through the POWER of our Testimony or Testament. If we find ourselves digressing in this formality, we have work to do in our *Proactive Family Portfolio*.

Just so we are crystal clear before moving on, God does not make mistakes, nor is any family totally perfect. There will always be a learning curve guiding us toward or away from the Kingdom based upon our free will choices. Listen, Bloodline is Bloodline regardless of whether we understand it or not, but there will always be hidden Lessons of many Blessings.

For example, God said to Abram (now called Abraham), "*Get out of your country, from your family and from your father's house, to a land that I will show you. I will make you a great nation; I will bless you and make your name great; and you shall be a blessing. I will bless those who bless you, and I will curse him who curses you; and in you all the families of the earth shall be blessed.*" Genesis 12:1-3. Are we not still living in the Blessings? Do we think God lied to him? Please allow me to answer this question with a scripture from this same Spiritual Covenant: "*God is not a man, that He should lie, Nor a son of man, that He should repent. Has He said, and will He not do? Or has He spoken, and will He not make it good? Behold, I have received a command to bless; He has blessed, and I cannot reverse it.*" Numbers 23:19-20. However, we must know this beyond a shadow of a doubt; if not, we can turn on ourselves without knowing it due to varying forms of Spiritual Blindness, Deafness, or Muteness.

How can we turn on ourselves, especially when living our best lives? The best life is a matter of opinion, predicated on our fruits, character, and motives. Why is it a matter of opinion? If our true Blessings appear as curses, we are wreaking havoc in the lives of others, we cannot recognize the difference between good and evil or positive and negative, or we cannot extract the win-win out of seeming defeat; we have work to do.

Suppose a parent cannot recognize their child's Giftings, Calling, Creativity, or Anointing, nor take the time to facilitate their expression of them. In this case, they have work to do as well. Why would they have work to do? Most often, if we cannot recognize something in our child, more than likely, we have overlooked the same traits within ourselves that our parents overlooked within us. All of these create a cycle of déjà vu in the Bloodline from a Mental, Physical, Emotional, Spiritual, or Financial perspective.

When being about our Father's Business, *As It Pleases Him*, if we engross ourselves in our Divine Blueprint with outright gratefulness, it will change the trajectory of our lives. How? It gives us the willpower to move forward in the Spirit of Excellence, uncovering what most overlook, releasing what most hold back, and thinking thoughts most are clueless about.

As parents, we believe in training our children in the way they should go according to Proverbs 22:6. But why are we missing out on training the Bloodline about credit building, leveraging, and maintenance? In my opinion, in certain cultures, we take our credit or financial portfolios for granted, not realizing the implications of not understanding our credit's true purpose, relevance, and how to leverage it accordingly. But of course, we all dream of owning homes, new cars, and taking our dream vacations, not realizing all of them will cost us something now or later.

Plus, this is where the enemy usually gains entry into our lives with an open invitation hidden under *Something Else*. Really? Yes, really! Is any of this Biblical? Here is what the Bible says, "*You shall teach them to your children, speaking of them when you sit in your house, when you walk by the way, when you lie down, and when you rise up. And you shall write them on the doorposts of your house and on your gates, that your days and the days of your children may be multiplied in the land of which the LORD swore to your fathers to give them, like the days of the heavens above the earth.*" Deuteronomy 11:19-21.

What if our children do not listen? If they have a deaf ear to us, we must find another way of communicating in their language, or we must master how to creatively share information on their level while living by example.

The bottom line is that communication is needed. The moment we cease communication with whomever we are in relations with, including family members, we leave an open door for the enemy to penetrate plots and plans of deceptive measures or embed hypocritical facades. At the same time, we avoid having tough conversations about finances, debts, spending habits, responsibility, and benefits, sweeping all of it under the rug as if the debt is not coming back to clean house. How do I know? Proverbs 13:22 says two things will happen:

1. A good man leaves an inheritance to his children's children.
2. The wealth of the sinner is stored up for the righteous.

Whether we are about our Father's Business or not, we decide which category we fit into. What is the purpose of deciding? According to scripture, *"Every kingdom divided against itself is brought to desolation, and every city or house divided against itself will not stand."* Matthew 12:25. If we think for a minute that this does not apply to our finances, we are sadly mistaken. Remember, the goal is to multiply, not divide! If one VALUES their family, home, or Bloodline, it is best not to divide it Mentally, Physically, Emotionally, Spiritually, or Financially.

Unfortunately, with all due respect, worldly individuals have mastered these Spiritual Principles while Believers lag behind in their efforts. To say the least, those who break free of the poverty chokehold usually learn their financial or credit-leveraging from individuals who want nothing to do with the Kingdom of God. Still, for some reason, the Believer who gleaned this information from a worldly system hoards these valuable principles from others to appear better, stronger, and wiser while pretending to be a brother's keeper.

Why is financial or credit-leveraging so important in or out of the Kingdom of God? Suppose we master the ability to leverage our credit and manage our finances. In this case, we can capitalize on low-interest rates on our purchases. We can also indulge in great reward programs to cover other things such as vacations, hotel expenses, airline tickets, and so on, freeing up money to invest in our Gifts, Callings, Talents, Creativity, and Purpose.

Turning worldly benefits inwardly, *As It Pleases God*, builds accountability and stewardship, allowing Him to trust us with Divine Provisions. More importantly, teaching and preparing our children to teach their children keeps the inheritance cycle going in a positive direction.

As a word to the WISE, if we were to show Believers how to tap into their Spiritual Reservoir or Divine Provisions, do we not know the underlying streams would eventually flow back to the Kingdom? Yet, we want whatever we want on the front end, not realizing the back end is where the treasures are. Unbeknown to most, the RIGHT NOW Blessings are not as powerful as the ones we wait on, prepare for, nurture, and put in the necessary work to obtain, sustain, and maintain, *As It Pleases God*.

In the same way that we say, 'We cannot beat God giving no matter how hard we try,' is why we should understand, 'We cannot beat God's Divine Teachings no matter how hard we try.' As Believers, the 'Each one helps another mindset' opens up our Spiritual Negev (the hidden water in the desert). Really? Yes, Really!

Here is the Spiritual Seal: *"And the LORD said to Abram, after Lot had separated from him: 'Lift your eyes now and look from the place where you are— northward, southward, eastward, and westward; for all the land which you see I give to you and your descendants forever.'"* Genesis 13:14-15. Do we think God changed His mind? The Ancient of Days wants us to know that everything we need is ALREADY! Blasphemy, right? Wrong! We must awaken from our slumber; better yet, we must stop slipping! Genesis 13:17 says, *"Arise, walk in the land through its length and its width, for I give it to you."*

Once again, everything we need is already inside of us, embedded in our DNA. Listen, our Spiritual Negev has been hidden within our Gifts, Callings, Talents, Purpose, and Divine Blueprint. Nevertheless, we must know it, apply Spiritual Laws, *As It Pleases God*, Spiritually Till our own grounds (put in the work), and not turn against ourselves Mentally, Physically, Emotionally, Spiritually, or Financially. Am I pulling for straws here? Absolutely not!

Here is King David's plea to God, *"Restore our fortunes, Lord, like streams in the Negev."* Psalm 126:4. What can this do for us? It will vary from person to person, situation to situation, culture to culture, bias to bias, and so on. For sure, if we repent and quote Psalm 126:4 daily, when it is all said and done, here are a few items that will help to gain our FLOW, but not limited to such:

- ☐ It helps us build a *Spirit to Spirit* Relationship with the Holy Trinity.
- ☐ It separates us from areas of disobedience and negative character traits.
- ☐ It helps us with the Fruits of the Spirit (Love, Joy, Peace, Patience, Kindness, Goodness, Faithfulness, Gentleness, and Self-Control).

- ☐ It provides a Spiritual Classroom of training, testing, molding, and commissioning.
- ☐ It activates the Law of Reciprocity, allowing God to give you more to help His lost sheep, ushering them in and out of the FOLD, *As It Pleases Him*.

So my question is, 'Why do we have to learn about managing finances later in life after making many mistakes, causing relational sabotage, or passing these mismanaging factors into our Bloodline?' God offers Divine Grace and Mercy for those deprived or not privy to certain financial information. How do I know? First, I am living proof. And secondly, amid frailties and flaws, know this: *"Though he fall, he shall not be utterly cast down; For the LORD upholds him with His hand. I have been young, and now am old; Yet I have not seen the righteous forsaken, Nor his descendants begging bread. He is ever merciful, and lends; And his descendants are blessed. Depart from evil, and do good; And dwell forevermore."* Psalm 37:24-27. To place a Spiritual Seal on this scripture, we must be willing to positively learn, grow, and sow back into the Kingdom with compassion and mercy when called upon while being about our Father's Business.

In my opinion, a properly governed and mentored Negev, *As It Pleases God*, will become a powerful force to be reckoned with! How do I know? My Spiritual Negev of Divine Wisdom has not stopped flowing yet! So, tell me, who is better able to share this Divine Information other than the one God is using as a Spiritual Negev to feed His sheep? No need for arrogance here; I just need you to tap into what is already within you and do as I am doing—Giving Back to the Kingdom in Earthen Vessel.

IN THE KNOW

In building a *Proactive Family Portfolio*, we will find that most couples in a relationship hide debt and discrepancies from each other, only to cause a big rift once they are married. For this reason, gaining control of your finances is imperative before engaging in a relationship where you must hide or become secretive about the fact that you are heavily in debt, overwhelmed with student loans, etc. However, if someone accepts you the way you are, then so be it. Hiding this information from a partner is a recipe for disaster, making it more challenging to leverage credit and have a bad relationship simultaneously, making things easier to spiral out of control.

How can we approach relational credit matters without becoming nosey or judgmental? In my opinion, if you are planning to marry a person, there is no such thing as being nosey about you or your partner's finances. Why do we need to put ourselves *In The Know*? According to scripture, "*A good name is to be chosen rather than great riches, Loving favor rather than silver and gold. The rich and the poor have this in common, The LORD is the maker of them all.*" Proverbs 22:1-2.

We must know what is in the lead, whether it is power, money, sex, status, fame, idolization, or God Almighty. Then again, we also must know if we are self-led or Spirit-Led. Whatever it is or is not, we must query ourselves and others without being intrusive, condescending, or judgmental. Here is a list of *NEED TO KNOW*, but not limited to such:

- ☐ You need to know and understand your spending habits and your relational partner's habits as well.
- ☐ You need to know how they spend money and how you spend it.
- ☐ You need to know how you and they feel about using credit cards, paying bills, and leveraging credit.
- ☐ You need to know how you both feel about the future.
- ☐ You need to know their goals and how they plan to attain them, as well as your own.
- ☐ You need to know how you both feel about setting goals, building plans, or achieving them.
- ☐ You need to know how you both feel about financial responsibilities.
- ☐ You need to know their mindset about accountability and responsibility while evaluating your own consistently.
- ☐ You need to know if you or they hide purchases, especially big-ticket items.
- ☐ You must evaluate the communication efforts regarding purchases and why.
- ☐ You must understand if they will keep their finances separate or if you will both operate as one team.
- ☐ You must know if you or they are in relation with you for the money or the long haul as a team.

What is the purpose of knowing this information? *"The steps of a good man are ordered by the LORD, And He delights in his way."* Psalm 37:23. If their steps are ordered by themselves or another outside of God Almighty, it is only wise to exercise caution with this individual, or kindly keep them at arm's length. Why should you exhibit caution without judging? It gives you enough time to bring God into the equation to prevent yourself from becoming unequally yoked.

Due to the omission of the *Spirit to Spirit* Relationship with our Heavenly Father, *As It Pleases Him*, the divorce rate is over a staggering 80% failure rate. Where are we erring in our relational efforts? Most breakdowns are due to the abuse of power, money, sex, and becoming unequally yoked for the fear of missing out or losing. Here is the kicker: Those who are unequally yoked know it. But they do not have the guts to tell their partner the yoke is not mixing properly. Or, it is causing a stinky spillage, creating a cycle of smelly or flaky stuff finding its way into their finances, home, or workplace.

Realistically, if you plan to embark upon the relational success rate, you must plan for it Mentally, Physically, Emotionally, Spiritually, and Financially. Psalm 112:5-6 says, *"A good man deals graciously and lends; He will guide his affairs with discretion. Surely he will never be shaken; The righteous will be in everlasting remembrance."* Do you think for a minute the Bible will lie to you about exhibiting discretion in our daily or financial affairs? No, the Bible will not lie to us.

On the other hand, our interpretations and perceptions will sway us according to our wants, needs, desires, fears, and traumas. Thus, when being about our Father's Business, we must trust Him in every aspect of our lives by building a *Proactive Family Portfolio* with Him at the forefront.

How do we begin to trust God, *As It Pleases Him*, especially when life is lifing? Trusting God begins with the worthiness of our Mind, Body, Soul, and Spirit based upon the Fruits of the Spirit and Christlike Character. Once we work on ourselves from the inside out, we can begin working on our finances and creditworthiness. Now, I have found that most of us begin with our finances and credit, leaving our psyche unkempt, which is not how God intended the natural flow of Divine Provisions to occur. Why is this so important? Money and credit do not make us Christlike, nor do they make our rotten fruits good.

Plus, what will we do when we need something that money or credit cannot buy? Do we become angry at God? Do we give up? Do we blame others? Do we run around with our tails in between our legs? Will we go to the dark side? Ultimately, we need to know what to do when currency cannot buy what comes from our Maker's Divine Hand.

Divine Potential

The goal of *Business is Business* is to unveil our *Divine Potential*, helping us to be about our Father's Business without meddling elsewhere. In addition, it is also designed to assist in building Spiritual Leverage Mentally, Physically, Emotionally, Spiritually, and Financially, *As It Pleases Him*, leaving no one on our path behind without having an opportunity to glean something, even if it is a smile.

Amid making many mistakes, wrong turns, bad decisions, and disobedience to the Will and Ways of God, I never want anyone to feel the sting of being rejected over a FICO score, as I once was, as my *Divine Potential* was overlooked. To say the least, although I am a great person with excellent character and a great heart, respectfully humble, possessing exceptional potential, and who owned up to her mistakes, it was not enough. Enough for whom? I was not enough for those seeking more than what I had to offer or were willing to sacrifice! God has been too good to me to lose my integrity, engage in idolatry, not operate with the Fruits of the Spirit, or opt not to behave Christlike, especially at this stage in the game.

After spending years working on and understanding myself from the inside out with a complete character overhaul from my Heavenly Father, it still was not good enough for those who refused to work on themselves, *As It Pleased Him*. Amid their rebellious assignment to break me, they attempted to overpower or manipulate me with money and sex as if I was going to become a sellout to the Kingdom of Heaven or turn away from God. Did they think I was NOT going to do what God called me to do, bring shame to my name, or use my body as a weaponized tradeoff because my FICO score did not meet their expectations? Come on...we have to do better than this!

How do I know my FICO score was not enough for them, or was I just being paranoid? I was told countless times that my credit score was not good enough, my health condition was not good enough, my status in life was not good enough to keep up with their lifestyle, I was not thin enough to be their trophy, it would cost them too much to keep me, and so on. Of course, they are not saying it now, but it was neglectfully voiced. Once we set our words in motion, we cannot retract them; therefore, we should choose them wisely before opening our mouths.

By the Grace of God, the EXCUSES to move on to other prospects appearing better did not make me unworthy as they hoped it would. Instead, it drove this backwoods country girl to get an understanding, *As It Pleased God*. And then present my case to the world through my ability to write like a champion, create a win-win situation out of a seemingly bad one, and help others to do likewise with proven results of profound and guaranteed impact.

Humbly speaking, if God Almighty TRUSTED me with Divine Wisdom, Secrets, and Treasures from the Kingdom, doing what most cannot, being enough was an understatement. I am MORE THAN ENOUGH without having to prove myself to those NOT connected to my Predestined Blueprint, or who COULD NOT hit a lick at a crooked stick. So, regardless of how the Vicissitudes and Cycles of my life appeared to the naked eye, I kept it moving in the Spirit of Excellence.

As God had it, and being that I was a *Diamond in the Rough*, it was all training for a time such as this. As I became wiser, stronger, and more astute, those who rejected me, picked at me, or snubbed their noses could have helped, educated, or coached me on what to do and what not to do because I was teachable. But instead, they chose to attempt to crush me due to my mistakes and naivety, withholding information that could have helped me along my journey.

To my amazement, no one ever asked me, 'What happened? Where did you go wrong? How did you get yourself into such a situation? Or, how can I help you?' Instead, they chose to use, manipulate, bully, or intimidate me to get what they wanted or to outright pilfer what they needed. To add insult to injury, some made money with my ideas without my permission, nor giving back to the cistern in which they gleaned.

Amid all this, I did not give up on myself nor hold grudges. Why? FORGIVENESS is one of my SECRET WEAPONS in grabbing the lessons needed on my Spiritual Journey, keeping my heart from oozing all over the place. Once again, regardless of how my life appeared to the naked eye, here is the deal: I chose DIVINE WISDOM, Secrets, and Treasures over all else. While simultaneously making a vow to God to become a Vessel of the Kingdom, unveiling the *Divine Potential* in others, *As It Pleased Him*. Here are some of my vows, but not limited to such:

- ☐ I vowed to provide ACCESS or OPPORTUNITY to Divine Information from the Heavenly of Heavens, *As It Pleases Him*.
- ☐ I vowed to help others learn how to *Leverage Their Credit*.

- ☐ I vowed to help others to understand and build themselves from the inside out, *As It Pleases Him*.
- ☐ I vowed to help bring others *In Purpose On Purpose* according to their Divine Blueprint.
- ☐ I vowed to help others build an empire with the vital information I gleaned over the years, without having to make or accept excuses, as my GIVEBACK to the Kingdom.
- ☐ I vowed to be about my Father's Business, *As It Pleases Him*, bringing the *Business is Business* Concept to the forefront.

What is the purpose of making such vows? First, I KNOW Spiritual Laws, Principles, and Protocols without undermining or underestimating my *Divine Potential*. Secondly, I can use them to my ADVANTAGE if I place the Holy Trinity at the forefront of my life, use the Fruits of the Spirit, operate with Christlike Character, remain humble, repent, forgive, learn, grow, sow, give thanks, and follow the Voice of God. Really? Yes, really!

Do all of this work? Judge for yourself…if you find someone who can authentically emulate my Predestined Blueprint, please let me know. It is not going to happen, not now or not ever! Why? We are all UNIQUE in the Eye of God, and this is what sets our *Divine Potential* apart from that of the next man.

My Spiritual Vows and Seals changed the trajectory of my life with no shame attached. And then impacting the lives of others through the Power of my Testimony. With all humility, I know I am Blessed to be a Blessing.

How can I be so sure that I am Blessed to be a Blessing? First, we all are…no one is exempt from this GIFT; we only falter at using it, *As It Pleases God*, opting to please ourselves instead. Secondly, based upon the Law of Reciprocity, if I keep open communication with my Heavenly Father, He will provide PROVISIONS for my Spiritual Journey and pinpoint my underground Divine Cisterns or Spiritual Negev. As long as it aligns with my Divine Blueprint while building my *Proactive Family Portfolio*, the Spiritual Manna will not cease.

On the Spiritual Learning Curve, *As It Pleases God*, we need to know a few things before going any further. Matthew 12:35 gives us 3 Leveraging facts we should never forget:

- ☐ A good man, out of the good treasure of his heart, brings forth good.
- ☐ An evil man, out of the evil treasure of his heart, brings forth evil.
- ☐ For out of the abundance of the heart, his mouth speaks.

The Spiritual Sealing encapsulated in this scripture requires that we know the difference between good and evil, positive and negative, right and wrong, just and unjust, and so on. If one does not know the difference, it is time to do a little homework. Why? Unfortunately, with outright respect, most Believers do not know the difference between them, while pretending or assuming they do.

As the tables turned in my favor, those who proclaimed to be on top of their game, insulting me for not being on top of mine, are now asking me for help or advice. Due to my consistency and kindness, and doing more for the Kingdom of God with less, while they did nothing for the Kingdom with more, they (meaning many of them) openly admit they wished they had helped me more. At the same time, continuing to glean from my reservoir, pretending as if it is from their own.

Listen, FICO score or not, regardless of what we have, where a person is from, or what they do, do not mistreat or degrade anyone. Yet, at the same time, we must know what we will allow in our lives and what we will not, then govern ourselves accordingly without badmouthing others. Why should we exercise extreme caution in this area? It only takes a fraction of a second to go from excellent credit to bad, wealthy to impoverished, successful to struggling, and so on. On the other hand, if you are insulted for working on yourself to become stronger, wiser, and more astute, keep it moving in the Spirit of Excellence.

There are many things I did not learn as a child, Mentally, Physically, Emotionally, Spiritually, and Financially, that I wish I had learned earlier. However, it is my reasonable service to share this information with you. I hope it will resonate in your heart so that you can do more family finance sessions, *As It Pleases God*.

To begin on any level in life, a budget is needed. It is not just mom and dad's job; it is everyone's job to understand the family's finances. Why is it everyone's job? If something happens to the parents, the kids need to know how to budget their finances. If not, they will become subject to trial and error, which sometimes does not work out well. When I lost my dad at a young age, I was clueless. I was forced to learn about the wolves in sheep's clothing from the people closest to me as they hung me out to dry. For this reason, I never want a child to experience financial helplessness in such a manner.

For the record, a child is never too young to learn about finances. They learn good and bad habits, even if you think they are not paying attention or do not know any better. They are very impressionable, so it behooves us to include them.

Why should we include children in adult affairs? We are here to prepare our children to survive in the real world, where we pay bills and use credit. Unfortunately, whatever we do not know, learn, or understand, it is in our nature to abuse or become overwhelmed.

As a family, you must begin to have a credit conversation about privileges, abuse, and neglect. In my opinion, it is a viable way to build unified bonds of accountability. When your family is financially safe, it lessens the tension of aggression in the home, making them want to turn off the lights, turn off the television, use coupons when available, and so on. More importantly, when everyone plays a role in the family's success, many things will not be taken for granted.

By not learning how to use, balance, or budget, we tend to overspend or constantly play cleanup after the fact. The goal is to prevent debt and not recover from it. We must become proactive in our spending habits, develop a good rapport with our credit, or rebuild it correctly with a good understanding of intelligent usage, with a financial legacy outliving us.

What if your child cannot handle money? If you believe they cannot, then you are right! If you believe they can, you are still correct! Either way, they are going to find a way to spend. So, here are the choices:

- ☐ Teach them how to spend the right way with accountability.
- ☐ They will learn their own way, according to their rules or assumptions, from watching you.
- ☐ The world will eventually teach them their way through impulse buying with little or no accountability.

As a family, financial accountability must begin early. If not, you will find your children begging instead of negotiating or finding solutions to obtain their wants, needs, and desires. Even if you teach them not to beg, the desire does not go away; it manifests into *Something Else*. What that *Something Else* is remains to be known until the seed sprouts, revealing some form of jealousy, envy, pride, greed, coveting, or competitiveness. The inner or outer begging will always lead to a negative *Something Else* if it is not counteracted with positive solutions. What does this mean? Our children need a viable means of obtaining their desires without being on the TAKE.

Unbeknown to most, it is in our nature to take, primarily if we do not know anything else. For example, a baby does not know how to ask for what they want, so they cry to get our attention, hoping we can figure out their need. Soon enough, or a few months later, we will find a sweet, innocent baby taking what they want, saying 'Mine, Mine, Mine,' thinking everything belongs to them until we train them to do otherwise. Why does this happen? We have instinctual dominion flowing through our veins as if we own everything within our reach, positively or negatively.

From then to now, according to the Heavenly of Heavens, this instinctual desire does not go away; it only ADAPTS to its environment, culture, or conditioning, and it needs to become appropriately governed. Listed below are a few ways to begin to train our children financially, regardless of their age or stage in life, but not limited to such:

- ☐ Open a checking and savings account.
- ☐ Get a prepaid credit card with a preset limit. I suggest a BlueBird card.
- ☐ Keep track of spending.
- ☐ Keep track of receipts.
- ☐ Build a monthly budget and follow it.
- ☐ Establish weekly or monthly limits (Lunch, Snacks, Activities, Cell Phone Bill, etc.).
- ☐ Review spending habits weekly or monthly to track and monitor them.
- ☐ Document everything, including why they made the purchase. This approach gets them into the habit of thinking before purchasing.
- ☐ Teach them how to pay the balance in full monthly or only carry less than 10% of debt to the next month. If they carry more than 10% over to the next month, they cannot afford to make the purchase. Therefore, they must determine how to raise funds to complete the purchase or develop a plan of action.

The *Proactive Family Portfolio* aims to get everyone to become consciously aware of their habits, even if they do not have money or credit issues. The value of money must be established to avoid its abuse or the manipulative efforts associated. Why is this a big deal? Financial bad habits lead to covering up other bad habits, Mentally, Physically, Emotionally, and Spiritually, that may affect others.

Yet, with the proper balance positively in place, we tend to have fewer issues on the back end that we have to deal with. Although there is no perfect family; however, when everyone is doing their part as a whole, the family is better able to carry its own load without drowning in debt, playing pretend, or keeping up with the Joneses.

If we keep up with the Joneses, we will also find ourselves choosing financial stability and rotten fruits over charactorial stability and positive fruits. As a result, we will begin making excuses about our decisions for settling or eventually ending up in divorce court, with God nowhere in the equation. When it comes down to the family, we cannot omit God, period.

Overcoming The Gold-Digging Mentality

The gold-digging mentality on behalf of males and females has got us into a bunch of qualms with God. Why would He have qualms with us, especially when we have free will? First and foremost, we expect others to do what we are unwilling to do for ourselves. Secondly, we are secretly pimping God to get what we want. Thirdly, we expect Him to fix blunders we have not taken the time to learn from, while thinking everyone else is the problem when our motives are actually keeled. What does this have to do with family finances? We are teaching our children how to manipulate, connive, and scheme under the guise of God.

With all due respect, I am not discounting what anyone hears from God Almighty. However, when we proclaim God said this and that or told us this and that, and He did not say whatever we proclaim, He is calling this behavior out! How can we determine when He is NOT speaking to us? When our thoughts, words, desires, or actions are evil, rude, prideful, or manipulative, based upon the lust of the eyes, the lust of the flesh, and the pride of life.

Listen, God is calling our behavioral rotten fruits out from the four walls of the Church, our homes, the workplace, and within our very own psyche, primarily when our motives are predicated on power, money, and sex. Why is God calling this behavior out, especially when we are free to do whatever, whenever, and with whomever? People are going into debt because of power, money, and sex. And those who have power, money, and all the sex they need are manipulating those who do not. Really? Yes, really! You know it, I know it, and they know it too!

Here are a few examples of the real deal of current happenings we sweep under the rug, ignore, or pretend it is not happening. Some men prey on underprivileged women with a promise of a better life, but will not marry them because they do not meet the status quo. Or, he may keep a side chick to do what the trophy wife will not. In all reality, if he does not want relational ties, he may slip to the other side of town to pick up someone from the oldest profession known to man as his best-kept secret or risk factor.

Then again, some women prey on underprivileged men or go across the tracks to get their rocks off while returning to their husbands for the blanket of security. On the other hand, the underprivileged woman may get a sugar daddy on the side to finance the relationship with the one she truly loves. Or, she may engage in such a manner to finance the lifestyle her main boo cannot afford. Unfortunately, this behavior is all too real. How do we break the Gold-Digger Mentality? Listed below are a few tips, but not limited to such:

- ☐ Place God first.
- ☐ Focus on building genuine relationships.
- ☐ Respect yourself and others.
- ☐ Stop begging.
- ☐ Be honest and upfront about your intentions.
- ☐ Share your expectations from the beginning.
- ☐ Avoid flaunting your wealth or possessions to attract others.
- ☐ Look for partners who have similar values and priorities.
- ☐ Get to know the person beyond their financial status.
- ☐ Share your interests, goals, and personality.
- ☐ Be wary of those who only seem interested in your money or assets.
- ☐ Do not let someone else's financial situation dictate the terms of your relationship.
- ☐ Set boundaries and stick to them.
- ☐ Avoid lending or giving money to someone you have just met.
- ☐ Do not rush into a relationship.
- ☐ Avoid making big financial decisions without consideration.
- ☐ Keep your financial information private and secure.
- ☐ Avoid giving in to pressure or manipulation from others.
- ☐ Surround yourself with supportive people who have your best interests at heart.
- ☐ Be aware of red flags.
- ☐ Avoid someone who constantly asks for money.
- ☐ Take your time getting to know someone before making any big commitments.
- ☐ Communicate concerns.
- ☐ Be willing to walk away from a situation that does not feel right.
- ☐ Focus on building a fulfilling life outside of your relationships.
- ☐ Do not let fear or insecurity drive your decisions.
- ☐ Be confident in your own worth.

- ☐ Value yourself beyond your financial status.
- ☐ Remember that true love and happiness cannot be bought with money.

If we do not teach our children how to have their own and operate with integrity, they may settle. Settle for what? Anything! By not being in the know, they become prime targets for sex trafficking. Had I known what I know now, I would have proactively avoided a lot of bad relationships, abusive situations, and the manipulative efforts of internal predators hiding in sheep's clothing. All of these begin or end with the family and finances by empowering our children with knowledge, understanding, and know-how to develop financial maturity. We cannot continue to ignore this issue plaguing our children, or better yet, the inner child of grown folks!

The Stronghold Taboos

Although getting an education is extremely important, we must also develop a strategy for funding it. In protecting the *Proactive Family Portfolio*, it warns against student debt loans and credit card debt, especially when it comes to paying the loans back. Why? We are losing some of our children because they cannot bounce back from debt or find a job.

Then again, we have some opting to become career students to defer debt, only to become engrossed in it or plague their future or marriage. What does marriage have to do with this? Most often, it creates excuses and lies. For example, some refuse to marry into student loans or credit card debt, and others hide their debt until they get married, contributing to lies and excuses.

Inexperienced or placated usage of money, loans, and credit is a plague. How is it a plague? When money, loans, and credit are not managed or leveraged correctly, it causes overspending, continual spending, and splurging without developing a budget, plan of action, or preventative measures, and sticking to them.

According to the Heavenly of Heavens, God wants this plague to let His people go. In doing so, we must want to release it to Him. What does this mean? We must place our finances under the Blood of Jesus. Is this not a little taboo? Of course not! First and foremost, it is a Spiritual Taboo to ignore God while doing what we want to do without any form of Spiritual

Discretion. Secondly, not creating a learning ground to help ourselves and others become better, stronger, and wiser creates a sealable taboo.

How does a taboo become a factor in our lives, and why? To properly answer this question without offending anyone, please allow me to interject a few Biblical Questions from scripture, *"Will not all these take up a proverb against him, And a taunting riddle against him, and say, Woe to him who increases What is not his—how long? And to him who loads himself with many pledges? Will not your creditors rise up suddenly? Will they not awaken who oppress you? And you will become their booty."* Habakkuk 2:6-7. If you do not believe this, take a look around. Can you not see? If you cannot see what is in plain sight, keep playing around without God Almighty, your eyes will eventually open to reality!

With all due respect, and for the record, we have more Believers crying Holy, Holy, and buying more stock from Satan Himself, boosting His Worldly Kingdom without knowing it! Then again, we have some who know it, and as long as they get paid, they ignore it. In my walk of life, I have no qualms about someone doing what they need to do to get ahead, making their money how they see fit. But do not knock the little man amid their small beginnings, period! One should offer a come-up instead of a put-down, allowing their light to shine for the Kingdom of God, feeding His sheep.

What is the purpose of feeding God's sheep, *As It Pleases Him?* God weighs MOTIVES! Listen to me, and listen well; we will all have an Exodus Experience, but know this:

- ☐ We never know who God may use to BLESS us.
- ☐ We do not know when He will flip the script.
- ☐ We do not know when He will turn the tables in our favor.

In knowing these three Spiritual Pointers, we must always be ready, leaving no stone unturned and no teachable and willing person behind. Why must we stay ready in such a manner? The Voice of God and His Divine Nudges require us to be Spiritually Alert to His Divine Timing. If the Children of Israel had not accepted the gold from the Egyptians in the Exodus Experience, they would not have had provisions for wandering in their Desert Experience for 40 Years.

It does not matter if we are in our Egypt Experience, wandering in our Desert Experience, or basking in the Promises of God; we must stay ready with the Fruits of the Spirit fully activated with Christlike Character standing at attention. When building confidence in our Mental, Physical, Emotional, Spiritual, and Financial decisions, *As It Pleases God*, we will find the benefits flowing to us like a natural Spiritual Negev. What do flowing benefits have to do with our decisions? We will feel worthy of the incentives and benefits flowing in and out of our lives because we put in the necessary work to enjoy the Fruits of our Labor.

On the other hand, if we do not labor or till our own ground, *As It Pleases God*, unworthiness sets up rigor mortis in the human psyche by default. This is similar to how Adam and Eve used leaves to cover themselves from the Spiritual Death of the human psyche in the Garden of Eden. Blasphemy, right? Wrong! Whenever we expose ourselves to the lust of the eyes, the lust of the flesh, or the pride of life, some form of nakedness occurs within the human psyche, causing a symbolic cover-up or hiding behind our *Something Else*, regardless of whether we understand it. Please allow me to align accordingly, *"So when the woman saw that the tree was good for food, that it was pleasant to the eyes, and a tree desirable to make one wise, she took of its fruit and ate. She also gave to her husband with her, and he ate. Then the eyes of both of them were opened, and they knew that they were naked; and they sewed fig leaves together and made themselves coverings."* Genesis 3:6-7.

THE VOICE OF GOD

The human psyche knows what our flesh denies, which is why we need the Holy Spirit for self-correction on a moment-by-moment basis. More importantly, no one is exempt, even if we pretend we are. We are all a constant work-in-progress; we only need to know what we are working on and the reasons why.

What is the purpose of knowing or seeking our *What, When, Where, How, Why,* and with *Whom*? It keeps us from lying, turning on ourselves when deception is in our camp or within us, and hiding from our Spiritual Responsibilities as the Voice of God whispers.

Based on my experiences, distractions or deception are on the horizon when we are told not to query or seek God, or when we are pressured to make a quick decision. According to the Heavenly of Heavens, we should inquire with God, asking fact-finding questions in a REPENTANT, HUMBLE, and FORGIVING state of being, pleading the Blood of Jesus, and invoking the Holy Spirit. Plus, if Jesus asked so many questions to His disciples to keep them on their toes, what makes us think we are any different? We must ask questions to get answers, especially when it comes to being about our Father's Business, period!

Can we really hear God? Of course, just as Adam and Eve heard God walking in the Garden, we can hear Him if we pay attention. Here is the hidden secret we need to know: *"And they heard the sound of the LORD God walking in the garden in the cool of the day, and Adam and his wife hid themselves from the presence of the LORD God among the trees of the garden."* Genesis 3:8. How is this a big secret? We have forgotten how God communicates with us, yet the instructions are hidden in plain sight. If we connect ourselves back to NATURE, we will find the Voice of God speaking without saying one word, we will spend less money seeking fulfillment, and it will heal the psyche in ways money cannot buy. But what do we do? We fear nature.

Some of us figured out the connection back to nature; some are too good to get their hands dirty. But if we take notice, children will naturally gravitate to outdoor activities, getting dirty, or playing with animals, unless we teach them otherwise. If we lock them in the house all day, they will become somewhat disassociative or dysfunctional, while we think we are protecting them from the world. Then, we wonder why our children get buck wild when they leave home. All in all, connecting to nature saves us money, Mentally, Physically, Emotionally, Spiritually, and Financially, especially when dealing with the human psyche.

Why do we need to connect ourselves back to nature? Adam and Eve made a free will choice to disconnect from their Source, while everything else God made remained connected. Therefore, we must choose to connect back to the Source through the Sacrificial Lamb, Jesus Christ, and allow the Holy Spirit to govern us accordingly. If not, we will continue with the cover-up, deception, hiding, pretending, and blaming game contributing to Spiritual Blindness, Deafness, Muteness, Dullness, and a Stiff Neck without learning the Spiritual Principles associated with tilling...Spiritually Tilling, to be exact!

Are we really designed to till our own ground? Of course, Spiritual Tilling is mandatory to embrace Eternal Life in Earthen Vessel and to use our Gifts, Callings, Talents, Creativity, and Purpose the way God intended, according to our Predestined Blueprint. As I align, once again, here is the Spiritual Seal we must know: *"Then the LORD God said, 'Behold, the man has become like one of Us, to know good and evil. And now, lest he put out his hand and take also of the tree of life, and eat, and live forever'—therefore the LORD God sent him out of the garden of Eden to till the ground from which he was taken."* Genesis 3:22-23.

Upon opening the above Spiritual Seal, *As It Pleases God*, we must continually work on ourselves to become better, stronger, and wiser. The moment we stop learning and think we have arrived, the Divine Well of Wisdom or the Tree of Life residing within each of us becomes guarded again.

Here is what happens when we stop tilling: *"So He drove out the man; and He placed cherubim at the east of the garden of Eden, and a flaming sword which turned every way, to guard the way to the tree of life."* Genesis 3:24. Simply put, we will turn on ourselves, bringing forth rotten fruit, Mentally, Physically, Emotionally, Spiritually, or Financially.

When dealing with being about our Father's Business, *As It Pleases Him*, we cannot omit the Spiritual Principles associated with it. If we do, we will find ourselves with many personal issues that money cannot solve. Thus, let us learn about *Passionate Brainstorming* and how to query ourselves and create a win-win out of everything.

Chapter Six

Passionate Brainstorming

What is your PASSION? Are you connecting to it? Is it speaking and guiding you? Do you even know what it is or is not? Whether you are in the know or out of it, Passionate Brainstorming can help you become crystal clear about what is needed to PASS ON to the next in line. More importantly, by removing the 'I' from passion, understanding that it is not about you, eliminates selfishness while ushering in humility, teachability, flexibility, and shareability. Passion is all about the PASS ON, solidifying the difference between being great in our own eyes or operating in documented and legitimized GREATNESS. Simply put, the difference exists between being verified with a SEAL OF AUTHENTICITY or blowing smoke with vaporizing effects.

Whether operating with smoke or a seal, we are here to ask the RIGHT questions to bring FORTH or PROVOKE the Creativity of Greatness and be about our Father's Business! More importantly, in *Business is Business*, we are here to unveil that PASSION from within, helping you get out of your comfort zone and into your Divine Purpose or Predestined Area of Expertise.

Throughout years of being about my Father's Business, *As It Pleased Him*, I have found that *Passionate Brainstorming* will help you get your wheels turning in the correct direction, regardless of where you are, what you are doing, why you are doing it, how you got there, and with whom.

Now the question is, 'What is brainstorming?' Brainstorming on a personal level is a creative technique used to generate ideas, concepts, and solutions to problems. Frankly, it is a powerful tool used for generating new ideas, thoughts, and insights to develop creative solutions to complex issues. It involves one person or group sharing thoughts, concepts, and ideas on a particular topic without judgment or criticism.

The goal is to produce as many documented ideas as possible, regardless of how feasible or practical they seem. Here are a few examples of questions to ask when brainstorming success on a personal level:

- ☐ How do you define success?
- ☐ What are your top three career aspirations?
- ☐ What are your top three personal ambitions?
- ☐ What are your greatest strengths?
- ☐ What areas do you need to work on to improve yourself?
- ☐ What skills do you need to develop to achieve your goals?
- ☐ What motivates you to keep going?
- ☐ What are your core values that guide your decisions and actions?
- ☐ How do you stay motivated?
- ☐ How do you overcome challenges?
- ☐ How do you handle setbacks and failures?
- ☐ What steps do you take to accomplish your goals?
- ☐ What kind of support do you need to achieve success?
- ☐ What habits do you need to develop to become successful?
- ☐ What habits do you need to break to achieve success?
- ☐ What routines do you need to establish to achieve success?
- ☐ What routines do you need to eliminate to achieve success?
- ☐ What resources do you need to achieve success?
- ☐ Who can be your mentors or role models to help you achieve success?
- ☐ What risks are you willing to take to achieve success?

Brainstorming is a formal question-and-answer idea session that can be done in person or online, and it is often used in business, education, and other fields where innovative thinking is required. The process typically involves a facilitator who guides the discussion and encourages participants to build on each other's ideas, often called Business Brainstorming.

Nonetheless, if you must do it alone, make sure you develop a *Spirit to Spirit* Relationship with your Heavenly Father, invoke the Holy Spirit, and cover yourself with the Blood of Jesus before documenting. Why? It gives you Spiritual Leverage, connecting you to the SOURCE. In *Business is Business*, here is what to use to preface your *Passionate Brainstorming* session with: "*My heart is overflowing with a good theme; I recite my composition concerning the King; My tongue is the pen of a ready writer.*" Psalm 45:1. Why must we use this scripture? You do not have to do anything...you have free will to use it or not. I cannot force this upon you, nor should you force it upon someone else, especially when doing business.

Why must we separate business from personal? Businesses constantly face new challenges and obstacles that require innovative solutions. Plus, the querying sessions are different. Most often, they entail a collaborative process that leverages the power of a group to generate fresh ideas with unique, innovative, and breakthrough solutions. Meanwhile, on a personal level...only one person is needed.

Nevertheless, in *Business is Business*, we are going to focus more on the business aspects because we are being about our Father's Business. Simply put, we are teaming up with the Holy Trinity and the Heavenly of Heavens to brainstorm on a level, putting our internal or external enemies to boot.

How will *Business to Business* Brainstorming help us? With this book, we approach from a Spiritual Perspective, getting our mental juices flowing by adding PASSION into the equation. Doing so allows us to tap into the diverse perspectives, thoughts, and experiences of team players, and it creates a platform for Spiritual Growth and Development.

Unlocking new levels of recognized or unrecognized Passion provides a nest egg of creativity, sustainability, and productivity, enabling teams to achieve their goals and transform their company's success. By harnessing the power of collective intelligence, businesses can overcome challenges, achieve their goals, and thrive on a level that sets them apart from the rest.

In the Eye of God, *Passionate Brainstorming* is our way of jumpstarting the creative process used to generate ideas and solutions to a problem, product, event, task, or direction. It is a valuable tool for anyone, especially writers, designers, singers, business leaders, entrepreneurs, or anyone needing fresh, new, or reformed ideas. Here are some steps to follow when brainstorming:

- ☐ Set a clear goal or objective. Before brainstorming, ensure you know what you are trying to achieve. Please write down the problem or task you are trying to solve so you can keep it in mind as you generate ideas.

- ☐ Establish a secure setting. Brainstorming is often done in a group setting, but you can also do it alone. If you are working with a group, ensure everyone is clear on the session's goal and is on one accord.

- ☐ Establish an open floor, leaving their feelings at the door. Brainstorming works best when there are no rules or criticism of ideas. Encourage everyone to speak up and share their ideas, no matter how wild or unconventional they may seem.

- ☐ Encourage free thinking. This will help you and your team feel more comfortable sharing thoughts and ideas, no matter how unusual or impractical they may seem. When your mind is free, it will produce more radical thoughts that can be used now or later; therefore, do not despise the day of small thoughts, people of small thoughts, or the diamonds in the rough.

- ☐ Use a variety of techniques. You can use many techniques during brainstorming to TRIGGER the mind, such as mind mapping, road mapping, word association, or random word generation. Experiment with different approaches to find the best that works for you and your team.

- ☐ Generate and document ideas. Start by writing down as many ideas as possible without judging or evaluating them. Use a whiteboard or flip chart to capture all the suggested ideas, or designate someone to document on paper.

- ☐ Encourage the Build-An-Idea mentality. One of the benefits of brainstorming in a group is that you can build on each other's ideas. Encourage everyone to listen to each other and then build on or expand the presented ideas, repeating this process. With each repeat, the information, thoughts, beliefs, or ideas should become stronger and stronger. If not, it means the conveyance system is blocked. Freedom and comfort must be re-established with a TRIGGER word, thought, belief, or a relevant story. What does this mean? Reset the expectations and reconnect by telling a story with triggered, encouraging, and comforting words of motivation.

- ☐ Listen actively. Listen carefully to what others are saying and ask questions to clarify their ideas. Active listening will help ensure everyone is on the same page and prevent misunderstandings.

- ☐ Stay focused. It is easy for brainstorming sessions to go off on tangents, wasting precious time. For this reason, it is wise to stay focused on the objective while overcoming viable distractions. If the discussion goes off-topic, gently steer it back to the main objective.

- ☐ Use visual aids. Visual aids such as whiteboards or flip charts can help to organize ideas and keep the discussion on track. Being that we are visual beings, they can also help to stimulate creativity and encourage participation in those who are anti-social by nature.

- ☐ Take breaks. Do not be afraid to take breaks during brainstorming sessions. Sometimes, stepping away from the problem for a few minutes can help you come back with fresh ideas and a renewed perspective.

- ☐ Refine and evaluate. Once you have generated a list of ideas, start evaluating them. Look for the ones that are most promising and refine them further. You can also combine ideas to create something new.

- ☐ Take action. Once all the ideas have been generated, they can be evaluated and refined to determine the most viable or practical. Once done, decide on a plan of action and assign tasks to team members, if necessary.

When being about our Father's Business, *As It Pleases Him*, will take time and practice. According to the Heavenly of Heavens, do not be afraid to experiment and try new techniques to encourage free-flowing, spontaneous thinking, and to explore all possibilities and develop viable solutions, even those that may seem far-fetched or impossible.

Why is this so important in *Business is Business*? Storming the Brain is crucial because it allows people to think inside, outside, around, through, over, and under the box and develop innovative ideas as building blocks to create a whole. When broken down into stages, it helps break down mental barriers without criticism or judgment in multiplicity forms.

For example, this analogy is similar to fixing a car; something must be broken down or removed to fix the issue, and then put back together to complete the job. The mind is the same way; some form of dissection must occur to enhance, repair, or fix someone or something, from the least to the greatest or vice versa. Therefore, when someone says, 'They have it all together,' or 'They do not have anything to work on,' I know it is not true, because deception is one of the greatest downfalls of humanity. For this reason, it is to our advantage to develop a work-in-progress mentality, enabling productive and fruitful growth.

The work-in-progress mentality also helps build team cohesion and improves communication among ourselves and others. When people work together to brainstorm, they learn to listen to each other's ideas, respect different perspectives, and collaborate to find the best solutions. Doing so helps to create a positive environment and fosters a sense of unity and shared purpose, developing our innovative people skills.

When properly governing your leverage and being about your Father's Business with *Passionate Brainstorming*, if you dare to take this up a notch to incorporate positive mind-storming, thought-storming, word-storming, action-storming, and character-storming, it will make you uniquely UNSTOPPABLE. Whether doing so alone or with someone else, it is a powerful tool guaranteed to revolutionize your life. Here are the benefits of brainstorming in conjunction with your mind, thoughts, words, actions, and character, but not limited to such:

- ☐ Increased Creativity
- ☐ Improved Communication
- ☐ Enhanced Problem-Solving
- ☐ Increased Motivation
- ☐ Greater Productivity
- ☐ Improved Decision-Making
- ☐ Increased Confidence
- ☐ Greater Sense of Ownership
- ☐ Increased Innovation
- ☐ Improved Problem-Identification
- ☐ Increased Teamwork
- ☐ Enhanced Learning
- ☐ Increased Engagement
- ☐ Improved Time Management

Sparking your creative juices from within and with others is one effective technique to encourage free association, allowing ideas to flow freely without judgment or evaluation. However, it is imperative to lock in on the win-win instead of the cynical lose-lose. What makes this so important when increasing our capacity? The win-win mindset expands your capacity, whereas the lose-lose mindset restricts and binds. Even if you are dealing with the appearance of losing, the WIN is hidden amid it, them, or you.

Stimulating creative thinking leads to unexpected insights, especially in this ability and agility process. Another strategy is to approach the problem from different perspectives. The approach can involve looking at the issue from the perspective of multiple or mirrored views, diverse participants, opposing forces, and so on. Just keep it positive and non-problematic, or without causing harm.

For example, for a cop to catch a criminal, he must think like a criminal to outsmart or catch them for the greater good or prevent further harm to the innocent. If not, a cop will 'get got' by the brainstorming of criminality, looking like boo boo the fool for not doing their homework. When it comes down to thinking proactively, they are held to a higher standard, and so are you.

Incorporating playful, fun, or unconventional elements into the brainstorming process is ideal, promoting stimulative interaction. Doing so may involve using games, puzzles, or other activities to stimulate creative thinking. By approaching the problem in a playful and lighthearted manner, you can help break down mental barriers and foster a more creative and innovative mindset.

Even if someone tries to convince you that your communicative efforts do not matter...well, let me be the first to say, 'It does matter!' The art of communication is a vital skill that everyone needs to master. At its core, communication requires a combination of verbal and nonverbal skills, emotional intelligence, and an understanding of cultural differences. Artful communication allows you to choose the right words to convey your message, become mindful of your tone, body language, and communication style, and adjust your approach accordingly.

Why must we go through all of this to be about our Father's Business? Once again, we do not have to do anything. We always have free will to opt out of doing His Business and do our own thing. Nonetheless, to be more adaptable and resilient in the face of challenges, you must be able to think on your feet instead of flat on your face.

By learning to identify and address problems, you become better equipped to confidently handle unexpected situations and navigate your way through complex and uncertain environments. More importantly, you can easily use a Mind Map from your documented information or create a vision for the future that aligns with your values, purpose, and higher self, *As it Pleases God.*

MIND MAPPING

Mind Mapping is a way to take the mind on a journey to some sort of accomplishment or a *Win-Win*. In addition, we can also associate Mind

Mapping with building, dismantling, revamping, or regrafting our thoughts, ideas, concepts, precepts, and so on.

Using a Mind Map enhances our ability to visualize strategically, instead of allowing the mind to wander aimlessly or ungoverned. If the mind is not governed correctly, it creates illusions, be it true or untrue, giving way to our perceptions, biases, traumas, conditioning, or limitations. By allowing this to happen, we unawaringly transfer our God-Given Rights for our psyche to take over. However, with a Mind Map, we can rationally document while understanding the *What, When, Where, How, Why,* and *Whom* formational questions.

A Mental Mind Map is crucial, helping us deal with more facts than fiction. Clearly, a little fiction is necessary to break the ice, create a little humor, or develop our momentum. Still, the underlying foundation must be built upon factual information. Why? If a Mind Map is predicated on the Seeds of untruth, then the Harvest will eventually follow suit. We often do not think questioning ourselves is essential, but let me be the first to say, 'It is."

In pursuing the *Win-Win* of our *Passionate Brainstorming* Sessions, a Mind Map is ideal in helping us to envision the vision. How can we make this make sense, especially being new to this practice? It helps us to hone in on our imaginative efforts from the inside out. What is the difference between vision and envision? The vision is an outward manifestation, and envisioning is an inside one. In all simplicity, vision refers to the ability to perceive the physical world through the eyes. Frankly, it is the act of seeing things as they are in the present moment. On the other hand, envisioning is the ability to perceive things beyond the physical world, seeing things in the mind's eye that do not yet exist in the physical realm as of yet.

So, for the sake of being about our Father's Business, a Mind Map helps us to bridge the gaps between the two, or it can also assist us in unblocking them as well. Still, amid all, we must understand the underlying desire for whatever or whomever. What does this mean for us? We must know the '*Why*' behind our efforts. It limits our sincere efforts if we fail to understand this one fact.

How can we limit ourselves when we are putting in the work? If we fail to connect to the PASSION from within, it cannot connect to us. Nor can it feed us the necessary information to fuel our inner drives or tap into its infinite potential. For this reason, most people give up; they may jump from one thing to the next or live their dreams through someone else. The bottom line is that if we fail to connect relationally, we will find ourselves doing the right things for all the wrong reasons, creating disconnects from the inside out.

On the other hand, if we properly connect ourselves using the *Business is Business* approach to Mind Mapping, there are no limits to what we can achieve. Really? Yes, really! Listen, a Mind Map is a Spiritual Tool of simplicity, allowing us to structure or restructure based on our present-day information. What does this mean? The instructions may change based on the level of our understanding, environment, conditioning, training, teachability, comprehension, resistance, and so on. All in all, we must PAY ATTENTION, period.

According to the Heavenly of Heavens, we cannot allow any form of frustration to detour us from our Spiritual Journey. Our Mind Map serves as a tangible source of information, getting us back on track when we suffer a detour and recalling what we may have forgotten when placed under pressure. Of course, we will all have our moments, so when it does happen, do not feel bad. We simply must dust ourselves off, jump back on the path, and keep it moving toward Greatness in the Spirit of Excellence.

When using a Mind Map, if we redirect our focus to PURPOSE or our Divine Blueprint, we will have less time trying to please, coax, or cater to those who are not a part of the plan, who are wreaking havoc, or who are intentionally sowing discord. As a result, we have more time to provide a service, solve problems, or regraft negatives into positives, creating a *Win-Win* for all we come in contact with.

When developing a Mind Map, we must find one that caters to our unique Blueprint. Listed below are a few ways to create one that will work in our favor, but not limited to such:

- ☐ We must place the goal, idea, thought, purpose, or concept in the center of the page to develop FOCUS on the SEED.

- ☐ We can use images, colors, symbols, or whatever we desire to keep us CONNECTED or CENTERED on the primary goal.

- ☐ We must create BRANCHES connecting us to the SEED, asking the *What*, *When*, *Where*, *How*, *Why*, and with *Whom* Formational Questions.

- ☐ We can have as many boxes as we like, providing different answers to each question. For some, a page will do, but for others, they may need a wall, depending upon the desired vision, goal, purpose, or whatever.

- ☐ We must document the Take-Away or Ultimate Achievement desired.

- ☐ Once done, for six days a week, we must provide the Reflective Thoughts regarding the primary reason for the Mind Map.

- ☐ We must use positive affirmations over the Mind Map, squashing all negative interjections. Mind Mapping for the *Win-Win* is a Positive Zone only!

- ☐ We must be willing to revamp often; no Mind Map is set in stone; it is a constantly evolving process of COMMITMENT. Why? Without growth, we are already symbolically defeated until we unblock ourselves.

If our Mind Map from the first day looks the same way a month later with the same information, this should be a RED FLAG of some form of stagnation or blockage.

A Mind Map can be used in any way we desire. So, outside of our goals or purpose, we may use a Mind Map for a few other things, but not limited to:

- ☐ Brainstorming.
- ☐ Projects or Presentations.
- ☐ Studying or Research.
- ☐ Relationships or Marriages.
- ☐ Self-development.
- ☐ Decision-making.
- ☐ Power moves.
- ☐ Family or Event planning.
- ☐ Problem-Solving.
- ☐ Inner Growth.
- ☐ Note-taking for writing an article, book, script, and so on.
- ☐ Unveiling our hidden Gifts, Callings, Talents, Purpose, or Creativity.

Regardless of how we use a Mind Map, it will prevent whatever we are doing from becoming messy or disorganized while we become crystal clear about *'What'* we are doing and our reasons *'Why.'* Most often, it is the power behind our *'Why'* that makes the *Win-Win* GREAT, creating an overflow of Blessings.

So, if we need to pinpoint the areas in need of revamping, additional questioning, or pruning, do it. Do not waste precious time wandering when you have the same opportunity to subdue, conquer, and WIN with the Spiritual Tools you already have in your hands.

By leading and Mind Mapping in outright humility, servanthood, self-control, diligence, love, and wisdom, we will not only become effective, but we can create *Win-Wins*. Yes, *Win-Wins* benefit the lives of others, creating Double and Triple-Portion Blessings. What does this mean? Putting in the work will not only benefit us, but it also BLESSES others to become a Blessing as well, causing our act of diligence to keep giving to create an overflow with a Legacy of Impact.

Here is the deal: it is always best to understand our Divine Blueprint. Why? It includes our prepackaged Gifts, Callings, Talents, and Creativity as the Spiritual Tools needed to facilitate our Divine Blueprint. If we do not have a clue, then it is our responsibility to become clued in on what is already within. So, it will take a little soul-searching on our behalf, but it is indeed well worth the effort. Why? Personally, I am not writing this book for us to get half of a portion; the goal is to receive FULL PORTIONS, period!

We are dealing with our *Win-Wins* and Divine Birthrights; therefore, we want all that God has already Predestined for us to have from the Beginning. Now, with or without a Mind Map, we can use the questions below to get the ball rolling on pinpointing our Spiritual Gifts:

- ☐ Make a list of WHAT we love doing.
- ☐ Make a list of WHY we love doing it.
- ☐ Make a list of WHEN we love doing it.
- ☐ Make a list of HOW we love doing it.
- ☐ Make a list of WHERE we love doing it.
- ☐ Make a list of WHO we love doing it with.
- ☐ Make a list of our 'TAKE AWAYS' for the Spiritual Unveiling.
- ☐ Make a list of our 'GIVE BACK' for the Spiritual Unveiling.
- ☐ Make a list of our POSITIVE FRUITS (Characteristics).
- ☐ Make a list of our NEGATIVE FRUITS (Characteristics).
- ☐ Make a list of the CONVERTED negatives to positives.

☐ Make a list of the WIN-WIN without setting limits on the mind.

Our lists will vary from person to person with different meanings and instructions; therefore, it is always best to put in the hands-on work ourselves first. Why should we complete these lists ourselves? It ensures that someone else's inner desires do not lead us. Plus, if they have not gone through the previous chapters, educating themselves from the Heavenly of Heavens on the *Win-Win* or being about our Father's Business, contamination can occur. So, exercise extreme caution when incorporating those who have not gone through Spiritual Processing or lack the understanding of the importance of having and maintaining a Positive Mental Mindset.

When Mind Mapping with our Divine Blueprint, we must follow the Spiritual Rules, exhibit Christlike Character, and be willing to move into our Purpose, utilizing our Spiritual Gifts, Creativity, or Talents. Furthermore, we must also correctly discern between right and wrong, positive and negative, just and unjust, as well as good and evil. Why? Without being able to discern people, places, and things properly, we can become an easy target of prey for the predators. So, we cannot be ignorant of the devices used to sift us Mentally, Physically, Emotionally, and Spiritually. What makes this so important? If we are all over the place in or out of our *Mind Mapping Sessions*, we can subconsciously compromise a few things, but not limited to such:

☐ Our Spiritual Connection or Receivers.
☐ Our Spiritual Queries.
☐ Our Spiritual Answers.
☐ Our Spiritual Astuteness.
☐ Our Spiritual Integrity.
☐ Our Spiritual Understanding.
☐ Our Spiritual Respectfulness.
☐ Our Spiritual Boundaries or Depth.
☐ Our Spiritual Protocol.
☐ Our Spiritual Compatibilities.
☐ Our Spiritual Fruits.
☐ Our Spiritual Journey.

Often enough, we take many things for granted, but when it comes down to our *Mind Mapping Sessions*, we should not play around. Why? It is the

Spiritual Tonic we need to satiate the inner thirst of the unnecessary, potentially debilitating issues of life. If we do not perfect this process to the point of having a direct connection to God in or out of our *Spirit to Spirit* Relations, we cannot fault anyone. We all have the same opportunity to receive all God offers; we simply need to get out of our own way.

We are all different, requiring something; yet, when it comes down to the Kingdom of Heaven and what it offers, there will always be an underlying Spiritual Perspective. Why? A Kingdom must have ordinances to remain. In contrast, the Kingdom of Heaven deals with Spiritual Ordinances to keep the Temple (the Body) from collapsing under pressure.

When doing our due diligence in Mind Mapping, it is imperative to step into its flow to gain access to the Secrets of Wisdom, Hidden Treasures, or Divine Insight. Plus, to better understand Spiritual Truths from God's point of view, we must also avail ourselves to the process. Listed below is a Mind Mapping Sample, giving us an idea of how to develop our own.

When Mind Mapping according to our Divine Blueprint, the Heavenly of Heavens wants us to double-check a few areas consistently:

- ☐ Double-check our thoughts.
- ☐ Double-check our emotions.
- ☐ Double-check our motives.
- ☐ Double-check our habits.
- ☐ Double-check our behaviors.
- ☐ Double-check our attitude.
- ☐ Double-check our decisions.
- ☐ Double-check our accountability.
- ☐ Double-check our idols.
- ☐ Double-check our lusts.
- ☐ Double-check our pride.
- ☐ Double-check our state of repentance.

If we need to do a Mind Map for each one, do not be afraid to do so. It is our responsibility to take charge of our relationships with ourselves, ensuring we can request help in the areas of need or lack. But if we are experts on ourselves, then congratulations! Nevertheless, those who desire to be their BEST self know what they have to do to achieve the *Win-Win* from within.

According to our Divine Blueprint, we must become a Spiritual Magnet when doing business, allowing others to gravitate toward us freely. Amid doing so, we cannot force our Divine Purpose on others, making them feel bad for not supporting us, or have our countenance fall when we do not receive what we expected. More importantly, once we master the ability to listen and obey instructions, we will find our lives doing an about-face, giving our magnets a little more pulling force.

A Mind Map is designed to keep us from living with regret by getting rid of the inferiority complex. Never allow the thoughts of you not being good enough, the perception of you not being an expert, the fear of making mistakes, or the idea of you not being famous enough to hold you back from succeeding. Of course, there very well may be someone better than you, but who cares? I made mistakes, and still do, but I do not allow it to stop me. Nor do I allow it to cause me to second-guess what I am good at or my Purpose. I simply understand, learn, make the corrections, share the wisdom, and move on as an EXPERT in my Giftings, Talents, and Calling with NO REGRETS! If you are dealing with this inferiority complex, open and honestly ask yourself and answer these questions:

- ☐ Who am I?
- ☐ Why am I here?
- ☐ What is my purpose in life?
- ☐ What do I really want out of life?
- ☐ What are my strengths?
- ☐ What are my weaknesses?
- ☐ What am I afraid of? Why?
- ☐ What are my values?
- ☐ What are my priorities?
- ☐ What motivates me?
- ☐ What discourages me?
- ☐ What makes me happy?
- ☐ What makes me sad?
- ☐ Am I honest with myself?
- ☐ Who do I need to forgive? Why?
- ☐ What type of effect do I have on others?
- ☐ What opportunities do I have available to me?
- ☐ What steps should I take to get what I want?
- ☐ How can I improve the quality of my life?
- ☐ How can I improve the quality of life for others?
- ☐ Are there any real roadblocks on my path? Why?
- ☐ What do I need to change about myself in order to grow?
- ☐ What are my responsibilities?
- ☐ Am I willing to live a fulfilled life of integrity?
- ☐ Am I willing to brand myself uniquely?

- ☐ What will be the difference in my branding?
- ☐ What is the desired outcome for my brand?

We are the brand that leaves a positive or negative stamp on a person's heart, determining our believability, genuineness, deceptiveness, insecurity, or fear. Remember, every story has three sides—your side, the other person's side, and the truth. When making decisions, we must evaluate all three; if not, we will make permanent decisions on one-sided information, or we may negatively judge what is designed to BLESS us.

Chapter Seven

Kingdom Alignment

Kingdom Alignment has been an overlooked commodity for many Believers since the Adam and Eve Experience in the Garden of Eden. Why is this such a big issue, especially when it was before our time, having nothing to do with us? According to the Ancient of Days, it does not matter if this information seems dated or not; it is Divinely Relevant for a time such as this. After the fall of man, we have become selfish by nature without realizing it. If we are not taught how to properly align the natural with the Supernatural, *As It Pleases God*, we will miss vital lessons, tests, and BLESSINGS, while going into a negative cycle of déjà vu.

Once in a cycle of repetitive déjà vu or operating outside of the Will of God, it becomes difficult for the mind to understand the difference between natural (worldly) and Supernatural (Spiritual). Instead, we feel dumbfounded as if Spirituality is a fairytale unless one has an out-of-body or near-death experience. Yet, when in such a state, we do not have the guts to admit the lack of understanding, only to find ourselves going all the way to the left with the pretense of being more than we are with money, designer labels, cars, houses, and material things. Some cannot afford to live life in such a manner, but do it anyway on credit or rob Peter to pay Paul. Or, those who can afford it are trying to prove themselves worthy or impress those who appear less than them. Although God frowns on both character traits, however, with *Kingdom Alignment*, we can come to a place of accountable balance and worthiness, *As It Pleases God*.

What does *Kingdom Alignment* have to do with anything, especially if we have good credit and do not have a money problem? *Kingdom Alignment* is predicated upon a Godly Mindset, not worldly, but knowing this: *"God is Spirit, and those who worship Him must worship in spirit and truth."* John 4:24. If we lie and manipulate our finances to control, use, abuse, or degrade for selfish reasons, it could put a monkey wrench in our self-proclaimed appropriations.

For example, we have someone making $100,000 a year, spending everything, running up credit card debt, and borrowing money from everyone to keep up with the Joneses. With this type of behavior, their life begins mimicking the son spending his father's money for riotous living (the Prodigal Son) in Luke 13:11-32. Then, on the other hand, we have someone making $10,000 a year, saving $1000 on a budget, and still feeding those in need, Mentally, Physically, Emotionally, Spiritually, and Financially, out of what they have. Who is considered in *Kingdom Alignment* in the Eye of God?

According to the Heavenly of Heavens, *Kingdom Alignment* is not just about what we have on paper; it is also about what we have in the Realm of the Spirit. It is imperative to collide them both together, getting God involved, *As It Pleases Him*. How can we go about doing so? It works best when we incorporate Spiritual Principles...this does not mean we should get all holy and dignified as if we are better than the next person. It means humbly using the Fruits of the Spirit and behaving Christlike, adding the Holy Trinity into the equation with a Kingdom Mindset.

How do we know a Kingdom Mindset from a worldly one? It will vary from person to person, situation to situation, culture to culture, and bias to bias; however, it does not take a rocket scientist to know right from wrong, good from bad, love from hate, and so on. The only difference is that we IGNORE it to get what we think we want, desire, need, or lust after. Only after the fact, do we include God when we get hurt, traumatized, used, abused, betrayed, or dumped.

Placing God on the back end of anything or with anyone will NOT possess as much POWER as placing Him on the front end, *As It Pleases Him*. Even with grace and mercy at our beck and call, it does not mean we are heeding to Divine Order or our Predestined Blueprint. *"Therefore do not be unwise, but understand what the will of the Lord is. And do not be drunk with wine, in which is dissipation; but be filled with the Spirit, speaking to one another in psalms and hymns and spiritual songs, singing and making melody in your heart to the Lord, giving thanks always for all things to God the Father in the name of our Lord Jesus Christ, submitting to one another in the fear of God."* Ephesians 5:17-21.

How do we transform a worldly mindset into the Kingdom? For example, from a worldly mindset, we have a guy who has very deep pockets and is looking for a wife. In his prospecting endeavors, his person of interest needs status, a title, and something going on to hang on his coattail as a trophy. In pursuit of this caliber of woman, he spends $400 for a date night with someone to impress her, hoping she will be the one.

After spoiling her in such a manner, he realizes she is NOT the one because she only calls him when she wants to eat like a queen, shop like a boss, or vacation like an elite. Yet, at the same time, hiding the fact of living like a pauper, Mentally, Emotionally, and Spiritually, while being Physically, deeply in debt, looking for a way out or someone to pick up the slack. Despite having the audacity to limit the goodies with the *Making Him Wait Game*,' WITHOUT once saying, 'Thank you,' 'I had a great time,' or 'I appreciate you.' Instead, for the $400 meal, $1000 shopping sprees, and top-dollar vacations with claims of celibacy and a little peck on the cheek, she says, 'When can we do this again?'

Although this individual can afford the $400 dates every day of the week, shopping, and vacationing, he is a great budgeter and has an excellent credit score, but it does not get him the wife he needs. Yet, he trusts God for her. Nevertheless, if he dared to invest in *Kingdom Alignment*, God would give him the desires of his heart. How is this possible? When we use Kingdom Principles, we will receive Kingdom Results in time. For example, if he had taken the same $400 he spent on one meal and taken that same chick on a date, feeding people experiencing homelessness with a portion of the money, he would have saved more money and time in the long run. In addition, he would reap Kingdom Benefits, getting to know her character and motives, and determining if she possessed the gold digger mentality instead of Kingdom.

Would it be an insult to feed others on the first date? It depends upon your mindset, motives, or beliefs. In reality, it would be more of an insult to feed one person when you could feed ten or more, especially when knowing nothing about the character of the person you are trying to impress. Spending that type of money on a prospect, not a spouse or special occasion, can become very tricky with God.

Do we not have free will on how to spend our money? Of course, we do! But if we are trusting God for something or someone, we need to approach people, places, and things, *As It Pleases Him*, to avoid being in divorce court two years later. Remember, the 80% divorce rate is over the abuse, misuse, or hidden motives of power, money, and sex.

Listen, if we planned a budget of $400 for a date. Suppose we took 10% of this, which is $40. If we had prepared $40 worth of meals to feed the unfortunate or homeless, we would have leveraged Kingdom Principles, allowing God to do what He does or move in the situation, *As It Pleases Him*. According to the Heavenly of Heavens, this one simple task would tell you everything you need to know without saying one word. How? Why do you think the Fruits of the Spirit are called such a name? With the fruits (food), you can determine what's what without opening your mouth! Really? Yes, really! It is based upon this one Spiritual Principle, *"Either make the tree good and its fruit good, or else make the tree bad and its fruit bad; for a tree is known by its fruit."* Matthew 12:33. All we need to do is let their character do the speaking, and their mouth will do the talking, as we do the listening.

Is speaking and talking not the same thing? Yes, they are the same, functioning differently together. They are similar to our hand, having fingers and a thumb, connecting the whole hand to the wrist and then to the arm. In the Kingdom, speaking can come across audibly or inaudibly, similar to positive or negative mental chatter that may or may not make it into reality. Meanwhile, talking is the verbalization of what slips off the tongue out of the heart, creating a transfer from one person to the next with or without damage control intact. Before moving on, here is a viable question: *"How can you, being evil, speak good things? For out of the abundance of the heart the mouth speaks."* Matthew 12:34.

We can intercept or budget what we speak to ourselves by counteracting, repenting, correcting midair, or using scripture. However, we are accountable once the tongue releases whatever with whomever, regardless of the intent. *"A good man out of the good treasure of his heart brings forth good things, and an evil man out of the evil treasure brings forth evil things. But I say to you that for every idle word men may speak, they will give account of it in the day of judgment. For by your words you will be justified, and by your words you will be condemned."* Matthew 12:35-37.

In any given situation, *"Let no one deceive you with empty words, for because of these things the wrath of God comes upon the sons of disobedience. Therefore do not be partakers with them."* Ephesians 5:6-7. How do we know the difference, especially when they have a sweet mouth or are wolves in sheep's clothing? We must pay attention to their fruits and character without judging, but for DISTINCTION. Please allow me to place a Spiritual Seal on this: *"For you were once darkness, but now you are light in the Lord. Walk as children of light (for the fruit of the Spirit is in all goodness, righteousness, and truth), finding out what is acceptable to the Lord."* Ephesians 5:8-10. When we know what God expects from us, we can better determine what we need to work on and why. Plus, when doing so, we will also know what we will allow into our circles while budgeting our time accordingly, especially when having a desire for Spiritual Illumination, *As It Pleases God.*

When dealing with Spiritual Illumination, some of the most significant character development moments with Jesus surround food imagery. Whether we believe the food analogies or not, they are profound in building our charactorial fruits, *As It Pleases God*. Here is what we should know: *"For everyone will be seasoned with fire, and every sacrifice will be seasoned with salt. Salt is good, but if the salt loses its flavor, how will you season it? Have salt in yourselves, and have peace with one another."* Mark 9:49-50.

If we choose not to work on ourselves, *As It Pleases God*, we subject ourselves to the vileness of the world. Really? Yes, really! As a Believer, Divine Illumination should be your PORTION.

When being about our Father's Business, if darkness is permeating or prevailing, we must check our salt (method of operation), flavor (presentation), or fruits (actions, thoughts, and beliefs). Is this Biblical? I would have it no other way: *"You are the salt of the earth; but if the salt loses its flavor, how shall it be seasoned? It is then good for nothing but to be thrown out and trampled underfoot by men. You are the light of the world. A city that is set on a hill cannot be hidden. Nor do they light a lamp and put it under a basket, but on a lampstand, and it gives light to all who are in the house. Let your light so shine before men, that they may see your good works and glorify your Father in heaven."* Matthew 5:13-16.

Although proper seasoning does not make us perfect, it makes us perfectly usable if we keep the Mindset of Jesus. Why are we usable and not perfect? Through the mind, the enemy will plant seeds of deception, giving us the ability to repent, pray, use scripture, and so on, similar to how Jesus was tempted in Matthew 4:1-11, after fasting forty days and forty nights.

Amid the Temptation of Jesus, He drops a Spiritual Nugget of Wisdom, saying, *"It is written, 'Man shall not live by bread alone, but by every word that proceeds from the mouth of God.'"* Matthew 4:4. This lets us know God has the last say with anything or anyone, giving us a few choices:

- ☐ Play by God's Rules, *As It Pleases Him*.
- ☐ Play by our own rules as it pleases us.
- ☐ Play by the enemy's rules as a puppet.

Are there other Spiritual Nuggets hidden within the Temptation of Jesus? Absolutely! There are many Spiritual Nuggets engrafted in the Temptation of Jesus, but this chapter deals with the human psyche and character development, *As It Pleases God*. According to the Ancient of Days, we are dealing with the FIRST temptation of a BLOODLINE weakness, which lies within food, leading to our *Something Else*.

Our *Something Else* depends upon our partaking of a forbidden fruit, Mentally, Physically, Emotionally, Spiritually, or Financially, that no one is exempt from. Still, we do ourselves further damage by pretending we are. For this reason, we have the Blood of Jesus to help us through the Vicissitudes and Cycles of Life, preparing us to do what we are Divinely Predestined to do.

To prevent the psyche from wallowing and complaining, Jesus said, "*I am the bread of life. He who comes to Me shall never hunger, and he who believes in Me shall never thirst.*" John 6:35. What is the purpose of knowing this information? From the Garden of Eden until now, the enemy's method has not changed; WE HAVE!

For example, to get a woman, a man should feed her nicely, pamper her, and provide a blanket of security, treating her like a Queen taking care of the home front. To get a man, a woman should cook for him, feed him like a King, and take care of his needs, wants, and desires to turn a house into a home. Amazingly, they both work according to our human nature. But without God, how long will it last? How long will they last without the Fruits of the Spirit before turning on each other? Without Christlike Character, how long will it take before jealousy, envy, pride, greed, coveting, or competitiveness provides a chokehold of control or manipulation? How long will it take without budgeting before debt becomes an issue for keeping up with the Joneses or pretending as if we have a happy home for show? By not having a Spiritual Mindset, *As It Pleases God*, we will find that our *Something Else* will become more than we bargained for, in or out of the Kingdom.

Everyone's *Something Else* will not be the same, so it is always best to redirect everything and everyone back to the Kingdom, not as an excuse, but as Divine Order. Listed below is the Spiritual Mindset of Jesus for His disciples to understand how to adjust their thinking process, *As It Pleases God*.

- ☐ "*In the meantime His disciples urged Him, saying, 'Rabbi, eat.' But He said to them, 'I have food to eat of which you do not know.'*" John 4:31-32.

- ☐ "*Therefore the disciples said to one another, 'Has anyone brought Him anything to eat?' Jesus said to them, 'My food is to do the will of Him who sent Me, and to finish His work.'*" John 4:33-34.

With this Spiritual Mindset, we can understand why Jesus said to the Woman at the Well, *"Whoever drinks of this water will thirst again, but whoever drinks of the water that I shall give him will never thirst. But the water that I shall give him will become in him a fountain of water springing up into everlasting life."* John 4:13-14. Listen, if we are grateful for the Breath of Life or are given a second chance at living, we are more willing to give life to another without being selfish, condescending, or unmerciful.

THE WOMAN AT THE WELL

Unbeknown to most, KINDNESS is a Spiritual Weapon, especially when being about our Father's Business. Nonetheless, we tend to lay it to the side based on how people treat us, our biases, and our belief systems. Amid someone's unkindness toward us, it brings us down to their level if our unkindness is left unrepented. Really? Yes, really.

Even if the assumption of our Spiritual Elitism or worldly protégé does not agree with being kind to ourselves or others, it does not make unkindness right. According to the Heavenly of Heavens, when using the Fruits of the Spirit as conferred in Galatians 5:13-23, it says, *"Against such there is no law."* So the next time we think it is cool to lawlessly pop off, bring shame to another, brainwash, or insult the innocent, we could assassinate our character or turn on ourselves without knowing it.

What places us at risk of turning on ourselves? Here is the Spiritual Decree: *"But if you bite and devour one another, beware lest you be consumed by one another! I say then: Walk in the Spirit, and you shall not fulfill the lust of the flesh."* Galatians 5:15-16.

What if we are justified in being rude, angry, degrading, or furious? In the Eye of God, justification is a matter of opinion, an excuse to do what we long to do in the first place, or to allow our hidden triggers to dominate. According to scripture, this is similar to how the Disciples of Jesus secretly judged the Woman at the Well for being a Samaritan. How do I know? First, they were surprised Jesus was talking to her. Secondly, they did not say a mumbling word or ask a fact-finding question about what He was doing, like they always do. Thirdly, they tried to force Him to eat amid doing the Will of God as if she did not deserve the Gift of God like them, or an opportunity to make a disciple out of her.

What is the big deal about the disciples inquiring about the Woman at the Well? Even the Samaritan woman knew how to ask the right questions to receive the desperately needed answers and confirmation from Jesus. If she had kept her mouth closed or ignored Him, being selfish, arrogant, rude, or disobedient, she would have missed out on her greatest Blessing. Nor would she have been able to use her Testimony and Testament as a Biblical Narrative until the end of time. All of which places a Spiritual Seal on this scripture: *"And those who are Christ's have crucified the flesh with its passions and desires. If we live in the Spirit, let us also walk in the Spirit. Let us not become conceited, provoking one another, envying one another."* Galatians 5:24-26.

Who knows if the disciples learned anything from this story because Jesus says in John 4:44, *"For Jesus Himself testified that a prophet has no honor in his own country."* Was this for the people in His circle or those outside of it? Regardless of the answer or intent, I gleaned the information needed for this chapter, doing my part for the Kingdom. Please read it for yourself in John 4:1-42; it will change the trajectory of your life.

If one needs a little help extracting and converting the Woman at the Well story, please allow me to ask a few questions. If Jesus picked the disciples up from where they were, why could He not do the same for her?' 'Does she not deserve character reformation, as they are currently receiving?' Regardless of where we are or what we are going through, we should not deprive anyone of *Kingdom Alignment*, nor should we hinder someone from sharing their faith or distracting God when He is doing the work. We should do what we are called to do, being about our Father's Business, and keep it moving in the Spirit of Excellence, leaving no one who is WILLING behind, even when provoked.

God has given us all the Fruits of the Spirit for a reason, and if or when we become provoked, we should take a minute to breathe, pray with our inside voice, repent, forgive, give thanks, and think about what we are doing before doing the deed. Is this not a lot to do, especially when we need help right now? At first, it may seem like a lot, but once it becomes a part of our character, it only takes a fraction of a second without saying one word. By doing so, God will fill our WELL with Divine Wisdom, the right words to say, or questions to ask, just like the Woman at the Well. Can God really do this for us? Of course, especially if we trust Him to do so without making excuses or allowing negative people to turn us into a frenzy.

SCOUTING MIRACLES

Do you remember when Jesus changed water into wine in John 2:1-11? God will always use us as a Blessing to BLESS others, filling some form of lack or solving a problem in the life of another. If we fail to transition or use our Blessings on ourselves without God's permission, we can render our GIFTS useless, or we must go to the dark side. So, Beware.

Similar to the fish haul in Luke 5:1-11 and John 21:1-14, God will use our place of lack to show Himself GREAT. However, we must listen, learn, trust, and obey, *As It Pleases Him*. When doing so in such a manner, He will let us know when to drop our nets and when to pull back, creating an OVERFLOW when the time is right. God knows where our Divine Provisions are! Who is better at guiding us to what is already ours?

Also, with the feeding of 5000 in Matthew 14:15-21 and then 4000 in Matthew 15:32-39, the food analogy prevails once again. The budgeting or rationing of food while feeding another causes it to multiply, building our belief system. When looking at people, places, and things with the natural eye, we become seriously limited in our thinking, becoming, obeying, and doing, causing us to become dull or stiff-necked individuals. However, when we follow Spiritual Principles and Protocols with compassion and mercy, we will find everything working in our favor with a Divine Lesson, Blessing, or Wisdom attached.

When Jesus caused the fig tree to wither in Matthew 21:18-22, it lets us know that we are designed to produce using our God-Given Gifts, Callings, Talents, Creativity, and Purpose according to our Divine Blueprint. If not, or if we lack faith in what is already within us, atrophy will set in, causing us to digress using our natural talents (worldly talents) instead of progressing using our Spiritual Talents (innerborn talents from God). While at the same time, turning on ourselves, exhibiting fear, with courage nowhere in sight, and running around with our tails in between our legs as if God is not who He says He is.

We have Martha and Mary in Luke 10:38-42, where Jesus shows them how to place Him first, while listening to the Voice of God before doing what we do. For the record, we need to stop siccing God on people if they are not doing what we think they should. Or, for Him to rebuke them as if He does not know what is happening, especially if we have not taken the time to place Him first, seek Divine Instructions, or align ourselves with His Will and Ways, *As It Pleases Him*.

With Spiritual Obedience in mind, to avoid Spiritual Error on our behalf, it is always best to seek direction or correction from within ourselves first, without going to God like a crybaby, a tattletale, or pointing the finger. Why should we self-check ourselves first? Most of the time, the problem is not with them; it is hidden within us. Here is a scenario where a father looked within himself for the healing of his son: *"Jesus said to* him, 'If you can believe, all things are possible to him who believes.' Immediately the father of the child cried out and said with tears, 'Lord, I believe; help my unbelief!' " Mark 9:23-24.

What provokes, plagues, or yokes one person may not be the same for someone else; therefore, before looking around to find fault, we should look within for solutions, answers, or resolutions, with God at the center of it all. Why should we place God amid our frailties? First, He has our Divine Blueprint. Secondly, He created everything. And thirdly, He said to them, 'This kind can come out by nothing but prayer and fasting.' " Mark 9:29. So, if we do not know or understand the KIND (Issue), then it is always best to query God, *Spirit to Spirit* to get an understanding, place it under the Blood of Jesus, and allow our Spirit to become ONE with the Holy Spirit.

To properly or Spiritually Align our feelings, emotions, or desires, we should take our qualms to God by saying or asking questions such as, but not limited to such:

- ☐ Please help me with _____?
- ☐ Please help me understand _____?
- ☐ What do I need to learn from _____?
- ☐ Why am I feeling like _____?
- ☐ What is the lesson hidden in _____?
- ☐ Where do I go from here with _____?
- ☐ How do I move on from _____?
- ☐ What is my next step out of or into _____?
- ☐ Lord, I feel like _____?
- ☐ Lord, show me the way _____?

The moment we master the ability to align ourselves Mentally, Physically, Emotionally, and Spiritually, budgeting ourselves from a financial standpoint will not be hard to do. We simply need to know WHAT to do and WHY, similar to the information in this chapter.

SPIRITUAL TABLE MANNERS

Then we have the Last Supper, the Passover Declaration, which gives the breakdown of things to come in Matthew 26:17-30, with our Spiritual Table Manners. What are Spiritual Table Manners? In or out of the Kingdom, as Believers, we are held to a HIGHER STANDARD because we are Spiritual Beings first, which means Christlike Character is already within us. We cannot get to the table, acting as if we do not have home training, or become shy about using the Fruits of the Spirit, because we may appear weak. Let us go deeper.

We must always do a checkup from the neck up because deception is always outside us and within. Therefore, a mirror or self-analysis must become our portion because the pressure of the human psyche is nothing to play around with. People can betray us, but before betrayal can happen, we will betray ourselves first by ignoring the warning signs given by our Heavenly Father.

When deception is at the table, we will know it unless paranoia gets the best of us. What does this mean? The Table of Deception has a lot of cousins involved, all based upon the *Something Else* charactorial factors, hitting us right where it hurts. Be it in our Bloodline, relationships, or pockets—just remember, a whammy is a whammy, and it is nothing new.

If we have a desire for it, whatever it is, to Passover, we must know what it is or is not before placing the Blood of the Lamb on the DOORPOST of our lives. Why? If we do not know the *What, When, Where, How, Why,* or with *Whom* of the personalized Passover, we can become subjected to anything, for not being *In The Know*. For example, but not limited to such when dealing with paranoia:

- ☐ A Deceptive Spirit is paranoid about being deceived. While at the same time, using others before becoming used to or a victim of what they fear.
- ☐ A Lying Spirit is paranoid about a liar. While openly or secretly violating the privacy of others without reasonable cause, with the '*Get you before you get me*' mentality.
- ☐ A Hateful Spirit is paranoid about haters while looking for love in all the wrong places.
- ☐ A Chaotic Spirit is paranoid about chaos as their mental chatter is doing a work on them.
- ☐ A Jealous Spirit is paranoid about jealous people who find themselves nagging or complaining a lot.
- ☐ An Envious Spirit is paranoid about envious people, wanting or taking what does not belong to them out of spite, while ruining the lives of others.
- ☐ A Greedy Spirit is paranoid about greedy individuals or people getting over on them.

A Spirit knows its kind, positively or negatively, good or evil. In so many words, Spirit knows Spirit, even amid paranoia! Paranoia is derived from the root of fear, arrogance, or disobedience, causing us to wage war against ourselves and then against others. What does this mean? We turn on ourselves from the inside out, taking it out on others.

Due to the fear of being found out, we tend to avoid people like us to prevent our masks from coming off or avoid risking the discovery of our rotten fruits. Paranoid or not, before we go any further, we all have a lot of different character traits on the table, we all have triggers, and we all have something that will rock our boat from time to time. In my opinion, this is similar to when Jesus calms the storm, causing the winds and waves to obey Him in Matthew 8:23-27. We must also understand:

- ☐ FAITH and LOVE conquer all.
- ☐ Fear and lack of faith FUELS.

Now, with this in mind, let us go deeper. How do we know if we are operating with paranoia? God warns us, similar to the warning of Judas in Matthew 26:21, "*Assuredly, I say to you, one of you will betray Me.*" Judas had ample time to change his mind, deal with his shame, or alter his behavior. Yet, according to his free will, he chose not to do so or repent. If we operate, *As It Pleases God*, He will help us with any type of paranoia, keeping us at peace and reversing it into PRONOIA.

What is pronoia? It is the opposite of paranoia. Instead of everything working against you with paranoia, pronoia is a mindset of having everything work in your favor, regardless of how it appears to the naked eye.

Is there anything Biblical about pronoia? Of course, here is the Spiritual Mindset according to scripture, "*And we know that all things work together for good to those who love God, to those who are the called according to His purpose.*" Romans 8:28. If one does not believe this, say it for 40 days; every time you do, breathe in the Breath of Life, then send me your Testimony about what worked in your favor. The Power of Expectation works positively or negatively, and if you consciously choose to add God into the equation, *As It Pleases Him*, things will change in your favor. I am living proof, and I would not mislead anyone on a path I have not traveled myself.

In the Kingdom, knowing the opposite of everything is crucial, especially if it is negative, unfruitful, unproductive, or disengaging. What if we are not smart? God does not require us to be smart; He requires us to become wise enough to use GOOGLE and the worldly or Spiritual tools He has placed in the palm of our hands for our Kingdomly Benefits.

What if we do not want anything to do with worldliness? Please do not limit yourself. God will use anyone or anything to accomplish His Divine Will, and if you do everything, *As It Pleases Him*, then why are you paranoid? Do you think God DID NOT use my worldliness to equip me? How do you think I know the difference between worldly and Kingdom for such a time as this?

Unbeknown to most, God uses worldly events, circumstances, situations, traumas, or whatever to train or smoke us out with a fiery furnace, like Shadrach, Meshach, and Abednego in Daniel 3. As Believers, when the heat is on, we have three options:

1. We can exhibit no faith, bowing down or breaking Mentally, Physically, Emotionally, Spiritually, or Financially.
2. We can allow God to stand in the fire, knowing He will deliver us regardless of how it appears to the naked eye.
3. We can leave Him out of the equation, burning in a pool of negativity, deceit, and rotten fruit, as the enemy sets us up to do.

Listen, the Spirit of Deception is real, regardless of what we think, feel, or believe. At five years old, my Grandmother began to teach me Romans 12:2 through my actions, thoughts, behaviors, character, and engagement with God, myself, and the world.

As a child, I developed my Spiritual Table Manners without knowing how to read, write, or articulate scripture with a level of Divine Creativity beyond human reasoning. I was an adult when I realized she taught me this scripture: *"Do not be conformed to this world, but be transformed by the renewing of your mind, that you may prove what is that good and acceptable and perfect will of God."* Did I just get lucky? No, my mindset was trained, disciplined, and creatively cultivated at age five. My siblings, whom the family highly favored, never had a chance to learn what my Grandmother taught me, which caused a character variance like night and day.

Even when I became a little disobedient, or better yet, very disobedient, doing what I wanted to do, I still knew how to get back on track. As a matter of fact, I had limits on how far I would go to the left before the Rod of Correction would stop me, until my day of RECKONING came. Did I push the limit with God? Yes, I did. Owning my Spiritual Erring and repenting did not justify my disobedience because I knew better.

However, I ensured my Testimony was worth it for the Kingdom of God, helping others to avoid pitfalls that easily beset us.

As babes in Christ, we play around, testing the limits or seeing how far we can go. If someone says they have not pushed the limits, they are lying. We do not go from sinner to saint overnight; it is a process. When God develops and molds us into a Spiritual Elite, we must turn in our worldly player's cards. Why must we choose? We do not have to choose; we have free will to do whatever we like with whomever. For me, I cannot risk my Spiritual Gifts, Treasures, Wisdom, Anointing, and Commissioning of the Kingdom of God, especially when possessing what money cannot buy.

For the record, once on Spiritual Assignment, we are accountable for doing what we are called to do in Earthen Vessel according to our Divine Blueprint. If we fall short, we are accountable for being about our Father's Business, similar to how Jonah ended up in the belly of a fish in Jonah 1:17. More importantly, we are accountable for what we present at our Spiritual Table to our Bloodline. Listed below are a few examples, but not limited to such:

- ☐ If we teach our children faith or fear, they will learn it from our *Spiritual Table Manners*.
- ☐ If we teach our children love or hate, they will learn it from our *Spiritual Table Manners*.
- ☐ If we teach our children happiness or sadness, they will learn it from our *Spiritual Table Manners*.
- ☐ If we teach our children desire or disgust, they will learn it from our *Spiritual Table Manners*.
- ☐ If we teach our children patience or impatience, they will learn it from our *Spiritual Table Manners*.
- ☐ If we teach our children peace or chaos, they will learn it from our *Spiritual Table Manners*.
- ☐ If we teach our children kindness or unkindness, they will learn it from our *Spiritual Table Manners*.
- ☐ If we teach our children goodness or abrasiveness, they will learn it from our *Spiritual Table Manners*.
- ☐ If we teach our children faithfulness or unfaithfulness, they will learn it from our *Spiritual Table Manners*.
- ☐ If we teach our children respect or disrespect, they will learn it from our *Spiritual Table Manners*.
- ☐ If we teach our children humility or pride, they will learn it from our *Spiritual Table Manners*.

- ☐ If we teach our children self-control or lasciviousness, they will learn it from our *Spiritual Table Manners*.
- ☐ If we teach our children contentment or greed, they will learn it from our *Spiritual Table Manners*.
- ☐ If we teach our children thankfulness or ungratefulness, they will learn it from our *Spiritual Table Manners*.
- ☐ If we teach our children obedience or disobedience, they will learn it from our *Spiritual Table Manners*.
- ☐ If we teach our children hope or despair, they will learn it from our *Spiritual Table Manners*.
- ☐ If we teach our children how to manage, save, or spend money, they will learn it from our *Spiritual Table Manners*.
- ☐ If we teach our children to pay or avoid paying bills, they will learn it from our *Spiritual Table Manners*.
- ☐ If we teach our children to leverage, manage, or abuse credit, they will learn it from our *Spiritual Table Manners*.
- ☐ If we teach our children to create a win-win or lose-lose, they will learn it from our *Spiritual Table Manners*.

Regardless of where we are or what we are doing, our *Spiritual Table Manners* matter. Plus, we need the Blood of Jesus to cover us amid living life or before partaking of anything with anyone. In the simplicity of it all, what we bring to the table can determine what we leave at it...thus, we must become cognizant about what we are doing and why, especially when being about our Father's Business.

BUDGETING SAINTS

So, let us move from the Spiritual Realm to reality, bridging the gap between *Kingdom Alignment* and worldly budgeting. A budget is nothing more than developing a plan for success in your finances, similar to having a plan to succeed in life, incorporating:

- ☐ Self-budgeting
- ☐ Family budgeting
- ☐ Business budgeting

Budgeting helps us analyze where we are, where we are going, how to get there, and sometimes why, depending upon those involved. We do not need to become mathematicians; having a good spreadsheet is all we need, and it can do the calculations for us. Here are a few tips:

- ☐ Use bill pay through your bank for easier record-keeping with fewer benefits.

- ☐ Pay bills on your credit card with more benefits and rewards, and make one payment to your credit card every month. If you do not trust yourself to do so, use cash!

- ☐ You need to know your income, monthly bills (utilities, mortgage, loans, car payments, etc.), monthly expenses (toiletries, food, gas, entertainment, etc.), credit history, and goals.

In exercising wisdom in your finances, safety is paramount:

- ☐ Please do not give your credit or debit card or account number over the phone or to someone soliciting you unless you are 100% sure about them. If you must give a credit card number, use a prepaid card such as Bluebird or PayPal for the transaction. Or, with Capital One, you can set up a virtual card for online purchases with Eno, keeping your main account number safe.

- ☐ When using a website, make sure the web address begins with https:// and DO NOT use sites that do not have encryption with a lock in the web address box.

According to the Heavenly of Heavens, *Kingdom Alignment* builds confidence, helping us to set long-term and short-term financial goals. Why is this so important? We use money to purchase the tangibles in life; therefore, if we can adequately manage the tangibles, we can better handle the intangibles with a bit of training and guidance.

How can we compare the two? Simply put, with wisdom comes the management of our finances, which are interchangeable. Even if we make mistakes from time to time, we must know and understand our point of erring to keep our Spiritual Negev flowing in our favor. Really? Yes, really!

Please allow me to align: *"Wisdom is good with an inheritance, and profitable to those who see the sun. For wisdom is a defense as money is a defense, But the excellence of knowledge is that wisdom gives life to those who have it. Consider the work of God; For who can make straight what He has made crooked?"* Ecclesiastes 7:11-13.

The ultimate goal is to gain BALANCE, period. Whether we are rich, poor, or somewhere in between, there is no need to self-destruct, especially when the power hidden in our humility is at our beck and call.

What does the lack of humility have to do with self-destructing amid budgeting? For the record, all life issues will point back to the abuse of power, money, and sex, and no one is exempt; it is a part of the Cycle of Life. The goal is to listen, learn, and understand from them all; if not, we can become our worst enemy instead of our best asset. Ecclesiastes 7:16-18 says, *"Do not be overly righteous, nor be overly wise: Why should you destroy yourself? Do not be overly wicked, nor be foolish: Why should you die before your time? It is good that you grasp this, and also not remove your hand from the other; For he who fears God will escape them all."*

In avoiding financial temptations, it is best to develop a budget, *As It Pleases God*. Why? To keep everything in its proper perspective, without things getting out of control, while allowing our credit to work for us in our favor. The AIPG Budgeting Charts are designed to help us stay on track with our finances and manage our debt-to-credit limit ratios. It also helps us keep track of our payment histories and confirmation numbers to contest any discrepancies on our credit reports. What is the purpose of having the details documented? Mistakes happen.

Keeping control of our finances gives us the governing ability needed to transition from employee to employer status easily, without becoming overwhelmed. What does this mean? Having a personal budget prepares us to deal with and understand business budgeting. If we do not begin on a personal level, it will become extremely difficult when starting a business. Thus, it forces us to have someone else do it without us understanding what we are looking at and why. Unfortunately, this is how many entrepreneurs and business owners 'Get Got!'

The principle of budgeting helps us not to overspend, govern our spending, or understand when we need to cut back. More importantly, tracking our finances will keep us consciously aware of what is going on Mentally, Physically, Emotionally, Spiritually, and Financially. What is the purpose of grouping them together? They all work together as a whole, even if we do not think they have anything to do with each other.

According to the Heavenly of Heavens, provision comes with the Cycle of Life. If we do not positively appropriate and become grateful for what we are given, we will place ourselves in a position to use masks to cover up our *Something Else*. This massive cover-up causes us to point the finger or play the blaming game without assuming total responsibility, making it difficult for us to repent, forgive, self-correct, or save money, *As It Pleases God*.

SAVING MONEY

In today's time, economic hardship has touched individuals and families alike. As a result, we are left scrambling for ways to save money or stretch our dollars as much as possible. The ultimate purpose of *Kingdom Alignment* is to give us a better understanding of how to maximize our savings without becoming a victim of impulsive buying. For the record, saving money is not designed for us to become a miser; it is designed for us to become WISER.

Some are afraid or ashamed to save money or use coupons in or out of the Kingdom of God. I am ashamed to pay full price, especially when we have Google in the palm of our hands to price check or compare items. Saving in such a manner does not mean hopping over dollars to pick up a nickel. It is designed to maximize the ability to know and understand what we are buying and why, activating the highest and best use of our money. Plus, it helps us to exercise a cooling-off period before making purchases without sacrificing quality.

Even the wisest person has something to glean by maximizing their ability to cut back, cut down, or outright budget. Plus, if we really want to find or save money, once again, we will be dealing with food. Why would most of our savings be on food? With or without buying items on sale or using coupons, think about how many expired items we have to throw out monthly. Better yet, think about the unused and unaccounted-for money sitting on our shelves. My point exactly! The money for someone's utility bill is sitting on the shelf or hanging in the closet.

In *Kingdom Alignment*, we must develop our own system, providing a benefit for us. Why must we find our own way of saving money? It will eliminate excuses such as:

- ☐ I do not have enough time.
- ☐ I forgot my coupons at home.
- ☐ My coupon has expired.
- ☐ I cannot keep track of my money.

- ☐ I am too busy.
- ☐ I cannot find any good deals.
- ☐ I would rather pay full price.

We are not just focused on saving money; we are focused on saving time as well. Time is money, and if we are saving money, then we cannot waste time! For some stores, they are now advertising the available coupons in their sales ad, and all we need to do is read it and download the digital coupon.

There are many different ways to save money, especially if we become consciously aware of where we can cut back. Here are a few items to include in the budgeting process, but not limited to such:

- ☐ Look for bargains.
- ☐ Use coupons, especially with groceries.
- ☐ Buy sale-priced items.
- ☐ Eat at home.
- ☐ Stay away from impulsive buying.
- ☐ Price compare.

When learning the average price of items, we can determine whether we are paying too much. Now, with *Business is Business: As It Pleases God*, the best way to keep up with what you are saving is to keep a logbook. Every time you save any money, write it down. In my opinion, it is wise to save money for other essential things, such as:

- ☐ Spending quality time with your family.
- ☐ Taking your family on vacation.
- ☐ A new home.
- ☐ A new car.
- ☐ Debt reduction.
- ☐ Emergency Funds.
- ☐ Starting a new business.
- ☐ Donating to your favorite charity.

In my opinion, this is an incentive to keep the money you give away at your local grocer or retailer, to do something else, or to focus on your ultimate goal.

According to *Kingdom Alignment*, when managing our finances, 'going with the flow' or 'winging it' is not part of our vocabulary. We operate with a plan! What does this mean? It means we do our homework; we must have our shopping list in hand, pulled coupons, have an idea of what we are looking for, and so on. For the record, blind shopping is a recipe for getting got!

To become a good steward over our finances, *As It Pleases God*, we must research and know what to do, how much we will spend, and what the takeaway is. Why? It prevents us from walking into a store to save money and walking out spending 1000% more. For example, if I went to save $5.00 and impulsively spent $50.00 more than I came to buy, I impulsively overspent 1000% more without calculating or projecting the cost. The bottom line is that AWARENESS is the first key, and APPLICATION is the second in Kingdom Alignment, *As It Pleases God*.

From now on, when you walk into a store, your ultimate goal is to save money without sacrificing quality! When this mindset is developed, you will start looking at your purchases differently. In *Kingdom Alignment*, this is not a matter of being cheap. It is a matter of maximizing your potential, saving money, and becoming a good steward of what you have. At the same time, it helps to *Bridge The Gap* between where you are, where you are going, and being about your Father's Business.

CHAPTER EIGHT

Bridging the Gap

From *Kingdom Alignment* to *Bridging The Gap* between where we are and where we are going, requires proactive awareness of our finances. Whether we think it is relevant or not, it is a need to have in the Eye of God. Why? It is connected to every aspect of our being, Mentally, Physically, Emotionally, and Spiritually. Unfortunately, this is why when we are distraught in any of these areas, we opt to spend on our pleasures surrounding power, money, sex, habits, and illusional lies, even if we do not have it like that!

As we go a little deeper, we often think our Spirituality has nothing to do with our finances and vice versa, but I beg to differ. God is concerned about us, our behaviors, fruits, and character. He is also perturbed about how we cover it up with power, money, sex, and lies without learning how to *Bridge The Gap* properly with the Spiritual Seals from the Ancient of Days until now.

As we all know, 'Money answers everything,' including the secrets to our wisdom, folly, and hidden glitches that it cannot buy. How do we make this make sense? Unfortunately, this is where most Believers get confused. In all simplicity, money can provide ANSWERS without having the CAPACITY to purchase without God Almighty involved or being about His Business. Nonetheless, I will go deeper later in this chapter, but to glean the information in its purest form, we must know it is there for us, or it is available to get an understanding.

Spiritual Seals are not for the faint of heart. Why is it reserved for some and withheld from others? It requires us to query God, ourselves, and others, as well as the situation, circumstance, or event causing the gap, Mentally, Physically, Emotionally, Spiritually, or Financially. In addition, it also requires us to understand the Spiritual Principles or Conditions associated with what we are doing and why we are doing so, *As It Pleases God*. I know it seems like a lot, and it is for some, thus is the reason for Spiritual Seals being opened by only a few.

Unbeknown to most, Spiritual Seals have the potential to RESTORE our Spiritual Negev, primarily if we learn how to use money as God intended or when we are about our Father's Business. Really? Yes, really! "*Men will buy fields for money, sign deeds and seal them, and take witnesses, in the land of Benjamin, in the places around Jerusalem, in the cities of Judah, in the cities of the mountains, in the cities of the lowland, and in the cities of the South; for I will cause their captives to return, says the LORD.*" Jeremiah 32:44.

Listen, everyone has a Spiritual Negev (underlying Gifts, Callings, Talents, or Creativity) facilitating their Predestined Blueprint, causing us to FLOW in whatever with whomever naturally. If we are forcing the flow or we are blocked, it may NOT be our Spiritual Negev, especially if we find ourselves becoming a copycat or stealing to keep up an appearance. By not embarking or focusing on our own Spiritual Negev, we will find ourselves easily influenced or bouncing from one thing to the next, especially when power, money, and sex are involved.

If this way of living works for you, continue in your folly. But, according to the Heavenly of Heavens, if you desire to unleash your Divine Blueprint, you must go Spiritually Till your own grounds. Here is the Spiritual Seal you need to adhere to: "*Let him who stole steal no longer, but rather let him labor, working with his hands what is good, that he may have something to give him who has need. Let no corrupt word proceed out of your mouth, but what is good for necessary edification, that it may impart grace to the hearers. And do not grieve the Holy Spirit of God, by whom you were sealed for the day of redemption. Let all bitterness, wrath, anger, clamor, and evil speaking be put away from you, with all malice. And be kind to one another, tenderhearted, forgiving one another, even as God in Christ forgave you.*" Ephesians 4:28-32.

The Spiritual Reservoir of others is designed to inspire, motivate, encourage, TRIGGER, or get our wheels turning in the right direction, similar to putting oil in our cars to keep the engine running properly. The moment the car decides it does not need oil or has a leak, it will begin to fail because it is not designed to produce oil. More importantly, a car needs to stay in its lane of being a car, doing what it is designed to do, and getting the maintenance or updates designed by its MANUFACTURER to function correctly. With this analogy, the same applies to us; our Spiritual Manual or Negev is within us; we do not need to take it from anyone—it is already.

Now, it is my JOB to TRIGGER or UNBLOCK the flow, allowing you to tap into what is already. Plus, by Divine Design, you are the only one who can do something about it or naturally FLOW in it, whatever your 'it' is.

How can we tap into our Spiritual Negev if we are not triggered or remain blocked? Please allow me to present an analogy of an underlying Negev (Spiritual Well). In the same way, oil is extracted from the earth, fruits, or vegetables; it knows what it has without doubting. We will never find the earth, fruits, or vegetables saying, 'I think I have oil.' It is a KNOWING hidden within *Something Else*, and it is our job to locate it and then capitalize on it. If not, it does not change the fact of the hidden commodity. It simply keeps recycling itself (Cycle of Déjà vu) until we EXTRACT the oil or awaken from our slumber.

Remember, the Well of Wisdom does not discriminate! Suppose we extract the Lesson, Blessing, Testing, or Revelation, converting it as we should. In this case, *As It Pleases God*, our Spiritual Negev will run over, getting everyone drenched with our Gifts, Callings, Talents, Purpose, or Creativity. What does this mean? They will multiply through others.

For example, the ocean branches out into other bodies of water, such as the seas, rivers, lakes, streams, lagoons, creeks, and so on. All of them are affected by the Law of Gravity, flowing together to create a rhythmic systemic cycle of motion. When movement ceases, the body of water becomes septic unless it is a frozen glacier moving under its own weight as a form of LEVERAGE. What does water have to do with us? Our bodies are 60% water, sometimes a little more, but the Universal Laws applicable to water will also apply to us.

Our Gifts, Callings, Talents, Creativity, or whatever is designed to create a lifeline for *Something Else*. Now, with it, *As It Pleases God*, it allows us to FLOW or give us LEVERAGE above or beneath whatever, with whomever. Here is the deal: If we are NOT flowing or gaining leverage, then what are we doing? If you do not know, then it is time to get *In The Know*!

What is the best way to EXTRACT and CONVERT in any area of our lives? We need faith, hope, trust, belief, humility, and obedience. Once understood or willfully applied to the best of our abilities, God Almighty will provide what we need to fill in the gap to keep our Spiritual Engines running with oil flowing from the Fruits of the Spirit.

Are faith, hope, trust, and belief not the same thing? In the Kingdom, they work together as a whole but function differently, predicated on our *Something Else*. For example, we can have FAITH that a chair will hold us up when we sit down; however, we do not TRUST the person who tends to snatch the chair from behind us. So, based upon this one action of contempt or deceit, we do not BELIEVE they have our best interests at heart; therefore, we opt not to sit down at all, HOPING that our paranoias, experiences, or traumas are not exposed.

Suppose we redirect our faith, hope, trust, and belief, incorporating the edifices of the Holy Trinity with humility and obedience. In this case, our instinctual nature goes on high alert, allowing us to extract the win-win, move proactively, positively address the issue, or LEVERAGE the chair before sitting, causing all things to work in our favor, even when appearing to go wrong. According to Proverbs 30:4-5, *"Who has ascended into heaven, or descended? Who has gathered the wind in His fists? Who has bound the waters in a garment? Who has established all the ends of the earth? What is His name, and what is His Son's name, If you know? Every word of God is pure; He is a shield to those who put their trust in Him."*

Amid our imperfections, it does not deface the fact that our *Spirit to Spirit* Relationship with our Heavenly Father is available to all. He is ready, willing, and able to assist us, especially if we play our cards right. What does this mean? As my ear has been to the ground, listening, learning, and understanding, we have come to a place where we live by what others say, through our biases, or we consume our minds with vile superstitions. When we avoid taking the time to consider what God says, reveals, or decrees, by default, we will expect others to read our mail (life story) instead of reading our own based upon our fruits, character, and the Word of God.

If we desire Spiritual Balance, *As It Pleases God*, here is what we need to know when dealing with tangibles: *"Because of laziness the building decays, And through idleness of hands the house leaks. A feast is made for laughter, And wine makes merry; But money answers everything."* Ecclesiastes 10:18. Money is used for tangible items we can see, feel, hear, touch, taste, or experience, all of which cater to our senses. Although we do not think about this much, it is so real beyond what we could ever imagine.

According to the Heavenly of Heavens, money cannot buy the intangible items dealing with the Spiritual aspects of our being, connecting us to the psyche or our soulish nature. What does this mean? We cannot buy what we cannot connect our senses to, and we cannot become lazy about putting in the work, Spiritually Tilling the unseen manifestations of who we are in Earthen Vessel. For example, we cannot buy thoughts. We can attempt to manipulate them as much as we like, but they are free moral agents, coming and going as they please. Therefore, we must put in the work for ourselves, tilling the ground of our mindsets and putting in the right information to receive the desired results. If not, they remain in control of the human psyche without us realizing they are pulling our strings.

The same applies to our Spirit, instincts, emotions, desires, health, beliefs, character, Fruits of the Spirit (Love, Joy, Peace, Patience, Kindness, Goodness, Faithfulness, Gentleness, and Self-Control), and so on.

It is often said, 'Money can buy love.' Well, in my opinion, money can buy a simulation of love called infatuation, which leads to *Something Else*, positively or negatively. When someone buys the illusion of love, do they not realize they are buying it? Of course, they do! For this reason, they will seek to control someone or something through material gain, gaslighting situations, or becoming an outright narcissist, capitalizing on the weaknesses of their prey. Then, as soon as the material aspects are gone, so is the predator who coaxed a temporary fix, as the prey miraculously becomes wise all of a sudden.

On the other hand, we also have those who spend their hard-earned money and time destroying the lives of others. Why would they do such a thing? Mismanaged emotions, rotten fruits, corrupt character, untreated trauma, or wayward conditioning associated with jealousy, envy, pride, greed, coveting, or competitiveness. Unfortunately, this behavior is happening among Believers, and those who proclaim to be Heaven Sent but operate as wolves in sheep's clothing. Is this really happening? Absolutely!

For example, my books have changed many lives, including my enemies. Only to have them (proclaimed Believers) attempt to spread rumors intentionally, trip me up, openly slander me, cause some form of ill-will, or lay traps to discredit me to bring shame to my name. Do we think God will bless this type of behavior? For the record, God condemns it.

Why would God condemn their behavior, especially if they are justified and it is the truth? Once again, God deals with MOTIVES and INTENTS. According to scripture, here is what we must know: *"The preparations of the heart belong to man, But the answer of the tongue is from the LORD. All the ways of a man (MOTIVES) are pure in his own eyes, But the LORD weighs the spirits. Commit your works to the LORD, And your thoughts will be established."* Proverbs 16:1-3.

As I redirect this back to myself, according to my Divine Blueprint, I intend to build, help, and nurture others for the Kingdom with Spiritual Leverage. What gives Spiritual Leverage? We can develop Spiritual Leverage by MASTERING our ability to place a Spiritual Seal (Covenant) on whatever we do, say, or become, *As It Pleases God*. If this is real, how do we go about doing so? It is accomplished by having a *Spirit to Spirit* Relationship with our Heavenly Father, covering ourselves with the Blood of Jesus, becoming ONE with the Holy Spirit, using the Fruits of the Spirit, behaving Christlike, and being about our Father's Business while operating in outright humility.

What is the purpose of having Spiritual Leverage and placing Spiritual Seals? It helps us gain the COURAGE and PEACE needed to move forward in the Spirit of Excellence without experiencing over-exaggerated fear. Here is the Spiritual Seal: *"Many nations shall come and say, 'Come, and let us go up to the mountain of the LORD, To the house of the God of Jacob; He will teach us His ways, And we shall walk in His paths.' For out of Zion the law shall go forth, And the word of the LORD from Jerusalem. But everyone shall sit under his vine and under his fig tree, And no one shall make them afraid; For the mouth of the LORD of hosts has spoken."* Micah 4:2;4.

How can we apply this in our daily lives without dropping the ball? If we make our best attempts NOT to operate in Spiritual Error, *As It Pleases God*, we have the legitimate right to say, *"No weapon formed against you shall prosper, And every tongue which rises against you in judgment You shall condemn. This is the heritage of the servants of the LORD, And their righteousness is from Me, says the LORD."* Isaiah 54:17.

Now, getting back to the example from above, my enemies intended to tear down, discredit, and bring shame with worldly means of manipulation while, at the same time, gleaning from my Spiritual Well. In this case, they CANNOT use the Blood of Jesus on what is already covered under the BLOOD to do evil. They must go to the dark side to carry out evil deeds and make their own sacrifices; once again, it CANNOT be covered under the Blood of Jesus. But, it also comes with a curse, yoke, bondage, or a gash in the human psyche, so beware when engaging in debauchery against those who truly have Spiritual Leverage.

To add insult to injury, if they do not behave Christlike, they will begin to turn on themselves while appearing right in their own eyes with rotten fruit all over the place. By NOT doing the Will of God according to their Divine Blueprint, they will automatically lose Kingdom Credibility regardless of whether they are Believers or not. Is this Biblical? Once again, I would have it no other way. *"Now hear this, You heads of the house of Jacob and rulers of the house of Israel, Who abhor justice And pervert all equity, Who build up Zion with bloodshed And Jerusalem with iniquity: Her heads judge for a bribe, Her priests teach for pay, And her prophets divine for money. Yet they lean on the LORD, and say, 'Is not the LORD among us? No harm can come upon us.' Therefore because of you Zion shall be plowed like a field, Jerusalem shall become heaps of ruins, And the mountain of the temple Like the bare hills of the forest."* Micah 3:7-12.

What if we are covered by grace, repenting continually, and tithing often? We can hide under grace, repenting, and tithing until we are blue in the face. It is a whole new ball game if we are causing God's sheep to stray from the FOLD or ripping people apart with our words, actions, thoughts, deeds, and beliefs. How can we interpret this? We symbolically change the trajectory of grace, repenting, and tithing, especially when we think it is only for us. Do we not think it is also for God's innocent or lost sheep who need help or guidance without it costing them what they do not have? What is more, do we think it is okay to be insulted, manipulated, abused, or discriminated against for not having?

Does discrimination happen under the guise of grace, repenting, and tithing? Absolutely! For example, I have had dignified Believers whisper false lies in my presence as if I would not hear them or discern their deceptive measures. To add insult to injury, they did not wait for me to leave; they spoke gossiping lies in my space as if I did not have Spiritual Ears to hear. Nonetheless, I politely gave the two gossiping women a sexy side-eye, smiled, and nodded without saying one word. Why? I wanted them to know I heard them and am highly tuned to my environment. Where is the discrimination in this story? Jealousy, envy, and coveting are forms of discrimination, producing justified or unjustified biases based on an individual's experiences, traumas, conditioning, and mindset.

The two so-called Believers who proclaim to operate in grace, openly repent as if they can do no wrong, and faithfully tithe did not exercise Spiritual Discernment when spreading lies to destroy the credibility of someone, which happened to be me. The front or backstage gossip can cause us to miss the Spiritual Mark or Cue. How? If the two women were operating in the Holy Spirit as they proclaimed, He would have told them to exercise extreme caution regarding the rumors they were spreading, especially when I was on assignment for the Kingdom of God. Or, they would have asked fact-finding questions to avoid operating in Spiritual Error.

Due to this issue of hiding under grace while operating in Spiritual Error, here is what God is bringing to the forefront of our lives: *"And I said: 'Hear now, O heads of Jacob, And you rulers of the house of Israel: Is it not for you to know justice? You who hate good and love evil; Who strip the skin from My people, And the flesh from their bones; Who also eat the flesh of My people, Flay their skin from them, Break their bones, And chop them in pieces Like meat for the pot, Like flesh in the caldron.' Then they will cry to the LORD, But He will not hear them; He will even hide His face from them at that time, Because they have been evil in their deeds. Thus says the LORD concerning the prophets Who make my people stray; Who chant 'Peace' While* they chew with their teeth, But who prepare war against him Who puts nothing into their mouths: 'Therefore you shall have night without vision, And you shall have darkness without divination; The sun shall go down on the prophets, And the day shall be dark for them. So the seers shall be ashamed, And the diviners abashed; Indeed they shall all cover their lips; For there is no answer from God.'" Micah 3:1-7.

It costs us nothing to be kind to the rich, poor, or indifferent. If we feel needy or tempted to use our finances waywardly, here is what we should know to avoid cursing our hands or Bloodlines. "*Everyone who thirsts, Come to the waters; And you who have no money, Come, buy and eat. Yes, come, buy wine and milk Without money and without price. Why do you spend money for what is not bread, And your wages for what does not satisfy? Listen carefully to Me, and eat what is good, And let your soul delight itself in abundance.*" Isaiah 55:1-2.

When *Bridging the Gap*, we cannot overlook the walls of our finances to indulge in foolery. "Thus says the Lord GOD: '*Woe to the foolish prophets, who follow their own spirit and have seen nothing! O Israel, your prophets are like foxes in the deserts. You have not gone up into the gaps to build a wall for the house of Israel to stand in battle on the day of the LORD.*'" Ezekiel 13:3-5.

Bridging the Gap provides a Biblical Roadmap toward our Divine Blueprint, even if it does not appear as so. Why would a Biblical Roadmap not appear as such? We need trust and faith to follow or download Divine Instructions or Principles from a *Spirit to Spirit* Connection. Why? Because distractions will come, similar to how Eve was distracted in the Garden of Eden.

Now, just as distractions come, they will go. Still, we must have staying power to follow the Voice of God, getting rid of the negative chatter and building checklists catering to our needs, wants, desires, discrepancies, and what to do Mentally, Physically, Emotionally, Spiritually, and Financially. What can this do for us? It helps to keep us *In The Know* of our assets and liabilities, or our credits and debts, in or out of the Kingdom of God. "*Therefore you shall be careful to do as the LORD your God has commanded you; you shall not turn aside to the right hand or to the left. You shall walk in all the ways which the LORD your God has commanded you, that you may live and that it may be well with you, and that you may prolong your days in the land which you shall possess.*" Deuteronomy 5:32-33.

Bridging the Gap in such a manner allows us to document our personal Biblical Roadmaps, Mindmaps, or Checklists. For example, here is what we need, but not limited to such:

- ☐ Mental Roadmap, Mindmap, or Checklist.

- ☐ Physical Roadmap, Mindmap, or Checklist.
- ☐ Emotional Roadmap, Mindmap, or Checklist.
- ☐ Spiritual Roadmap, Mindmap, or Checklist.
- ☐ Financial Roadmap, Mindmap, or Checklist.

When structuring ourselves, our family, goals, finances, or whatever, we must ask fact-finding questions in the *What, When, Where, How, Why,* and with *Whom* formation. All of which help us develop the Spiritual Elements of Responsibility and Discipline in querying. Plus, it assists in keeping us on track, especially when having a busy lifestyle; it is easy to forget things. Therefore, documenting, *As It Pleases God*, will keep us standing tall without falling short.

╲AIPG GIVE ╲BACK ╲BRIDGE

The Divine Prescription to *Bridging the Gap* is hidden in your GIVE BACK, breaking the poverty mentality and strengthening your backbone. What makes this so important? God does not want to open up the Windows of Heaven for you and is not able to use you as a VESSEL to open up the Windows of Heaven for someone else.

What is the big deal about giving back as Believers? God uses people to accomplish His wondrous works. If He Blesses you, and you are **NOT** able to Bless someone else, that one Blessing stops at YOU, which means you robbed Him! I believe God needs people who will keep tithing on what He is Blessing to keep the Blessings in motion.

Most people think tithing is just money, and it is NOT! Let me repeat, 'It is N.O.T.' Most people do not want to hear the truth, but I am not most people. Tithing is one of the rules of the Covenant that most of us do not really understand, yet it is the MOST MANIPULATED and ABUSED. As a part of the Covenant, a Tithe means you are partnering with God to accomplish a specific Mission in which you both have a vested interest.

Being about our Father's Business is indeed the Highway to Heaven...but why are so many of us missing the bus on this? Well, someone has to answer this question, so it may as well be me. We often talk about losing our SALVATION, but what about salvaging it? Reclaiming what rightly belongs to us is not losing it! Although it may feel as if we have lost it, once the Wrath of God is upon us. Still, what Jesus did on the CROSS for us is SEALED in the Heavenly of Heavens.

When most speak about losing our salvation, it is more like having it lie dormant, similar to the Holy Spirit lying dormant within us. Due to our lack of understanding, we are quick to condemn and throw someone into the Pit when we do not know what God is using to train, teach, test, or chastise, unless the Holy Spirit reveals it to us. For this reason, we must evaluate and work on our fruits and character when being about our Father's Business.

According to the Heavenly of Heavens, you must invest (Tithe) back into your Spiritual Negev to keep it flowing, similar to how water evaporates from the earth and gives back to it through the rain. In reality, I do not know of one bank that would finance a company with nothing vested or that is unwilling to invest in its potential! Then we sit around mad at God for not doing what we neglect to do for ourselves, not Spiritually Tilling our own grounds. We want our dreams to fall out of the sky and not have to work for them. Well, let me advise: It is not going to happen! We must put in the work because *"To whom much is given, much is required."* Luke 12:48.

What we desire in life is not going to come to us by luck; it is going to come to us by SKILL; therefore, if we can piggyback off the Wisdom of God for only 10%, I think it is well worth the investment.

The type of Covenant Partnership between you and God may vary from person to person, so do not allow others to put you in a box or brainwash you. However, whatever is agreed upon is used for Kingdom Purposes to further the growth of souls, character building, help those in need, make this world a better place, and so on. You can enter this Mission with God on your own, or someone can set the Mission for you to follow. Once this is accomplished, He will empower you with the wisdom, instincts, provisions, ideas, concepts, and know-how to accomplish the Mission, which means the meat in the storehouse. You will have all of these benefits for a 10% Tithe on the profits.

Most of us think God will pay us back in money if we Tithe. Well, this rationality has no formal truth to it. Why not? God's currency may appear as intangible, which are things money cannot buy. Listen, the meat (benefits) from the Tithe is more powerful than any form of currency known to man. To become Divinely Wise, to bring forth the Genius from Within, to have Spiritual Strength, to have Supernatural Guidance, to have Internal Peace, to have a Spiritual Covering, and to have what money cannot buy are worth every bit of what you give back to the Kingdom of God.

The truth is that we can be wealthy and not pay a single Tithe a day in our lives; therefore, we must stop with the lies we tell ourselves about wealth. I know many wealthy people who live the good life, wanting for nothing while laughing at those who pay Tithes. However, their Spiritual life is not as it should be. What does this mean? Without adding God to our wealth, prosperity, or life's equation, be it wealthy, poor, or anything in between, we will suffer an internal void within the human psyche. Regardless of one's financial status or mindset, here is what can happen or what to watch out for when taking the Holy Trinity out of the equation, but not limited to such:

- ☐ We will suffer some form of longing from within the human psyche.
- ☐ Our mental state may become unstable, negative, reactive, or warped.
- ☐ Our emotions may be all over the place or conjectured, allowing our mental chatter to get the best of us.
- ☐ Our physical well-being may be the only thing we would appear to control to a certain extent, causing us to adorn ourselves outwardly while leaving ourselves unkempt from within.
- ☐ We will have a void from within that all the money in the world cannot fill, while possessing rotten and mangled fruits.
- ☐ Our character will become geared toward power, money, and sex, causing our habits to get out of control.
- ☐ We will have bouts of Spiritual Blindness, Deafness, and Muteness, not knowing if we are coming or going.
- ☐ We will possess a stiff neck, battle with dullness, or the inability to connect effectively with people.
- ☐ We will become chaotic, gullible, selfish, or lack confidence.
- ☐ We may confuse humility with a weakness rather than a hidden strength.
- ☐ The lust of the eyes, the lust of the flesh, and the pride of life will have a chokehold, causing us to turn on ourselves secretly or openly.
- ☐ We may become consumed with idolatry while appearing justified in our own eyes.

In *Business is Business*, or when being about our Father's Business, we are held accountable for the acknowledgment and use of our Spiritual Gifts. We are also responsible for sharing them, which brings me to the second part of the Spiritual Covenant with our Heavenly Father, the OFFERING. Here again, we often associate Tithe and Offerings with church services as we should; however, we are oblivious to the fact that we must have a Tithe and an Offering for our Spiritual Negev.

For example, I will use myself…To become the writer I am today, breaking open my Underground Cistern of Wisdom. I had to invest heavily in my writing and articulation skills without settling for defeat. While simultaneously learning and creating a win-win out of everything, regardless of how it appeared to the naked eye.

According to the Heavenly of Heavens, each person is accountable for their OWN Tithe and Offering to their Spiritual Gifts so they can become true moneymakers or provide Divine Provisions when the timing is right. Until then, we must work on them. How?

- ☐ Work toward them with a plan of action, mind map, or contingency plan.
- ☐ Work on them through our querying sessions.
- ☐ Develop them using the Fruits of the Spirit.
- ☐ Polish them by putting them into action or practicing with the Law of Use.
- ☐ Master them by developing consistency and accuracy.
- ☐ Share them by activating the Law of Reciprocity.
- ☐ Cover them with the Blood of Jesus.
- ☐ Invoke them by becoming ONE with the Holy Spirit to fulfill our Divine Destiny.
- ☐ Most of all, RESPECT them by becoming thankful, merciful, compassionate, and repentant.

Remember, you must share your Spiritual Gifts from Within and the proceeds of overcoming a lesser law with a GREATER ONE. Why? It is God's capitalizing way of getting your Mental, Physical, Emotional, Spiritual, and Financial Systems flowing through you. Here are some rules that will help you safeguard your blessings while being *'In PURPOSE on Purpose'* or Intentionally Purposeful:

- ☐ Do not take from something, and do not give back.
- ☐ Do not take from a person, and do not give back.
- ☐ When you receive a Blessing, Bless someone else.
- ☐ If you need a Blessing, create a Blessing for someone else.
- ☐ When entering a person's house as a visitor, Bless them with a gift.
- ☐ When someone visits you, Bless them with a gift before they leave.

Although these rules seem so simple, they are continuously overlooked. These few rules have so much power I cannot begin to tell you about...you must experience it yourself. God is very strategic, and He has designed everything to reproduce after its own kind. Nevertheless, there are a few things we often forget:

- ☐ We must take care of it.
- ☐ We must nurture it.
- ☐ We must prepare it.
- ☐ We must respect it.
- ☐ We must share it.

Whatever our 'it' is, we cannot ignore it because it will not get resolved, or it will create a life of its own without our permission due to our ignorance or lack of understanding. For this reason, we must own our truth regardless of whether it is good, bad, or indifferent.

Establishing documented information gives us a reference point of contact with the Heavenly of Heavens instead of committing everything to memory. What makes this so important? We symbolically establish a covenant with what we have in our hands or the tools God has Divinely Blessed us with. For example, when someone begins to brag about what God is doing within them or around them, I prefer for them to show me instead of telling me. Why is showing better than telling? The mouth can say anything; therefore, our actions will always speak louder than words, positively or negatively. In the Kingdom, when *Bridging The Gap*, we use words to confirm or convey, not to convince. For example, in a court case, it is not what we assume or think; it is what we can prove!

In *Bridging The Gap*, suppose we dare to use our words as butter (Smooth) or honey (Sweet) while being about our Father's Business, using the Fruits of the Spirit and Christlike Character. In this case, we will become a force to be reckoned with in or out of the Kingdom while understanding that *Business is Business*.

Chapter Nine

Business is Business

The invincible layer of security is at our beck and call, causing us to question whether *Business is Business*, or whether it is more suitable to be about our Father's Business, *As It Pleases Him*. In the Eye of God, we all can do business, even if we are not considered to be businesspeople. Regardless of whether you handle your business, their business, His Business, minding your business, or staying out of other folks' business...*Business is Business*, despite how you label it. In this chapter, we will discuss the *Glitches* associated with not recognizing business for what it is.

Business in the Eye of God is our occupation. Most view their occupation as a job. However, our Heavenly Father views our occupation as our Spiritual Gifts, Skills, and Tools, regardless of whether we use them or not. In the NKJV, it says, *"So he called ten of his servants, delivered to them ten minas, and said to them, 'Do business till I come.'"* Luke 19:13. In the KJV, it says, *'Occupy till I come.'* Whichever version we choose, still, *Business is Business*. Irrespective of how we view the Parable of the Minas from Luke 19:11-26, the servants were given something to work with to do business, to occupy their time, or to fulfill their purpose and contribute to the world in a meaningful way.

When the nobleman returns, he finds that some of his servants have made good profits with their minas (talents or units of money), while others have not. The nobleman rewards those who made profits and punishes those who did nothing with his mina, saying, 'To everyone who has, more will be given, but from him who does not have, even what he has will be taken away.' This parable teaches us about the importance of using our talents and resources wisely for the benefit of our MASTER or the Kingdom. All in all, we will be held accountable for how we manage what has been entrusted to us. Finding purpose, meaning, and fulfillment in one's work, skills, or potential, using it as a way to serve others and for the greater good, is what is required of us.

According to the Heavenly of Heavens, using our Spiritual Gifts and Abilities to be about our Father's Business is what He has in mind for us. If we fail to do so, *As It Pleases Him*, the consequences will result in some form of GLITCH.

Still, we determine how long our Glitches last by how we think, believe, speak, behave, and resolve conflict Mentally, Physically, Emotionally, Spiritually, and Financially. Our *Glitching Outcry* entails every part of our being, even if we pretend as if it does not. Why do we become consumed? We cry out to God as if He created the problem when we are oppressed. When we become suppressed, we cry out even more as if we are the victims.

The moment depression has a chokehold, we shift the blame, attempting to place how we think, feel, or believe on the next person as if their *Something Else* is the same as ours, causing us to misjudge without asking fact-finding questions. Then, when we become yoked to the core, we point the finger as if it is someone else's responsibility to fix us or that we demand God to fix it or them.

In all actuality, it is our duty to take responsibility, putting people, places, and things into their proper perspective. So, the question is, 'Is our outcry becoming a GLITCH in or out of the Kingdom because we are putting our business above God's Business?' Better yet, what we should be saying is, *"Why did you seek Me? Did you not know that I must be about My Father's business?"* Luke 2:49.

To eliminate our Spiritual Indebtedness Mentally, Physically, Emotionally, Spiritually, and Financially, we must become proactively involved with our Predestined Blueprint, *As It Pleases God*. How do we eliminate this type of debt? The first step is to understand what they are. If not, they will pass us by while taking over our lives like a thief in the night.

What does our Glitching Outcry have to do with a thief in the night? The moment we begin fazing in and out between light and darkness (wishy-washy), we are considered Spiritual Thieves who are combative, confrontational, deceptive, dull, stiff-necked, lukewarm, or loose-lipped to cover up the reality or truth. Really? Yes, really! Is this Biblical? Unfortunately, it is! *"Whoever is a partner with a thief hates his own life; He swears to tell the truth, but reveals nothing. The fear of man brings a snare, But whoever trusts in the LORD shall be safe."* Proverbs 29:24-25.

A Spiritual Thief caters to others based on their lies; they are constantly whitewashing everything for their benefit, or they are consumed by ignoring the truth to get what they want, need, or desire and seek control. In *Business is Business*, we must understand that Spiritual Thieves target what we cannot see with our physical eyes.

Spiritual Thieves attempt to attack our thoughts, emotions, will, inner chatter, weaknesses, traumas, fears, and insecurities as a part of the indwelling of the human psyche, connecting or disconnecting us from the Spirit Man. Do they have that much power? They have as much as you give them, and if you are clueless about their method of operation, you can fall victim due to the lack of knowledge or understanding.

With our known or unknown *Glitching Outcries*, we must know what we want and why. If not, we will settle for anything, living with dissatisfaction, severe regret, uncontainable doubt, debilitating fear, or trying to make our wrongs right. Being in the know helps us do the proper research to make educated decisions in or out of the Kingdom of God.

What is the purpose of making educated decisions when having free will as Believers? Unbeknown to most, getting pre-approved Mentally, Physically, Emotionally, Spiritually, and Financially from the Heavens Above changes the trajectory of our lives.

As Believers, we most often use this concept as getting the Green Light or Go Ahead from God, *As It Pleases Him*. Yet, according to scripture, it is called the LORD's Release (7th Year Release) or the Year of Jubilee (50th Year Release). When dealing with the Lord's Release, we must know: "*At the end of every seven years you shall grant a release of debts. And this is the form of the release: Every creditor who has lent anything to his neighbor shall release it; he shall not require it of his neighbor or his brother, because it is called the LORD's release. Of a foreigner you may require it; but you shall give up your claim to what is owed by your brother, except when there may be no poor among you; for the LORD will greatly bless you in the land which the LORD your God is giving you to possess as an inheritance— only if you carefully obey the voice of the LORD your God, to observe with care all these commandments which I command you today. For the LORD your God will bless you just as He promised you; you shall lend to many nations, but you shall not borrow; you shall reign over many nations, but they shall not reign over you. If there is among you a poor man of your brethren, within any of the gates in your land which the LORD your God is giving you, you shall not harden your heart nor shut your hand from your poor brother, but you shall open your hand wide to him and willingly lend him sufficient for his need, whatever he needs.*" Deuteronomy 15:1-8.

Most would assume the above scripture is just about a monetized debt. But it also applies to the Mental, Physical, Emotional, or Spiritual Ties, linking our fruits and character to the debt owed. Why would this happen, especially when we have taken a loss? For example, suppose someone said they forgave a debt but continued to ponder over the debt with thoughts of being duped. In this case, it will negatively affect their thoughts, behaviors, attitude, and demeanor, secretly harboring the Spirit of Unforgiveness. Please allow me to align: "*Beware lest there be a wicked thought in your heart, saying, 'The seventh year, the year of release, is at hand,' and your eye be evil against your poor brother and you give him nothing, and he cry out to the LORD against you, and it become sin among you.*" Deuteronomy 15:9. For this reason, when releasing any form of debt, we must do a clean sweep from the inside out, detaching ourselves from any negative or debauched charactorial traits. For this reason, repenting and forgiveness are essential in being about our Father's Business, *As It Pleases Him.*

Now, when completing seven cycles of seven, which is forty-nine, the 50th year is the Year of Jubilee (the Ram's Horn), designed for the complete release of bondage. As it is already upon us, here is what we need to know: "*For it is the Jubilee; it shall be holy to you; you shall eat its produce from the field. In this Year of Jubilee, each of you shall return to his possession. And if you sell anything to your neighbor or buy from your neighbor's hand, you shall not oppress one another. According to the number of years after the Jubilee you shall buy from your neighbor, and according to the number of years of crops he shall sell to you. According to the multitude of years you shall increase its price, and according to the fewer number of years you shall diminish its price; for he sells to you according to the number of the years of the crops. Therefore you shall not oppress one another, but you shall fear your God; for I am the LORD your God.*" Leviticus 25:12-17. Is this not from the Old Testament? Absolutely!

Although we have changed, the Year of Jubilee has not, nor will it ever in the Eye of God Almighty, especially when the *Glitching Outcry* is among us. Blasphemy, right? Wrong. The Blood of Jesus has redeemed our debt of sin, but it does not make this Spiritual Principle of no effect. We need to know it and live accordingly, repenting and forgiving ourselves and others when falling out of alignment. Why must we do so? It helps us to realign ourselves, *As It Pleases God.* Once self-correcting in such a manner, it allows the Holy Spirit to do His part in guiding, protecting, and preparing us on a moment-by-moment basis.

In the Lord's Prayer, Matthew 6:11-12 says specifically, "*Give us this day our daily bread. And forgive us our debts, As we forgive our debtors.*" Do we think for a minute that Jesus did not know what He was advising us to do when praying? Of course, He knew, while at the same time allowing us to capitalize on our daily bread by getting rid of our indebtedness and taking responsibility.

With the Blood of Jesus and the outpouring of the Holy Spirit, we do not have to wait seven or fifty years to redeem ourselves. Unbeknown to most, every 24-hour Cycle is the LORD's Release or our Day of Jubilee, as the evening and the morning were the first day, the second day, and so on, from the Book of Genesis until now.

To change the trajectory of our lives, here is the MINDSET we must keep, regardless of how life appears to the naked eye: *"Through the LORD's mercies we are not consumed, Because His compassions fail not. They are new every morning; Great is Your faithfulness. 'The LORD is my portion,' says my soul, 'Therefore I hope in Him!'"* Lamentations 3:22-24. Once we get up every morning knowing this, we will find the human psyche bowing down to hopefulness, building our faith one step at a time.

From the Ancient of Days to the present moment, we can begin cleaning houses Mentally, Physically, Emotionally, Spiritually, and Financially. With a proposed seven-year training, tilling, and regrafting timeframe, we can become a Spiritual Powerhouse, putting our enemies to boot and changing the trajectory of our Bloodline in 50 years or less. Listen, if we DO NOT know this Divine Principle, we cannot Spiritually Enforce it as we should.

When Spiritually Enforcing the Word of God, what do our fruits, character, and debt release have to do with each other? They are all intertwined in the multiplicity and yielding of our seeds sown. In addition, it is also comprised of knowing when to sow, till, grow, and rest at the appropriate time, *As It Pleases Him*. The Bible says: *"So you shall observe My statutes and keep My judgments, and perform them; and you will dwell in the land in safety. Then the land will yield its fruit, and you will eat your fill, and dwell there in safety."* Leviticus 25:18-19.

Amid the *Glitching Outcry*, with any form of debt, we owe it to ourselves to add God into the equation to capitalize on this Spiritual Principle. If we take this same Spiritual Principle and apply it to our FICO Credit Scoring System, the seven-year release of debts also applies, except for in bankruptcy, which is ten years. Although this may seem far-fetched, I have been Spiritually Ordained to walk those willing through the process.

According to the Heavenly of Heavens, with good or bad credit, we do not have to remain in bondage; we can bring our MINDS out of bondage first. Secondly, we can bring our EMOTIONS out by uprooting and regrafting our input and output system of the human psyche. Thirdly, we can align our lives with the Holy Trinity in a *Spirit to Spirit* Relationship. Fourthly, we can put our FINANCES under the Blood of Jesus, according to our Divine Blueprint, while invoking our Spiritual Negev. By the time we MASTER these four elements in Earthen Vessel, our inner growth will align with our outer, making the PHYSICAL evident, without having to say one word.

Why not place Spiritual Development above all else? We have free will to place them in any order we like, depending upon whether we are on Spiritual Milk or Meat, our Walk with God, or if this is the beginning of a new journey. However, with the *As It Pleases God Movement*, we approach the human psyche, getting to the ROOT or SEED of our worldly development.

Why is the approach from the human psyche better? By humbly, truthfully, and repentantly approaching the Spiritual Classroom in such a manner, it brings one into the AWARENESS of what they are thinking, believing, saying, becoming, or creating from the inside out, *As It Pleases God* or as it pleases self. If we do not do a mirrored checkup from the neck up, we will approach Spirituality from our perspective, conditioning, or biases. While, at the same time, not knowing what we are doing or why, and with all types of uncorrected rotten fruits appearing good in our own eyes. So, *"Let us search out and examine our ways, And turn back to the LORD."* Lamentations 3:40.

Not being *In The Spiritual Know* from God's Divine Perspective, we will find ourselves getting more confused, misled, corrupted, and malnourished about Him, our PURPOSE, or our reason for being, without having the guts to express our aloofness. Unfortunately, this type of cluelessness causes indebtedness from the human psyche, spreading outwardly and preventing us from being about our Father's Business.

For example, the *Glitching Outcry* of the Children of Israel when enslaved to the Egyptians was loud and convincing in the Book of Exodus. The GLITCH is that their minds, emotions, and will were indelibly stuck in Egypt, which created a profound stronghold. It was so strong that it caused them to wander in their Desert Experience for 40 years, almost aborting their Promised Land Experience for their entire Bloodline. From back then until now, we have been no different from them. Our Egyptian Experiences are turned inwardly, spreading outwardly, impacting or affecting our SEEDLINGS or Bloodline, causing some form of malfunction.

Understanding a Genetic Glitch is a malfunction in our genetic code or Divine Design. It can come as a warning to self-correct, present itself as a yoke, a constant cycle of bad decisions, or as an intractable generational curse. How can this happen? There are many different reasons, but primarily due to idolatry, dullness, disobedience, pompousness, stiff-neckedness, or the failure to do something, behave, think, or believe, *As It Pleases God*. All of which can be revoked, managed, or canceled due to the Blood of Jesus by becoming ONE with the Holy Spirit, using the Fruits of the Spirit, exhibiting Christlike Character, aligning with our Predestined Blueprint, and being about our Father's Business, *As It Pleases Him*.

When dealing with or eliminating varying known or unknown *Glitches* or debts, we must know what they are and how they affect or infect us. What does this mean? We have Mental, Physical, Emotional, Spiritual, and Financial Glitches, and we must know what they are to counteract them or capitalize on them.

The Mental Glitch

Mental Indebtedness or Glitches are eliminated by knowing what we think and why. To keep people from getting into our heads or playing mind games, we must know what we are thinking, saying, or contemplating, right? Simply put, we must know what is firing off between our two ears to avoid our A-Game becoming our End-Game in the Eye of God.

Although mental chatter is real, and no one is exempt. We do not often take the time to evaluate our inner conversations, allowing our thoughts to chat on, positively or negatively. Without evaluating our thoughts, *As It Pleases God*, the mind can do a work on us, thinking whatever it wants or creating all types of false images, especially when left ungoverned.

How do we know if our thoughts are ungoverned? Our actions, reactions, and words reveal the mindset, even if we attempt to cover it up. Then again, our naivety can also cause a recipe for disaster as well. How is this possible? In this condition, we tend to overlook the truth, ignore the red flags, and not exercise our ability to say 'NO,' and mean it. While sometimes allowing counterfeits to enter our lives under the helpful guise of power, money, status, sex, or a potential career move, leading to compromise in the Eye of God. Here is what James 5:12 leaves behind for us to glean: *"But above all, my brethren, do not swear, either by heaven or by earth or with any other oath. But let your 'Yes' be 'Yes,' and your 'No,' 'No,' lest you fall into judgment."*

How we perceive something or someone is based upon our mental indebtedness, giving our minds the authority to create mental playbacks of what we are constantly chatting about, internally or externally, before the deposit is made into the human psyche. So, suppose we do not want negative feedback or chatter to become deposited into the soulish realm of our being. In this case, we must cancel it with a positive counteraction while Spiritually Sealing it with an applicable scripture.

Do we have the power to cancel negative thoughts? Absolutely. In the same way, we can cancel positive thoughts, affirmations, compliments, or inspirational self-talk with negativity; we can do likewise by canceling negativity with positivity. It may take a little practice to develop a positive or win-win mindset, canceling negativity at the drop of a dime or midair, but it is doable. Thus, we need to control our *Emotional Glitches*, neediness, and ego before we can become impactfully effective, living by example.

THE EMOTIONAL GLITCH

Emotional Glitches or Indebtedness are eliminated by knowing what we are feeling and why, in public and behind closed doors. When we allow our emotions to get the best of us, we will make permanent decisions based on temporary circumstances, provisions, or information while appearing right in our own eyes. For this reason, we must become careful about what we lay at the Doorpost of God.

Why must we exercise caution with God's Doorpost? There are times when the fear of being wrong will override our sense of good judgment. Why? To make our decisions appear right, especially when the ego has a secret chokehold, hanging us out to dry in turmoil or creating emotional fires! Now, according to scripture, two things will happen:

1. *"Every tree that does not bear good fruit is cut down and thrown into the fire."* Matthew 7:19.
2. *"Every branch in Me that does not bear fruit He takes away; and every branch that bears fruit He prunes, that it may bear more fruit."* John 15:2.

When dealing with ungoverned, glitchy, or desperate emotions, we can easily get Divine Instructions wrong, as the mind convinces us we are right. According to the Heavenly of Heavens, this is a prime reason we deal with Spiritual Blindness, Deafness, and Muteness in Earthen Vessels. Once we get into our emotions, excluding God Almighty, we symbolically invoke the Cycles and Vicissitudes of Life to do what they are designed to do. What are they designed to do? Help us self-correct before self-destructing with some form of GLITCH. What does this mean in layman's terms? Someone or something will break the heart of the glitcher, allowing them to heal properly or ooze profusely to open their eyes to reality. If they choose to ooze instead of healing, the cycle of déjà vu will be enacted until healing occurs or the lesson is learned.

Unbeknown to most, our *Emotional Glitches* can also be determined by our *Mental Glitches*. For this reason, once someone gets our emotions keeled or triggered, it then gets our minds operating on what is already there, giving us a mental playback of misfires. How can we emotionally or mentally misfire? Our thoughts and emotions contribute to the paralytic misfires or mixed signals within the human psyche, causing flare-ups of our hidden or open paranoias and traumas. In my opinion, this is similar to sparks from an electric socket when plugging in a cord.

More importantly, we often do not know this is happening because we have adapted to this condition, it has become our normal, or we are in denial. In all actuality, this is abnormal behavior in the Eye of God, contradicting the intended design from the Beginning. What makes this abnormal? Our emotions were designed to protect us from harmful situations, not put us in them. However, if they are overused or misused, it will affect our ability to think rationally, causing us to settle or operate in Spiritual Error.

From the Ancient of Days until now, to make a *Spirit to Spirit* Connection, *As It Pleases God*, we must MASTER the ability to remain calm and be at peace with ourselves and others. Why must we remain calm and at peace with others? To avoid short-circuiting, draining, or zapping ourselves. What is the purpose of comparing our being with electricity? We generate electricity, and it is only wise to make such a comparison. What we charge our cells with is what we will receive in due time. So, it behooves us NOT to charge ourselves with negativity. What is the big deal about what we energize ourselves with? In due season, we will give off this energy, even if we pretend to be positive.

Regardless of which side of the playing field we are on, positively or negatively, they both attract and repel. Negative energy gleans power from positive or negative sources. Positive energy gleans power from positivity and becomes depleted by negativity. So, we should exercise extreme caution when dealing with negativity, especially if we have not MASTERED the ability to recharge ourselves or extract and convert, *As It Pleases God*.

When I am out and about, I read the room based on the energy released. Consequently, when someone is putting on their A-Game, operating on their N-Game, I already know what I am dealing with. How? Their conversational words, demeanor, behavior, questions, or responses confirm their fruits and character, affording me the opportunity to read the room without saying one word.

When truly operating in the Fruits of the Spirit, it comes with Divine Illumination, allowing us to see what most cannot. Of course, not in judgment, but for REVELATION. The Bible says, *"Therefore by their fruits you will know them."* Matthew 7:20. To know what we are dealing with, in or out of the Kingdom, we must lay aside our *Emotional Glitches*, paying attention to our fruits and those of another.

What is the purpose of paying attention to our fruits? We may not recognize the fruits exhibited in others, especially if we do not know them or operate with the Fruits of the Spirit and Christlike Character for ourselves. More importantly, if we do not know the difference between positive and negative fruits, we will miss our Spiritual Cue when the Holy Spirit advises or warns us.

Once we are in Spiritual Alignment, *As It Pleases God*, it is imperative for us not to become reactive, abusive, or confrontational. Why? It can release negative energy. If we feel ourselves becoming provoked, we must change the trajectory of the energy immediately to a positive atmosphere. If we cannot change the atmosphere, we can also excuse ourselves by having a cooling-off period. Clearly, this is not to run away, but to deal with the provocation to avoid a *Physical Glitch* or reaction.

THE PHYSICAL GLITCH

Physical Indebtedness or Glitches are eliminated by knowing what we are dealing with and why. If we do not know by now, the outer manifestations of who we are in Earthen Vessel are objectively real, beginning from an internal seed of *Something Else*. In *Business is Business: As It Pleases God*, for this section, we are speaking of being indebted to people, places, and things, often having nothing to do with money, and more with yokes, bondages, and soul ties.

Most often, our *Physical Glitches* will show up in our people skills, even if we do not acknowledge them. Why would our people skills be affected as Believers? Everything in life is based upon relationships; if there is oversight or neglect on our behalf or that of another, we will find ourselves between a rock and a hard place when it ends, be it personal, professional, casual, substantial, or conditional.

How do we heal, *As It Pleases God*? It will vary from person to person, trauma to trauma, culture to culture, and so on. On a broader aspect of healing from the inside out...we must own our truth! We often fall short of our people skills due to the lies we tell while justifying them as our self-fulfilling prophecies. What does this mean? Simply put, we lie to ourselves while denying the truth about who we are, what we are doing, how we got there, when it happens, why we are doing it, and with whom! As a result, we assume a mask to portray ourselves in a certain way, contradicting ourselves and causing rifts in our relationships because they know we are in denial.

When dealing with our people skills, we may not realize most of our issues are derived from fear or anger, leading to *Something Else*. Listen, anger, and fear issues are real; therefore, it is best to engage in self-help or self-correcting techniques to assist in our self-control repertoire, regardless of the age group. We are never too young or old to begin mastering or managing our inherent fears or triggering fits of anger. If we do not learn how to cope with the two, our *Something Else* can create undue pressure.

To avoid *Physical Glitches* preventing us from achieving mental or emotional freedom, we must find a way to create balance within the human psyche. How can we obtain balance when we cannot see our way clearly? It is done by thinking good, positive, and fruitful thoughts while doing a few things, but not limited to such:

- ☐ FIND the problem, issue, or root cause.
- ☐ OWN your truth.
- ☐ UNDERSTAND the WHY.
- ☐ REPENT of how it affects you.
- ☐ FORGIVE yourself and others.
- ☐ RELEASE whatever it is or is not to God.
- ☐ DOCUMENT or journal the lesson, instructions, or nuggets of wisdom.
- ☐ ADD God into the equation of whatever, with whomever.
- ☐ COVER yourself with the Blood of Jesus.
- ☐ USE the Fruits of the Spirit
- ☐ INVOKE the Holy Spirit to guide, provide, and rearrange.
- ☐ GIVE thanks.
- ☐ SAY Amen.

This approach helps us pinpoint our thoughts, actions, and emotions to enhance our culpability and coping skills. What does this mean for a Believer? As Believers, it helps us to focus, problem-solve, negotiate, persevere, and become flexible in all things, *As It Pleases God*. If we omit the work-in-progress mentality, we will find ourselves having hidden or open bouts of anger, fear, resistance, and disobedience. Now, if we do not know what to look for when engaging in self-development or Spiritual Maturity, we will overlook the character traits God is looking for.

Whether trigger-happy or trigger-focused, our people skills are essential in becoming our best selves while avoiding people, places, and things that cause us to fall short. More importantly, when we think we cannot fall short, we subject ourselves to temptations easily besetting us. For this reason, it is essential to exhibit humility, *As It Pleases God*, and not our own version of humility.

What can humility do for our *Physical Glitches*? According to the Heavenly of Heavens, it allows us to become a Spiritual Remnant. What does a remnant have to do with *Glitches*? God uses the leftover remnants to Bless us to be a Blessing. Most often, we turn up our noses at any form of residue, but to say the least, in the Eye of God, the residue has a purpose, even if it does not appear as much.

When God takes away something, it is just as important as what remains. How do we make this make sense? Our perception causes us to overlook treasures to pick up or value trash. Also, overlooking the hidden treasures affects our people skills, causing us to second-guess ourselves or live with regret. How is this possible when we have free will to choose? Unfortunately, our free will is not the problem here; it is our ability to see the trash or treasure clearly, or to see it for what it really is. If we transform our mindsets with the Spiritual Remnant Mentality, we can indeed change the trajectory of our lives. Is this Biblical? Of course. *"It may be that the LORD your God will hear all the words of the Rabshakeh, whom his master the king of Assyria has sent to reproach the living God, and will rebuke the words which the LORD your God has heard. Therefore, lift up your prayer for the remnant that is left."* 2nd Kings 19:4.

When we are grateful for what we have left, we can better release the people, places, and things having nothing to do with our Predestined Blueprint to embrace the upward movement of the seeds sown in or out of season.

How do we know if we are releasing or embracing properly? Growth is the indicator; the lack of it lets us know we may be operating in Spiritual

Error. Please allow me to align accordingly: *"This shall be a sign to you: You shall eat this year such as grows of itself, and in the second year what springs from the same; Also in the third year sow and reap, Plant vineyards and eat the fruit of them. And the remnant who have escaped of the house of Judah Shall again take root downward, And bear fruit upward. For out of Jerusalem shall go a remnant, and those who escape from Mount Zion. The zeal of the LORD of hosts will do this."* 2nd Kings 19:29-31.

By refusing to look at people, places, and things as possible Spiritual Remnants, we can overlook our Divine Blessings, Testings, Lessons, Cues, Classrooms, or Promises. How is this possible? A REMNANT is a SEED, and if we refuse to plant or uproot, *As It Pleases God*, we may miss the appropriate timing of tilling, sowing, growing, and harvesting, *As It Pleases Him*. At the same time, we will inadvertently pick up negative feelings, thoughts, beliefs, and biases, causing us to turn on ourselves with *Physical Glitches*. Blasphemy, right? Unfortunately, ungratefulness or negativity prompts us to plunder the Promises of God from our Forefathers until now. Here is what we need to know before moving on: *"So I will forsake the remnant of My inheritance and deliver them into the hand of their enemies; and they shall become victims of plunder to all their enemies, because they have done evil in My sight, and have provoked Me to anger since the day their fathers came out of Egypt, even to this day."* 2nd Kings 21:14-15.

How can we avoid turning on ourselves? It will vary from person to person, situation to situation, culture to culture, bias to bias, issue to issue, and so on. Nonetheless, here are a few pointers:

- ☐ Return to God. *"Children of Israel, return to the LORD God of Abraham, Isaac, and Israel; then He will return to the remnant of you who have escaped from the hand of the kings of Assyria."* 2nd Chronicles 30:6.
- ☐ Avoid negative or wayward conditioning, thoughts, or beliefs. *"And do not be like your fathers and your brethren, who trespassed against the LORD God of their fathers, so that He gave them up to desolation, as you see."* 2nd Chronicles 30:7.
- ☐ Avoid disobedience. *"Now do not be stiff-necked, as your fathers were."* 2nd Chronicles 30:8a.
- ☐ Develop a *Spirit to Spirit* Relationship with God. *"But yield yourselves to the LORD; and enter His sanctuary, which He has sanctified forever, and serve the LORD your God, that the fierceness of His wrath may turn away from you."* 2nd Chronicles 30:8b.

What are the Spiritual Benefits associated with the four pointers? According to the Heavenly of Heavens, the four pointers are similar to respecting the Spiritual Four Corners, guiding us like a Divine Compass. Whereas in the Eye of God, compassion, grace, mercy, and redemption are our seeds, spreading to the Four Corners in Earthen Vessel. Really? Yes, really! *"For if you return to the LORD, your brethren and your children will be treated with compassion by those who lead them captive, so that they may come back to this land; for the LORD your God is gracious and merciful, and will not turn His face from you if you return to Him."* 2nd Chronicles 30:9.

What is the big deal about the Spiritual Remnants? There is a PROMISE hidden within the understanding and ownership of Divine Remnants, *As It Pleases God*. According to scripture, it says, *"And it shall come to pass in that day That the remnant of Israel, And such as have escaped of the house of Jacob, Will never again depend on him who defeated them, But will depend on the LORD, the Holy One of Israel, in truth. The remnant will return, the remnant of Jacob, To the Mighty God. For though your people, O Israel, be as the sand of the sea, A remnant of them will return; The destruction decreed shall overflow with righteousness. For the Lord GOD of hosts Will make a determined end in the midst of all the land."* Isaiah 10:20-23.

Unbeknown to most, with this time-sensitive Promise, God will use us to feed His sheep who are knowingly or unknowingly scattered Mentally, Physically, Emotionally, Spiritually, and Financially. Here is what we must know: *"Therefore, thus says the LORD God of Israel against the shepherds who feed My people: 'You have scattered My flock, driven them away, and not attended to them. Behold, I will attend to you for the evil of your doings,' says the LORD. But I will gather the remnant of My flock out of all countries where I have driven them, and bring them back to their folds; and they shall be fruitful and increase."* Jeremiah 23:2-3.

We do not want to play around with the Folds of God, especially when our people skills are not up to par. Why? Playing around in such a manner comes with a Spiritual Woe. *" 'Woe to the shepherds who destroy and scatter the sheep of My pasture!' says the LORD."* Jeremiah 23:1. God has a plan for His sheep or remnants; therefore, we must exercise extreme caution. Just because He does not reveal His Divine Plans or show us the invisible Spiritual Crown does not mean He does not have one on us or someone else. *"In that day the LORD of hosts will be For a crown of glory and a diadem of beauty To the remnant of His people, for a spirit of justice to him who sits in judgment, and for strength to those who turn back the battle at the gate."* Isaiah 28:5.

Before moving on to *Spiritual Glitches*, here is what we must know: "But everyone shall sit under his vine and under his fig tree, And no one shall make them afraid; For the mouth of the LORD of hosts has spoken. For all people walk each in the name of his god, But we will walk in the name of the LORD our God Forever and ever. 'In that day,' says the LORD, 'I will assemble the lame, I will gather the outcast And those whom I have afflicted; I will make the lame a remnant, And the outcast a strong nation; So the LORD will reign over them in Mount Zion From now on, even forever.' " Micah 4:4-7.

THE SPIRITUAL GLITCH

Spiritual Indebtedness or Glitches are eliminated by involving the Holy Trinity (The Father, Son, and Holy Spirit) in our daily lives. Why is this important for us to know? We are indebted to God; even if we do not claim Him or our Divine Blueprint, we are created in His Image. We can debate about the Holy Trinity all we like, but if we are not in Purpose on purpose or being about our Father's Business, my question is, 'What are we really debating?' Until we can answer this question in total transparency, there is no need to debate the Will of God, but to do His Will. If we do not know what it is or is not, we have bigger issues, causing *Spiritual Glitches*.

When dealing with *Spiritual Glitches*, everyone wants to be right about God, the Bible, and so on. Yet, we must remember that no one is 100% right or wrong, nor will we be 100% perfect. We will always remain on a learning curve as long as the earth remains and we have breath in our bodies. More importantly, if we do not know or understand something about God, the Bible, or Spirituality, we need to stop making up stuff and do our homework. I cannot tell you how often I hear people making up stuff on the fly, spreading untruths while convincing others the Holy Spirit is speaking.

How can I determine if they are making up stuff without judging? First and foremost, Spirit knows Spirit! Secondly, I can hear the insecurity in their voice pattern. How is this possible? The Voice of the Holy Spirit has a tenured vibration understood by those possessing it. Thirdly, I also know Spiritual Principles, Divine Character Traits, and the Fruits of the Spirit, which gives me the ability to Spiritually Align on the spot without saying one word, with zero judgment and complete understanding.

According to the Heavenly of Heavens, as the charactorial flaws remain from the Garden of Eden, so do our WHY factors. What do our WHY Factors have to do with anything? When we understand our WHY in all things, we become better equipped to deal with all other life factors with humility. For example, the reason WHY we have Kingdom Treasures, Wisdom, and Secrets is to avoid the egotistical abuse of what is Divine. The reason WHY Jesus shed His Blood on the Cross was for Spiritual Atonement on our behalf. One of the reasons WHY we have the Holy Spirit is to become our Spiritual Comforter. For the above reasons, it is WHY we need to Spiritually Till our own ground, *As It Pleases God*, with a work-in-progress mentality and being about our Father's Business.

What if we choose not to understand the WHY? We may get a few notches knocked off our belts, particularly when we think we have arrived. Why would this happen? We are designed to remain humble. Once humility ceases, it becomes a trigger for God, as if we are becoming stiff-necked, lukewarm, or dull.

Can we really trigger God, especially when advising us to have self-control as Believers? Absolutely! Self-control used when playing as a little god or being in the image of God and being IN CONTROL as the Supreme GOD of all things are two different playing fields. Overstepping or disrespecting our boundaries is often how *Spiritual Glitches* occur, causing us to stumble into idolatry without realizing it, similar to the King Saul Experience in 1 Samuel.

King Saul started good, but once he got a little power, money, and sex under his belt, he became disobedient, unruly, and conniving in the Eye of God. Based upon the lust of the eyes, the lust of the flesh, and the pride of life, here are a few character traits he dealt with that caused *Spiritual Glitches*, but not limited to such:

- ☐ **JEALOUSY**. Are you operating in jealousy, invoking the desire to control others?
- ☐ **ENVY**. Are you envious, causing a great divide internally and externally?
- ☐ **PRIDE**. Are you prideful, arrogant, disobedient, or operating with a proud look?
- ☐ **GREED**. Are you secretly or openly greedy, ungrateful, or shed innocent blood?
- ☐ **COVETING**. Are you coveting people, places, and things that do not belong to you?
- ☐ **COMPETITIVENESS**. Are you motivated by being competitive, superior to others, or devising wicked plans?
- ☐ **LYING**. Are you obsessed with lying to yourself or others?

- ☐ **CHAOS**. Are you moved or stimulated when engaging in evil acts and sowing discord?

Unbeknown to most, aside from not exhibiting the Fruits of the Spirit, these negative character traits will cause *Spiritual Glitches* within the human psyche, invoking unrest, emptiness, and drought from a Distressing Spirit. Please allow me to align based upon the King Saul Experience in 1 Samuel 16:14-15: *"But the Spirit of the LORD departed from Saul, and a distressing spirit from the LORD troubled him. And Saul's servants said to him, 'Surely, a distressing spirit from God is troubling you.'"*

Why would God allow a Distressing Spirit to oppress us? We will become distressed by default when we engage in debauchery without self-correcting, repenting, forgiving, or outright lying about it. Unbeknown to most, it is a natural alarm system within the human psyche, letting us know a harmful intruder is in our camp and allowing us to call for Spiritual Backup. If we do nothing, the seeds of the enemy we allow can gain entry.

When we do not listen, we will find ourselves *Glitching Out* or making a mess. Why would this happen? Spiritual Blindness, Deafness, and Muteness will do it to us every time, primarily when we think we have it going on. Eventually, the blinders, earplugs, and loose lips will become our portion by continuing in such a manner, soon causing *Financial Glitches*.

THE FINANCIAL GLITCH

When being about our Father's Business, we cover all the bases: Mentally, Physically, Emotionally, Spiritually, and Financially. What makes this so crucial in the Eye of God, especially when having free will? When dealing with the vitality of life, *As It Pleases God*, there are a few reasons to cover all of the bases and develop a positive mindset. First, this ensures you can stay on top of your game, hitting a home run or creating a win-win out of everything. Secondly, it helps you overcome any challenge without creating panic within the human psyche. Thirdly, to prevent you from leaving an open door, causing one to become unglued, angry, hateful, negative, negligent, or rude, resulting in some form of *Financial Glitch*.

What do *Financial Glitches* have to do with the other areas of our lives? Most often, our *Financial Glitches* are stimulated by our *Something Else*. With effective management from the inside out, we can pay our debts off significantly if we change how we approach our finances and gratefully leverage what is available to us. Why is this so important? Having money is not beneficial if we owe everyone in town, begging and using others, amid having a cash flow that is mismanaged, or when we are on the verge of bankruptcy, trying to keep up an image.

Building a golden calf for show is indeed idolatry; self-idolatry to be exact, hidden in the word, COVETING. Really? Yes, really! *"Therefore put to death your members which are on the earth: fornication, uncleanness, passion, evil desire, and covetousness, which is idolatry. Because of these things the wrath of God is coming upon the sons of disobedience, in which you yourselves once walked when you lived in them."* Colossians 3:5-7.

If we take a moment to understand WHY we do what we do thoroughly, we will find our motives will surround the lust of the eyes, the lust of the flesh, and the pride of life. All of this leads to some form of hidden or open jealousy, envy, pride, greed, or coveting, hidden underneath our *Something Else*, giving us more of a reason to pinpoint the money trail.

What is the purpose of following the trail of money? Our financial trails will often tell us what our mouths will not through our actions, truths, or lies. Whether our trail leads somewhere or nowhere, it has a meaning. If we take the time to understand the financial trail, it will change the trajectory of our lives. How? It varies from person to person, situation to situation, and bias to bias; however, most often, the trajectory will determine if we are doing something about it or if it remains the same with zero upgrades.

Financial Indebtedness or Glitches are eliminated by paying our bills on time and developing a mindset to manage our finances without becoming a victim of the poverty mindset. Whether we are in debt or not, we must have a plan of action, paving the way into our Spiritual Negev of Divine Provisions. If we omit a plan of action, we may find ourselves '*Robbing Peter to pay Paul*,' so to speak, without realizing it, while spending with zero benefits.

We all have bills to pay; there is no mistake about this. However, when paying bills on time and keeping our debts to a bare minimum, we must make the money spent work on our behalf. What does this mean? Our dollars spent should provide a reward for us, giving us an expectation of some form of benefit. If not, we will splurge when we should not, or not have enough when we need it, causing *Financial Glitches*.

What do we do if we have bad credit? It varies from person to person, situation to situation, and so on. Nevertheless, we should adhere to three basic things to avoid *Financial Glitches*. First, we must know where we stand with our credit analysis, credit score, and financial status. Secondly, we must begin paying our household bills on time. Thirdly, we must know we do not have to remain in this condition and commit to working on our credit from now on, up to the next seven years. Why seven years? Bad debt takes seven years to fall off our credit report, but it does not mean we cannot begin rebuilding it right now. For this reason, here is what we must know, but not limited to such:

- ☐ Getting pre-approved WITHOUT IMPACTING our credit scores when seeking a house, car, loan, or credit card is best. Doing so prevents excessive hard inquiries on our credit reports. If NO IMPACT is advertised, ensure a copy of the advertisement is kept. If it shows up on our credit reports, we can file a complaint with Experian, Equifax, and TransUnion to get it removed.

- ☐ Beware of credit repair agencies; the quick-fix schemes are out there. If we decide to take the shortcut without understanding our point of erring, we may end up getting got!

- ☐ When rebuilding credit, opt for secured credit cards (security deposit) with Citi, Capital One, and Discover instead of paying the high one-time fees, annual fees, and maintenance fees for other secured or unsecured credit cards. In rebuilding our creditworthiness, we should not waste money paying excessive fees. However, we should only use secured credit cards when we DO NOT qualify for unsecured ones with Chase, Citi, Capital One, American Express, Discover, Bank of America, or Wells Fargo.

Whatever we decide to do with our credit, the choice is ours to make, but make sure to exhibit *Credit Card Safety* when choosing. Regardless of where we are on our journey, we must avoid *Financial Glitches* in the American Dream. In all things, we must protect ourselves because thieves are among us. We cannot ignore this fact or pretend we are exempt. So, I encourage proactive safety to prevent undue trauma, stress, or mishaps. Listed below are a few tips to avoid *Credit Card Glitches*, but not limited to such:

- ☐ Keep your credit or debit cards in a safety pouch.
- ☐ Do not allow your credit or debit card out of your sight.

- ☐ Do not leave your credit card lying around.
- ☐ Do not use your credit or debit card on an unsecured website beginning with (http://). It must be secured with (https://).
- ☐ Do not keep your PIN with your card.
- ☐ Do not give your PIN to anyone.
- ☐ Make sure no one sees your PIN when withdrawing money from the ATM or purchasing an item.
- ☐ Question and verify suspicious emails with credit card companies or banks to avoid phishing scams.
- ☐ Keep your checkbook and cards separate.
- ☐ Report your lost or stolen cards immediately and place a freeze on your card.
- ☐ Do not leave your account numbers visible.
- ☐ Shred your credit card information when discarding it.

As we live our best lives, we do not often focus on doing business and *Leveraging Credit* until we need it. In my opinion, we should always remain in the proactive stage of building and protecting our credit. Why? An unknown credit glitch can cost us everything, especially when building a life of substance. Now, with more or less credit opportunities, here are the frowned-upon credit glitches, but not limited to such:

- ☐ Multiple credit applications or credit abuse.
- ☐ Late payments over 30 days.
- ☐ When we are in arrears on a mortgage or loans.
- ☐ Judgment for a debt owed.
- ☐ Repossessions.
- ☐ Recent and undischarged bankruptcy.

Why do we need to know this? When being about our Father's Business or *Leveraging Business*, we must monitor our credit and financial status, like getting our oil changed or maintaining our vehicles.

Listen, the *Glitching Outcry* does not have anyone's name on it. To avoid becoming a victim, we must proactively prepare, *As It Pleases* God, to facilitate our Predestined Blueprint, containing its own Spiritual Negev.

Chapter Ten

Leveraging Business

Our quality of life is crucial in the Eye of God; He does not want us to become overwhelmed with debt, overspending, drenched by a poverty mindset, or in a state of covetousness. According to the Heavenly of Heavens, our lives are more than dollars earned or spent; it is about becoming or doing what we have been called to do in Earthen Vessels, allowing our Divine Provisions to find us. When doing business or developing our credibility, *As It Pleases God*, in due season, "*A man's gift makes room for him, And brings him before great men.*" Proverbs 18:16.

As my give back to the Spiritual Negev, flowing to and through me, it is my reasonable service to provide tips or techniques to gain Mental, Physical, Emotional, Spiritual, and Financial freedom with organization and pristine clarity, *As It Pleases God*. What can this do for us? The commitment to leveraging ourselves in such a manner helps bring Divine Illumination with internal balance, humility, and growth that money cannot buy. While simultaneously becoming a fisherman of all men with a *Baited Hook* that packs a powerful punch.

Moving forward in *Business is Business*, and being about our Father's Business, self-control is needed. Why do we need self-control when establishing leverage? A superfluous ego is a recipe for disaster when left untamed or consumed by materialism. How do we know if we are pompous? Please allow me to counteract this question with another: 'Besides God, who knows us better than we know ourselves?' 'Besides God, who knows our WHY better than us?' Nevertheless, here are a few indicators, but not limited to such:

- ☐ If we feel as if we need trophies, titles, or recognition for doing what we do.
- ☐ When we are not tapping into our Divine Purpose or Passion, according to our Divine Blueprint.

- ☐ If we are easily triggered to become angry, rude, judgmental, or chaotic.
- ☐ If we are hateful, mean, or grouchy.
- ☐ If we are a gruesome complainer.
- ☐ If we look for fault in others without working on ourselves to become better, stronger, or wiser.
- ☐ If we are very unforgiving or unmerciful.
- ☐ If we are a fire starter or a gas lighter.
- ☐ If we find ourselves getting mad at others about their personal belongings.
- ☐ If we find ourselves using what we have done for another as a form of blackmailed or manipulation.
- ☐ If we find ourselves praying negative or harmful prayers without accounting for our debaucherous behaviors.
- ☐ If we do not listen to WISE counsel, especially when solicited, or we have to play cleanup afterward.
- ☐ If we find ourselves making a mess out of people, places, and things, Mentally, Physically, Emotionally, Spiritually, and Financially.

What does all of this have to do with *Business is Business: As It Pleases God*? If the internal balance is out of whack, our finances will reflect likewise. Even if our pockets are loaded, we have deeper than deep pockets or holes in them; in the Eye of God, it is still a leveled playing field for the human psyche. So, when playing by God's rules, we need LEVERAGE, period!

How do we obtain Heavenly Leverage in or out of the Kingdom? Having a sense of control helps the human psyche set limits and boundaries, allowing us to persevere under pressure to create a win-win, regardless of how it appears to the naked eye. Whereas, if we DO NOT have self-control, doing what we so desire, it is a possibility we may collapse or implode Mentally, Physically, Emotionally, Spiritually, and Financially under pressure when faced with a loss or when negatively triggered.

As long as we are not in debt, it is easy to point the finger, but is pointing the finger the right answer? Absolutely not. Our responsibility is to teach others the ropes of finances, even if it is one step at a time, instead of judgment. Why is it our responsibility, mainly when we are accountable for our own lives? We have all been on a learning curve; if not, keep living!

In or out of our curve of learning, there is no reason to crucify someone over finances when our psyche (soulish nature) is unstable. Nor should we degrade someone's intellectual condition or the lack thereof when our Spiritual Condition is ungodly, outright unkempt, or manipulative. Also, we should not downgrade others because we know something they do not; we should be more willing to share.

Why should we share, especially when having to work hard for everything that we have? Once again, God is looking for BALANCE in helping others through our experiences. By gaining balance in such a manner, *As It Pleases Him*, there are a lot of people, places, and things we will instinctively avoid to maintain our internal and external freedoms while placing value in its appropriate place. What can we do to help ourselves in this area? It varies from person to person, situation to situation, bias to bias, and so on; however, when it comes to our Father's Business, here are a few tips on how the convergence works according to Him:

- ☐ Develop a Plan of Action, Budget, or Tally Sheet and stick to it. This tip applies to any area of our lives. *As It Pleases God*, it assists in the emergence of discipline within the human psyche.

- ☐ Develop a spending limit to control the urge to overspend. *As It Pleases God*, it contributes to the development of self-control.

- ☐ Buy what we can pay for, living within our means. *As It Pleases God*, it keeps coveting from providing a yoke or snare within the Mind, Body, or Soul.

- ☐ Avoid impulsive buying, especially when feeling bored, upset, envious, or angry. *As It Pleases God*, it exercises the ability to say 'No' and mean it, based on what is good or bad, positive or negative, right or wrong, want or need, and so on, keeping the inner chatter at a minimum.

- ☐ Tally the amount we spend as we go, even if budgeting is not our thing. *As It Pleases God*, it helps us get into the habit of documenting and developing mind-eye and hand-eye coordination.

- ☐ Cross-check our spending limits with what is actually spent. *As It Pleases God*, it keeps us from lying or hiding things from ourselves.

- ☐ Pay the balance monthly if possible, keeping the overall debt below 10%. *As It Pleases God*, this causes us to proactively think about what we are doing before it is done, while heeding to a certain vision.

- ☐ Pay bills on time to avoid late fees, paying higher interest rates, or decreasing credit scores. *As It Pleases God*, it keeps us from developing selfishness or the user mentality, thinking everyone owes us something. In all actuality, we owe it to ourselves to "*Render to Caesar the things that are Caesar's, and to God the things that are God's.*" Mark 12:17.

- ☐ If carrying more than 10% high-interest credit card debt, consider a balance transfer to a card containing 0% APR for 6-12 months. Doing so gives us an opportunity to pay more toward the actual balance without interest. *As It Pleases God*, it helps us to become good stewards of our Divine Provisions.

- ☐ Opt for the no-annual-fee credit cards. *As It Pleases God*, it prevents us from wasting money when it is within our power to cut back.

Why should we adhere to this list? First, budgets help us manage and be aware of our debts. Secondly, we do not want bad habits to become an ungoverned lifestyle catering to our impulses, addictions, or traumas. How does this apply to us? Unbeknown to most, doing business is interwoven within the human psyche. For example, if a child grows up impoverished, once they become well-to-do, they buy everything to feed the childhood trauma of not having enough.

On the other hand, if a child grows up getting everything, throwing temper tantrums if they do not get what they want, they will become ungrateful for the simple things in life, wanting more, more, and more like a bottomless pit. Unfortunately, these affect and infect other areas of our lives, even if we cannot talk about or admit it. If we learn to do business, *As It Pleases God*, the other areas of our lives become easier to maintain.

What is the big deal, especially if we can afford our wants, needs, desires, and habits? Whether we can afford them or not, dissatisfaction and ungratefulness are the keywords here. Having bouts with dissatisfied or ungrateful thoughts, actions, behaviors, and beliefs will negatively impact the Mind, Body, Soul, and Spirit. To the detriment of the human psyche, they all lead to people-pleasing or needing validation from others to determine our worth, eventually showing up in our finances. Here is what we must know: "*Hell and Destruction are never full; So, the eyes of man are never satisfied. The refining pot is for silver and the furnace for gold, and a man is valued by what others say of him.*" Proverbs 27:20-21.

Using the above list makes us a better planner in other areas governing our peace; instead of having chaos or wishy-washiness leading us into *Something Else*. When we can handle our business Mentally, Physically, Emotionally, Spiritually, and Financially, it builds confidence naturally within the human psyche. How does confidence affect our finances? Our psyche knows the truth about us; it knows all the kempt or unkempt areas. So, if we lie to ourselves without repenting or engaging in a work-in-progress agreement with God or being about our Father's Business, it possesses the power we gave it, doing what it is designed to do.

THE BATTLE FOR THE MIND

What is the psyche designed to do? Rule over us with all types of impulses, deception, denial, and blaming until we awaken from our slumber, *As It Pleases God*. The more we ignore this one factor, the bigger the gap becomes between the ONE God of all, Who is within us all. In addition, it also impacts our thought patterns and how we communicate with ourselves from the inside out. The most prominent example is when the mind says one thing, the heart says another, and our conscience also weighs in, causing an internal battle or extreme exhaustion.

If we have not noticed by now, our tangible communication tools, such as our eyes, ears, mouth, and nose, are closer to the mind than the soul (the core of our being) for a reason. It allows us to rationalize or govern what is going on in the MIND, or evaluate our brainial functions before involving the intangible heart (soul).

On average, by using less than 10% of our brainial functions, if a soulish trigger occurs, it still allows us to interject positivity and rationale, or the negativity and defeat of our choosing based upon the mindset, as well as our people and problem-solving skills. All of these are based on what we see, hear, speak, taste, and smell before connecting the power of touch or engagement. Why do we need to know this? It gives us the ability to shut it or them down, safeguarding ourselves to be about our Father's Business, *As It Pleases Him*.

How is this possible when the soul(psyche) is one with the mind? Here is where Spiritual Erring takes place. Just as the body is one in itself, it has many members. If we go to the doctor, they do not treat the entire body; they treat the members of the body, such as the head, eye, arm, finger, heart, chest, leg, knee, foot, toe, and so on. Therefore, when dealing with the psyche, it is imperative to deal with the MIND separately. Why? It is where the Realm of Spirituality takes place, serving as a Spiritual Filter before depositing whatever or whomever within the soul or reacting on emotions. More importantly, it is where SCIENCE has not tapped into yet.

Why does science have limited access to the components of the mind? Spiritual Death from the Garden of Eden was not with the body, as most would think. It was through the Divine Connection back to the Kingdom of God in Earthen Vessel through our mental communicative capacity. Blasphemy, right? Wrong!

In Genesis 3, when the serpent beguiled Eve, he planted a seedful thought in her mind, and she had the choice to accept, reject, or ponder on it. Nothing happened to her Mind, Body, Soul, or Spirit until she put ACTION behind the seedful thought planted with a question of contempt from the most cunning beast of the field. As a result of her acceptance of the seedful thoughts, the cunned individual became cunning, feeling right or justified in her own eyes.

With the implantation taking effect with the same Seed of Deception, she gave the Forbidden Fruit to her husband to keep the cycle going. Once Adam took part in this act of disobedience, it changed the trajectory of how the Mind's Eye connects to the Mind of God and His All-seeing EYE as the cycle continues.

What does the cycle have to do with the Mind's Eye or Eye of God? In all simplicity, nothing has changed up until now with the Seed of Deception. It is still seeking its dominance and relevance, preventing us from being about our Father's Business, *As It Pleases Him*. However, the Blood of Jesus and the Holy Spirit are our RECONCILIATION and SALVATION factors, merging the two back together as ONE with Spiritual Conditions.

Moreover, it is available to all, making no one exempt as long as we meet the basis of the Covenantal Agreement from the Heavenly of Heavens. Thus, being that we do not fully understand this information, it causes *The Battle For The Mind* to occur within the human psyche and for the Believer to bogart, control, or prostitute God with deceptive intentions.

In the Eye of God, being that the cycle of deceptive measures has not stopped yet, therefore, it has Spiritual Laws, Protocols, and Principles protecting the Divine Access to certain Spiritual Realms, Wisdom, Secrets, Treasures, and Knowings, regardless of who we are or why we are. Really? Yes, really! Although God loves us all, for this profound reason, from the Ancient of Days until now, Spiritual Tilling must occur, *As It Pleases Him*. If not, we will have limited access, even if we go to the dark side to obtain the counterfeit version and suffer the consequences of this Spiritual Violation.

In moving forward in the Spirit of Excellence, even if someone says we do not have to do anything to become or remain a Believer, it is a LIE. We need God, the Blood of Jesus, and the Holy Spirit involved in our daily lives to unfold the reason for our being or unveil our Predestined Blueprint. More importantly, we need the Fruits of the Spirit and behave Christlike to gain Spiritual Access, *As It Pleases Him*. Why must we *Please Him* to gain Spiritual Access? Illegal Access comes with curses, yokes, and strongholds seeping into the Bloodline of the violators.

As a rule of thumb, we must work on ourselves to AVOID becoming deceitfully negative or cunning and to prevent people from getting into our heads. What is the purpose of doing so? The enemy will plot and set traps to ruin our credibility, especially in the minds of those who are gullible. Suppose we are not strong Mentally, Physically, Emotionally, Spiritually, or Financially. In this case, we can become consumed, crushed, or thrown under the bus by the cunning voices whispering in our ears, catering to our weaknesses, insecurities, lack, or traumas.

How do we know if we are being deceived? First, deception is recognized through the questions being asked, often creating doubt, the fear of missing out, or the attempt to dismantle our Spiritual Assignments. Secondly, it is known by the language spoken, whether it is positive, negative, intrusive, fact-finding, or illuminating light or darkness. Thirdly, it is identified in whether it leads us to the truth or lies about ourselves or others. Fourthly, whether it guides us to or away from the Fruits of the Spirit, Christlike Character, the Word of God, or straight into the PIT. And lastly, it prevents us from being about our Father's Business, *As It Pleases Him*.

According to the Heavenly of Heavens, the way to the Tree of Life within us and back to our Heavenly Father is HEAVILY guarded. Why? God's most precious commodities, such as gold, silver, diamonds, oil, etc., will always be hidden in plain sight, not appearing as such or causing us to work at unveiling them. From a human perspective, it is similar to Fort Knox, but with Divine Grace and Mercy attached, allowing us to forgive, repent, or change the trajectory of our conscious thoughts before seeding itself within, protecting our hidden treasures.

So, on the path to Fort Knox of the Kingdom of God, we must operate with the Mind, Body, Soul, and Spirit. What does all of this mean? How we THINK with the MIND can protect or destroy the Body and Soul, affecting our *Spirit to Spirit* Relationship with our Heavenly Father. For the record, and before moving on, just because we think right does not mean we are correct, and just because we are in right standing with God, it does not mean we are thinking right, *As It Pleases Him*. How would we know the difference? Simply put, it is noticed by what slips off our tongues, our hidden or open actions, and our internal or external reactions, which are predicated on our THOUGHTS and MINDSETS.

According to the Heavenly of Heavens, the problem with getting one-sided information from man's perspective, not from God's Divine Perspective, is that it leaves room for the *Something Else* of deceptive measures to gain a chokehold on our weakest links. The bottom line is that we must know where we are, Mentally, Physically, Emotionally, Spiritually, and Financially, to govern our next moves or Bloodline. Is any of this Biblical? It says, *"Be diligent to know the state of your flocks, And attend to your herds; For riches are not forever, Nor does a crown endure to all generations."* Proverbs 27:23-24.

Whether we have or do not have, we cannot lose ourselves amid whatever or with whomever. If we lose ourselves, deception is waiting to overtake us with negative thoughts, emotions, actions, behaviors, and beliefs. Really? Yes, really! This condition is why, when some people get a little taste of money, they become a force to be reckoned with in a bad way. How do we make this make sense? The negative character traits were already flowing through their veins, and money allowed them to become comfortable with cutting loose, removing the mask, or treating others as they were once treated.

In *Business is Business*, I suggest proactively working on our fruits and character before tasting the Promises and Blessings. Why should we work on our fruits and character if we are Believers? Regardless of who we are, where we are, or what we believe, the material gain associated with power, money, and sex MAGNIFIES who we really are at the core, eventually costing us in the long run. For the record, it can cost us Mentally, Physically, Emotionally, Spiritually, or Financially with a flaming arrow, especially if we do not find a way to add the Holy Trinity into the equation. Nonetheless, it behooves us to tread with caution. *"For I say, through the grace given to me, to everyone who is among you, not to think of himself more highly than he ought to think, but to think soberly, as God has dealt to each one a measure of faith."* Romans 12:3.

WEIGHTED ⟍BALANCER

According to the Heavenly of Heavens, without using the Fruits of the Spirit and Christlike Character as a properly *Weighted Balancer* of our faith, we subject ourselves to certain types of wrath, creating internal yokes, bondage, lost hope, and wavering faith. Why do we need a *Weighted Balancer*? It is not necessary, nor is it required. However, when using the Fruits of the Spirit and Christlike Character as a *Weighted Balancer*, it indeed provides benefits and privileges of the Kingdom. *"When you eat the labor of your hands, You shall be happy, and it shall be well with you."* Psalm 128:2.

How can we equate ourselves with a *Weighted Balancer*? Basically, it provides a symbolic Spiritual Anchor. For example, when fishing in strong currents, without a weighted sinker when casting, the fishing line will wind up all over the place, it will become harder to control, and it will reduce the anchoring ability. What does weighted or Spiritual anchoring have to do with anything? In the Eye of God, it has profound meaning if we dare to grasp the underlying, yet profound WISDOM connecting us to the Divine Oath.

Here is one of the Divine Oaths we need for *Business is Business*: *"For when God made a promise to Abraham, because He could swear by no one greater, He swore by Himself, saying, 'Surely blessing I will bless you, and multiplying I will multiply you.' And so, after he had patiently endured, he obtained the promise. For men indeed swear by the greater, and an oath for confirmation is for them an end of all dispute. Thus God, determining to show more abundantly to the heirs of promise the immutability of His counsel, confirmed it by an oath, that by two immutable things, in which it is impossible for God to lie, we might have strong consolation, who have fled for refuge to lay hold of the hope set before us."* Hebrews 6:13-18. How would this apply? It is Spiritually Enforcable if we know how to do so when being about our Father's Business or ALIGNING accordingly with our Predestined Blueprint. Now, if we use it to further our agendas, having nothing to do with Him and misaligning, then it is a different story.

I have always heard the cliché, 'Give credit where credit is due.' Who does not want to be acknowledged, right? Actually, due to our human nature, it feels good to receive credit, whether just or unjust. However, giving credit where there is no effort changes this cliché dramatically.

Out of all due respect, there is another cliché saying, 'Give a man a fish, and he will eat for a day; teach a man how to fish, and he will eat for a lifetime.' As a Spiritual Dimension of the Divine Oath, in or out of season, teaching others how to fish for their own substance is the most sustainable way to share the various scopes or the acknowledgments of our Spiritual Gifts, opening our Spiritual Negev.

In the south, where I am from, fishing for information, understanding, substance, or whatever, is when we STRATEGICALLY take what we have in or around us to solve a temporary or long-term problem. It does not matter whether or not the problem resides within us or with another; fishing for our own substance will help eliminate the victim mentality, calming the human psyche. It also gives us the upper hand in acknowledging our shortcomings and strengths, allowing us to do something about our situations, circumstances, or conditions, and building the necessary skills to up the ante on whatever, with whomever.

Regardless of whether we believe it or not, there is GREATNESS in everyone. More importantly, we must share what we have to help bring forth something positive in someone else while taking a step back, allowing them to shine. Listen, true leaders give credit where credit is due; they teach others how to fish for their own substance, expecting nothing in return.

In my opinion, you cannot go wrong in rightfully sharing, respecting, and serving others regardless of how they feel about you or vice versa. Yet, at the same time, if you never do anything to better yourself, nothing ever happens, or stagnation may occur, preventing you from doing your due diligence, *As It Pleases God*. According to the Spiritual Oath, here is what we must know with simplicity:

- ☐ We are designed to multiply. *"For when God made a promise to Abraham, because He could swear by no one greater, He swore by Himself, saying, 'Surely blessing I will bless you, and multiplying I will multiply you.'"* Hebrews 6:13-14.

- ☐ We must be patient. *"And so, after he had patiently endured, he obtained the promise."* Hebrews 6:15.

- ☐ We must stand on the Spiritual Oath without wavering, doubting, fussing, fighting, or complaining. *"For men indeed swear by the greater, and an oath for confirmation is for them an end of all dispute. Thus God, determining to show more abundantly to the heirs of promise the immutability of His counsel, confirmed it by an oath."* Hebrews 6:16-17.

- ☐ We must understand that God is not a liar, placing a Spiritual Seal on our faith. *"By two immutable things, in which it is impossible for God to lie, we might have strong consolation, who have fled for refuge to lay hold of the hope set before us."* Hebrews 6:18.

- We must anchor ourselves in the Holy Trinity, doing what needs to be done for Divine Order to avail itself at the right time, while Spiritually Sealing our hope. *"This hope we have as an anchor of the soul, both sure and steadfast, and which enters the Presence behind the veil, where the forerunner has entered for us, even Jesus, having become High Priest forever according to the order of Melchizedek."* Hebrews 6:19-20.

Amid our faith and hope, we are designed to sharpen ourselves and others. If we find ourselves cutting wounds into others as a pastime, we need to make a few charactorial adjustments surrounding our faith and hope. Why should we make changes, especially if we are comfortable with who we are, while being faithful and hopeful? I am not here to discount anyone's hope or faith; I am here to feed God's sheep from His Divine Perspective.

Here is the deal: First and foremost, we are designed to learn, grow, and sow back into the Kingdom. Secondly, if we are dealing with stunted growth, *As It Pleases God*, the psyche wallows in unrest by default, hidden under masks, doubt, lies, and deceptive measures. Thirdly, if rotten fruits are spoiling the bunch, it makes us and others uncomfortable by default, even if we choose not to admit it. Please allow me to align before moving on: *"As iron sharpens iron, so a man sharpens the countenance of his friend."* Proverbs 27:17. The type of iron needed will vary from person to person, situation to situation, condition to condition, mindset to mindset, and so on. Frankly, this is more of a reason to establish a *Spirit to Spirit* Relationship with our Heavenly Father, cover ourselves in the Blood of Jesus, and allow the Holy Spirit to guide us on our *Iron Sharpening Journey*.

Unbeknown to most, our *Iron Sharpening Journey* will often become grafted into our finances. Nonetheless, we do not know how it may appear; therefore, it is essential to pay attention to overspending, underspending, selfishness, financial abuse, the rod of judgment, using others, manipulation, or when becoming a miser. They all mean something; if we miss the lesson, it creates an imbalance in other areas.

Spending more than we make is bound to catch up with us sooner or later; therefore, we must find a way to offset where we have overspent to keep our budgeted balances in check. The moment we begin to control our finances, *As It Pleases God*, we will find Him helping us understand our mistakes, causing us to self-correct, reflect back to awaken us, and identify the problem immediately. This approach provides us with a *Baited Hook*, allowing us to sharpen our iron from the inside out.

BAITED HOOK!

Whether we teach others how to fish, fish for ourselves, or when doing business, *As It Pleases God*, baiting the hook is mandatory. Why must we provide bait? It is in our nature to become drawn to some form of lure, attraction, or temptation instigated by our wants, needs, desires, or the lack thereof. All of these are governed by the Gravitational Pull, which is based upon our Divine Blueprint, how far we are straying away from it, or what is inside the core of our being.

More importantly, everyone's BAITED GATE will not be the same. Why? One man's treasure is another man's trigger, and the other man's trigger is the treasure for the next person. Listen, we are all created differently with varying fingerprints, footprints, and mind prints, even if we pretend to be alike. If we do not master this Divine Principle, our enemy gains leverage to capitalize on our weaknesses as we pretend to be strong. Why would this happen? Humility is our true strength. When we exhibit overzealous strength or become a know-it-all, the enemy can set traps to trip us, proving we are NOT who we say we are to create doubt, disbelief, or insecurity.

On the other hand, if our hidden strengths have a *Baited Hook* of humility, *As It Pleases God*, the enemy's tricks become a Lesson, Blessing, Testing, or Nutrition for the Kingdom of God. Really? Yes, really! For this reason, in a *Spirit to Spirit* Relationship with our Heavenly Father or in a Spiritual Classroom, we must document, document, and capture the information for His sheep. Not our sheep, not their sheep, but HIS sheep!

Why must we know about the *Baited Hook* and God's sheep? Simply put, we have Believers praying wicked, deceptive prayers or trying to become Spiritual Bosses over other people's stuff not belonging to them for the come up, while insulting His sheep behind their back. After all, they think this behavior is rightfully justified, whereas it is NOT in the Eye of God. Why? It is based upon deceptiveness. We do not need anyone to tell us when we are behaving in such a manner; the psyche knows, overriding our sense of good judgment, leaning toward what appears right in our eyes without TRUTHFULLY involving the Holy Trinity. How do we know the difference? If there is any form of selfishness, untruths, or biases in this equation, more than likely, the Father, Son, and Holy Spirit may not be involved, and repentance needs to occur.

Why must we repent if we feel deceived or ousted? According to the Heavenly of Heavens, deceptiveness is derived from jealousy, envy, pride, coveting, or greed. For the record, being deceitful is an act, whereas feeling deceived or thinking we are getting the short end of the stick is a matter of perception. Unfortunately, this is one reason we operate in Spiritual Error without knowing it. For example, repentance must occur when we say one thing as being pro-holy, and our behaviors, demeanors, words, thoughts, or beliefs prove otherwise. Without self-correcting, we will turn on ourselves, getting the short end of the stick while appearing right in our own eyes.

Let us go deeper, or better yet, deeper than deep. A non-correcting and non-repenting mindset will cause us to turn on ourselves from the inside out. Why would we turn on ourselves, especially when we are pro-self? Although the psyche is very fickle, it keeps account of the good and bad, right and wrong, just and unjust, as well as our indifferences and avoidances. Unbeknown to most, to negatively turn on others without compassion or mercy, we must turn on ourselves first from the inside, spreading outwardly, even if we proclaim to love ourselves.

What is the purpose of the psyche keeping track of what we do or do not do? It contributes to us walking uprightly, *As It Pleases God*, or meandering with a topsy-turvy effect as it pleases self. Listen, the psyche has an internal file cabinet waiting for the right moment to gain leverage, especially when we do not know how to release our *Something Else* to God Almighty. It also happens when we are clueless about how to Spiritually Counteract our negatives into positives using the Word of God and the Fruits of the Spirit. Without taking the time and energy to pray, repent, self-correct, or invoke our Spiritual Gifts, Divine Blueprint, Spiritual Provisions, or Supernatural Alignment regarding our own stuff, *As It Pleases God*, it will cause us to feel like a victim or pretend as if we are one.

Then again, if we do not walk in the LIGHT, it may cause us to operate in Spiritual Error or opt for a grab bag full of tricks, causing the *Baited Hook* to become a pruning hook instead. Please allow me to align: "*Many people shall come and say, 'Come, and let us go up to the mountain of the LORD, To the house of the God of Jacob; He will teach us His ways, And we shall walk in His paths.' For out of Zion shall go forth the law, And the word of the LORD from Jerusalem. He shall judge between the nations, And rebuke many people; They shall beat their swords into plowshares, And their spears into pruning hooks; Nation shall not lift up sword against nation, Neither shall they learn war anymore. O house of Jacob, come and let us walk In the light of the LORD.*" Isaiah 2:3-5.

When walking in the LIGHT or becoming Spiritually Illuminated, if we do not take the initiative to exhibit the Fruits of the Spirit or use Christlike Character, only sharing the victim mentality, we will have issues with ourselves and God. Why? Siccing God on others or pimping God to appeal to our illusional visions, bogus paybacks, or the downfall of another, we will fall short Mentally, Physically, Emotionally, Spiritually, or Financially. Unfortunately, with the *Baited Hook* becoming a pruning one, it will bring forth after its own kind, baiting the bait for another to satiate the longing hidden within the psyche.

What is the big deal about pruning hooks? A pruning hook can become dangerous, especially before the season of harvest. Here is what we must know before moving on: *"For before the harvest, when the bud is perfect And the sour grape is ripening in the flower, He will both cut off the sprigs with pruning hooks And take away and cut down the branches. They will be left together for the mountain birds of prey And for the beasts of the earth; The birds of prey will summer on them, And all the beasts of the earth will winter on them."* Isaiah 18:5-6. For this reason, it is imperative to ensure the psyche is not secretly sour or repulsive amid the growth process. Why? When the cutback occurs, we do not want to ooze all over the place, trying to hold on to dead people, places, and things, getting caught in our self-made snares.

As a Word to the Wise, when we bait our hooks to ensnare the RIGHTEOUS, we can become an Enemy of God, so beware. Why must we exhibit caution? When the Holy Spirit leads, He will advise us when to be extremely cautious with the thoughts of casting ill will, misguiding, or setting a trap of doom and gloom over someone He is using for Kingdom Purposes, or it is unjustified. In addition, He will also send a warning when attempting to lead them into Spiritual Error intentionally. When this type of warning goes out in the Realm of the Spirit, the cautionary Spiritual Decree goes out to the person we are attempting to mislead as well. Sometimes they get it, and sometimes they may not, due to some form of Spiritual Blindness, Deafness, or Muteness. However, the question is, 'Would we want to risk our plots backfiring?'

For the record, when engaging in a *Spirit to Spirit* Relationship with our Heavenly Father, the Holy Spirit will not warn us without warning them, and vice versa. Why would God inform anyone of a deceptive *Baited Hook*? First, it allows us to suit up with the Whole Armor of God to withstand the enemy's wiles. Why? He knows, *"We do not wrestle against flesh and blood, but against principalities, against powers, against the rulers of the darkness of this age, against spiritual hosts of wickedness in the heavenly places."* Ephesians 6:12. Secondly, He advises them to stand down, allowing them to retreat, rethink, repent, recalibrate their mindset, forgive, or add Him into the equation. Thirdly, if any involved parties miss their Spiritual Cue or Warning, with or without the *Baited Hook*, they are still accountable!

Although, as a Child of God, we should NOT behave as if we do not have home training, try to ensnare others, or prey upon their weaknesses. However, if we decide to behave in such a manner, here is what can happen: *"Because you have forgotten the God of your salvation, And have not been mindful of the Rock of your stronghold, Therefore you will plant pleasant plants And set out foreign seedlings; In the day you will make your plant to grow, And in the morning you will make your seed to flourish; But the harvest will be a heap of ruins In the day of grief and desperate sorrow."* Isaiah 17:10-11. I do not wish grief and sorrow upon anyone. Therefore, I am giving you the information to decide whether the seedling is sown in or out of season.

In building leverage, *As It Pleases God*, we will all have our moments in the learning process or when in a Spiritual Classroom. And this is where the Holy Spirit will correct or recalibrate us, leading us into forgiveness and a state of repentance. Why do we need the help of the Holy Spirit when on a learning curve? It helps us to avoid pridefulness, worldliness, turning on ourselves, or self-destructing. All the curvature behaviors we unawaringly overlook may cause us to become stiff-necked, dull, lukewarm, a flaming sword, consumed with idolatry, or esteeming ourselves on power, money, or sex.

Unbeknown to most, the enemy's *Baited Hook* categorizes everything under the lust of the eyes, the lust of the flesh, and the pride of life, hidden in our *Something Else*. Unfortunately, these are the contributing factors to becoming the Enemy of God. Is any of this Biblical? Once again, I would have it no other way; we need to know this because it does not make sense how some of us carry ourselves in the Name of God. *"Where do wars and fights come from among you? Do they not come from your desires for pleasure that war in your members? You lust and do not have. You murder and covet and cannot obtain. You fight and war. Yet you do not have because you do not ask. You ask and do not receive, because you ask amiss, that you may spend it on your pleasures. Adulterers and adulteresses! Do you not know that friendship with the world is enmity with God? Whoever therefore wants to be a friend of the world makes himself an enemy of God."* James 4:1-4.

We must set aside our differences for the Kingdom of God, coming together as ONE, being about our Father's Business. But, for some reason, the *Baited Hook* for the Kingdom has become downtrodden by those designed to uphold it. What does this mean? The character traits of worldly individuals supersede those of the Kingdom of God.

As I move about, I have to shake my head in dismay. Asking God and myself...Where is the kindness? Where is the love for one another? Where is the respect? Where is self-control? Where is it, where is it, where is it?

Have we totally lost ourselves in the whitewash? Please, someone, tell me...the *Spiritual Hook* is seriously bent! Over what? Jealousy, envy, pride, greed, coveting, competitiveness, pompousness, and revenge.

While writing this book, *Business is Business: As It Pleases God*, my eyes have seen much from both sides of the spectrum. Believers throw each other under the bus without exhibiting the Fruits of the Spirit or Christlike Character. Thus, when I see worldly individuals controlling their temper, working together, staying calm, resolving conflict amicably, and joining forces against Believers to take them down, I am flabbergasted. What is the reason for being shocked? Should this not be what they should do? Of course, we should all behave Christlike, but when watching the Kingdom Seekers openly spread curses, talk down to others, and mistreat God's sheep. While at the same time excluding people based upon certain biases, conditioning, or terminology, as if this is normal, I have to shake my head in dismay.

For example, if one person uses the word luck instead of Blessing, they are ousted. In all actuality, they have the same meaning, according to the dictionary. Whether we feel lucky or Blessed, they are both POSITIVE words. Meanwhile, the ones who are ousting those using the word luck do not know the difference between positive and negative affirmations, period! While at the same time, speaking negatively, knowing nothing about the use of the Fruits of the Spirit, gossiping like cackling hens, throwing innocent people under the bus, placing people in superstitious categories based upon their negative mindset and background, and looming curses over people who believe differently.

Listen, I do not make it a secret; I am a backwoods country girl who uses the word luck or Blessings as a part of my vocabulary, depending on who I am speaking with while doing what I do. Yes, I speak eloquently in public, but when I am with my family, I speak our countrified language. For the record, and *As It Pleases God*, the upbringing He chose for me makes my SPIRITUAL BAIT and HOOK potent.

To have someone insinuate I am less than a Child of God using a positive word as such, especially when I have ten toes in the Kingdom, was a blasphemous insult and an ancestral dig at my cultural background. I am who I am for a reason, and I could not believe what my ears were hearing, especially from someone who claimed to be led by the Holy Spirit.

What is the big deal, especially when everyone is entitled to their opinion? They were asking me for help, not the other way around! Out of the kindness of my heart and upbringing, I was sharing the Spiritual Gifts granted to me by my Forefathers to help them. How dare they insult me when speaking my own tongue and gleaning from that same Spiritual Reservoir simultaneously, right?

For the record, before we release negative, condescending words into the atmosphere, we must know who we are speaking to before setting them in motion. Why must we exhibit such caution? They may become a part of someone's story, just like now. If the Holy Spirit had been leading, He would have advised them to tread carefully and not to insult the hand that was helping them. So, being that the issue is on the table, we must address it for such a time as this.

As Believers, we must RESPECT the culture or upbringing of another without labeling, calling them names, or insulting them. The point is that God loves us all, regardless of our creed, deed, breed, or language. More importantly, He confounded the language and scattered us abroad from the Tower of Babel incident in Genesis 11:4-9 for a reason. And now, in the Kingdom of God, we must exhibit RESPECT. Besides, who are we to shun someone for their native tongue? We have to do better than this!

In the *As It Pleases God Movement*, when it comes down to words, we simply need to know whether it is positive or negative—THAT IS IT! We can play on words all we like, but God deals with Fruits, Character, and Motives. All of them are hidden within the human psyche, governing our mindset, thoughts, beliefs, and biases, creating a SEED.

Suppose we are working with negative seeds or do not know the difference between positive or negative, right or wrong, and so on. In this case, it behooves us to start reading more, looking up the opposite of the words in our vocabulary, and searching out new positive words to add to it. How can this help us? It helps our mindset. Think of it like this: When we open our mouths, it becomes a *Baited Hook* on behalf of the Kingdom of God or a baited snare, yoking us to the core.

When drawing out of our Divine Provisions or our Spiritual Negev, we must put something in based on the Spiritual Law of Seedtime and Harvest. For example, a SEED must be planted to harvest produce, plant a tree, or bring forth human life. When fishing, we must bait a hook to cause the intended target to feed a need, want, or desire. Now, if we choose not to bait the hook, we must lower a net to capture or trap our supply of fishery provisions. All in all, we must do something or avail ourselves to usher in provisions.

Most would think a *Baited Hook* is negative, but if we view it from God's Divine Perspective, it will change the trajectory of our lives. As we approach this topic, *As It Pleases Him*, the BAIT will become the Word of

God, and the HOOK must become the Fruits of the Spirit and Christlike Character.

By knowing the Word of God without the Fruited HOOK, we will find ourselves offending or repelling people, places, and things without realizing it. If we DO NOT submit to the Word of God, use the Fruits of the Spirit, and exhibit Christlike Character, our seeds can become tainted, mangled, or wormy, costing us in the end. If we desire good seeds, we must be intentional about what we are sowing, tilling, and harvesting. Why? The *Baited Hook* consists of them; if we bait our lives with the wrong things, the *Baited Hook* can become a Spiritual Yoke.

How can our lives become Spiritual Yokes as Believers? It happens all the time, especially when turning on ourselves without knowing it. Then again, it also occurs when we know we are severely yoked but choose not to do anything about it or outright hide it from others.

- ☐ If we DO NOT submit to God, our Heavenly Father, the *Baited Hook* will become tainted.

- ☐ If we resist God and DO NOT resist the devil, we will become misdirected, deceived, and easily manipulated.

- ☐ If we DO NOT consciously attempt to operate with clean hands and a pure heart, we will become double-minded, chaotic, and contradictory.

Is this Biblical? Absolutely! According to scripture, *"Therefore submit to God. Resist the devil and he will flee from you. Draw near to God and He will draw near to you. Cleanse your hands, you sinners; and purify your hearts, you double-minded."* James 4:7-8.

When dealing with the Hook, Line, and Sinker, *As It Pleases God*, He will let us know when the time is right to launch into the deep and drop our nets for the extensive haul, according to our Predestined Blueprint. When doing so, we must exercise *Proactive Management*, listening, learning, becoming good stewards, and being obediently humble while washing our nets.

What does washing our nets have to do with anything? According to the Ancient of Days, it is similar to Spiritually Tilling our own grounds, giving off a Spiritual Actionable Cue of Readiness. Sitting around doing nothing, gossiping, complaining, and eating bonbons in the Spirit of Laziness will cause our boat to become overlooked.

Here is the Spiritual Seal to keep in mind when being about our Father's Business with a *Baited Hook* or Spiritual Net, *As It Pleases Him.* "*Then He got into one of the boats, which was Simon's, and asked him to put out a little from the land. And He sat down and taught the multitudes from the boat. When He had stopped speaking, He said to Simon, 'Launch out into the deep and let down your nets for a catch.' But Simon answered and said to Him, 'Master, we have toiled all night and caught nothing; nevertheless at Your word I will let down the net.' And when they had done this, they caught a great number of fish, and their net was breaking. So they signaled to their partners in the other boat to come and help them. And they came and filled both the boats, so that they began to sink.*" Luke 5:3-7.

Every time you think about quitting, read this Spiritual Seal before making a permanent decision based upon a temporary feeling. Why do we need to read about a fish haul? When being about your Father's Business, He will always ask you to do something, or He will ask a question, testing your response or the lack thereof. Therefore, we must develop our Spiritual Eyes to see, Ears to hear, and Tongue to speak on behalf of the Kingdom while patiently waiting on the Spiritual Cue. If we hear nothing in our *Spirit to Spirit* Relationship, keep learning, training, understanding, and documenting, *As It Pleases Him,* developing the Fruits of the Spirit and Christlike Character while on standby.

What is the purpose of standing by, waiting on God? It builds Spiritual Leverage, *As It Pleases Him,* getting rid of the impatience and selfishness secretly residing within the human psyche. Really? Yes, really! When someone says God is speaking, I sit back and watch their method of operation, and it tells me who is really speaking. How is it possible to see this? First, I know Spiritual Principles. Secondly, God deals with obedience through the ability to listen, learn, grow, apply, and give back. Thirdly, if one rejects my advice of what is evident or in plain sight, I sit back, watching the story play out to glean the information for the Kingdom.

What is the purpose of sitting back and watching? God will always send us a warning. More importantly, we have free will to heed or reject it. I am not here to judge anyone; I have had my share of disobedience, but I thank God for the second, third, and fourth chances, or as many as I needed to get it right with Him and complete my Divine Mission.

Taking A Chance

For those who do not believe in chances, opting to use the word grace or mercy as a play on words, if we do not take a chance to forgive or repent, amid using grace or mercy, do we not change the trajectory of the two? Do we not render grace and mercy useless to the human psyche if we fail to repent or forgive? Of course, we do.

Grace and mercy are available to all, but if we do not take a chance on our Spiritual Gifts and Predestined Blueprint or be about our Father's Business, they will remain dormant. In contrast, using grace and mercy as an excuse to sit on our hands doing nothing for the Kingdom is not wise, and grace and mercy do not support or endorse this behavior. How can I say such a thing, right? Most often, we pretend we are doing something for the Kingdom of God, but we are really doing it for ourselves, for a show, to stroke our egos, or for the money.

As Believers, we are called to be active participants in the Kingdom, being about our Father's Business. In addition, we are also called to love and serve others, share the gospel, and use our talents and resources for the glory of God, not to glorify ourselves. However, some Believers may use the concepts of grace and mercy as an excuse to exist or wallow in folly, breathing in the Breath of Life as if they do not need to do anything in return. Based upon this misconception, in *Business is Business*, we pride ourselves on this Spiritual Principle: *"Freely you have received, freely give."* Matthew 10:8.

Grace and mercy are not a license to be lazy or complacent, and not to take chances. Here is the deal: Grace is the unmerited favor of God, given to us despite our sins and shortcomings. Mercy is the compassion of God, shown to us even when we deserve punishment. These concepts are not meant to be an excuse for inaction but rather a MOTIVATION for us to live out our faith and serve Him with all that we have, being about His Business first.

Why must we place God first, especially when He has given us free will? If He served us what we deserved, we would hang our heads down in shame. Better yet, if He released the skeletons hidden in our closets, we know that we would get a severe side-eye. Instead, we can walk in boldness and confidence that He has our backs with our heads held high...thus we should never come with the 'woe unto me' mentality in this lifetime or the next.

Furthermore, the Bible teaches us that faith without works is dead in James 2:17. We cannot simply claim to believe in God and then do nothing to show it, or see a fallen brother or sister and not help them back up, kick them when they are down, plot their demise, or spitefully air out their dirty laundry, especially when we have our own. In the Eye of God, our faith must be accompanied by ACTION, positive action to be exact. Even Jesus himself said in John 14:15, '*If you love Me, keep My commandments.*"

With that out of the way, let us get back on track. We must consciously choose to Spiritually Till our own grounds, taking a RISK on ourselves, according to our Predestined Blueprint. Why? Every seed planted in or out of season must take a risk at living, and we are no different in Earthen Vessel.

When someone says to me, 'I do not believe in chances.' I am like, 'Speak for yourself!' I believe in them because I am living proof of several occurrences. If one has never experienced making a conscious choice to come back from the other side to complete their Divine Mission, it becomes easy to judge what we do not understand. More importantly, if I had not taken a chance at writing with my flaws and all of my idiosyncrasies, pushing beyond my self-imposed limitations, we would not have this TIMELY information to be about our Father's Business.

What is the big deal about grace, mercy, and taking chances? We need them all. When taking a risk or chance, we will need grace and mercy working on our behalf. For those opting to use grace and mercy without taking a chance, it is like buying an 'As Is' product without a warranty; come on...this manipulation of Believers must stop. As long as grace and mercy remain, so will the element of risk.

Our Forefathers took risks for us, and we should never forfeit the element of chance. Why? There is a time and season for everything under the sun; whether we are given another chance at living, as I have been given, or we take a chance on something or someone as a formal risk, it is indeed a chance!

Before ending this chapter on a note of chance, please allow me to Spiritually Align this squeamish debate: "*Whatever your hand finds to do, do it with your might; for there is no work or device or knowledge or wisdom in the grave where you are going. I returned and saw under the sun that—The race is not to the swift, Nor the battle to the strong, Nor bread to the wise, Nor riches to men of understanding, Nor favor to men of skill; But time and chance happen to them all.*" Ecclesiastes 9:10-11. So, what do we have working in our favor aside from grace and mercy? TIME and CHANCE! Let me share how to work on it in the next chapter with *Proactive Management*.

Chapter Eleven

Proactive Management

According to the Heavenly of Heavens, most of our issues lie in the lack of *Proactive Management* of our tongues, saying God is speaking when He is not. And with our superfluous envisioning process, we create false illusions, saying it is Him when it is not. When dealing with the MIND and TONGUE, we must become very strategic in this approach. Why is a strategy necessary? We do not want to become contradictory, creating all types of false doctrines and causing reproof from our Heavenly Father, especially when being about His Business, *As It Pleases Him*.

When the mind is creating whatever it wants or allowing all types of chatter, if not managed properly, all types of things will begin to roll off the tongue without any form of restraint. All of this will be proclaimed in the Name of God, but it is indeed for selfish reasons. In short, we cannot begin making up stuff and serving it to God's sheep as palatable information from the Heavens Above with the ulterior motive of controlled manipulation.

People are going into DEBT based on the information we are feeding them to fulfill our wants, needs, and desires, not that of the Kingdom of God. What does this mean, especially when people have free will to believe or do what they want? Instead of putting people in debt, it is our responsibility to get them out of it, Mentally, Physically, Emotionally, Spiritually, and Financially! If we cannot do this, be honest about our intentions without deceiving them.

When we create rifts and gaps, dismantling the walls with false propaganda misleading God's sheep, He may have a problem with us that needs rectification. Where does it say this in the Bible? I am so glad this question is on the table: "*You have not gone up into the gaps to build a wall for the house of Israel to stand in battle on the day of the LORD. They have envisioned futility and false divination, saying, 'Thus says the LORD!' But the LORD has not sent them; yet they hope that the word may be confirmed. Have you not seen a futile vision, and have you not spoken false divination? You say, 'The LORD says, but I have not spoken.'*

Therefore thus says the Lord GOD: 'Because you have spoken nonsense and envisioned lies, therefore I am indeed against you,' says the Lord GOD." Ezekiel 13:5-8.

Why would our issues lie in our management abilities, especially when we all have issues? Regardless of what issues we have or do not have, when we refuse to READ books, especially the Word of God, as building blocks to keep the Well of Wisdom flowing on our behalf, governing our input and output capacity, we will become blocked. Such blockages cause us to indulge in frivolous foolery, manifesting inwardly and then spreading outwardly, often noticed in our finances. Is this Biblical? Of course. *"And the word of the LORD came to me, saying, 'Son of man, prophesy against the prophets of Israel who prophesy, and say to those who prophesy out of their own heart, 'Hear the word of the LORD!' Thus says the Lord GOD: 'Woe to the foolish prophets, who follow their own spirit and have seen nothing! O Israel, your prophets are like foxes in the deserts."* Ezekiel 13:1-4.

Is foolery not a matter of opinion? From one's human perspective, it is. On the contrary, from God's Divine Perspective, it is a matter of fruits, character, and intents. Really? Yes, really! All the information we digest is based upon wisdom or folly, depending on what we do with the information. We can take negative information and make it positive, productive, and fruitful. Or, we can take positive information and make it negative, unproductive, and unfruitful based on intentions.

For example, the internet is pumping hot with juicy information, where we read more comments than edifying information. Such engagement tells me we can read and are reading, but we lack the *Proactive Management* of WHAT we are doing and WHY with limits.

With *Proactive Management*, we must ask ourselves, 'Are we learning without listening?' 'Are we listening without learning?' Or, 'Are we responding without listening, learning, growing, or sowing back into the Kingdom, *As It Pleases God*?'

As my ear has been to the ground, I have noticed people taking more time to comment about the life of another without reading or proactively writing their own script. While at the same time thinking God is failing them and not asking these questions, 'Are they failing God?' Or 'Are they being about their Father's Business?"

God has expectations for us, and if we do not take the time to *Proactively Manage* ourselves from the inside out, we can miss the mark. After continuously operating in this manner, the next thing we will know is that gray hair is coming out. Then, we find ourselves asking:

☐ Where is the Gift?

- ☐ Where is my Talent?
- ☐ What am I CALLED to do now?
- ☐ Have I lost the Gift?
- ☐ Has my Gift given up on me?
- ☐ How long will it wait?
- ☐ Am I too old?
- ☐ Is it too late?

How can we miss the mark, especially if we must live our own lives and God does not make mistakes? Missing the mark is a matter of perception, not *As It Pleases God*. Some would say, 'I am exactly where I need to be.' And one would be correct; however, we must ask ourselves, 'What are we doing with or learning from our current situation?'

What is the purpose of querying ourselves in such a manner? We may be in a cycle of déjà vu with little or no progress, but the longing or thirst within the human psyche tells our story without our participation.

On the other hand, if we hoard our Spiritual Gifts, they will become dormant, or we may lose them altogether. Now, if the CALLING is strong, it is essential to Global change, or it is time-sensitive, God will shut our lives down until we heed the CALL. Will God really shut our lives down? Absolutely! Unfortunately, this means nothing will work as it should until we get on the right track.

Once we get on the right track, everything will begin to fall into place. Until then, this individual will feel like Jonah in the Belly of the Fish in Jonah 1:17. As a word of caution, if you are walking with a serious Spiritual Calling on your life, it is better not to run from the calling. It is better to run toward it with a work-in-progress mentality. Why? You will never have peace, causing the psyche to remain in a state of unrest with a cloud hovering over you, penetrating your environment in due time.

For example, we have a lot of people wanting to write books but have not taken the initiative to do so. To add insult to injury, they consistently post on social media, then turn around, proclaim or complain that they do not have enough time. Or, they refuse to take the time to document their *Spirit to Spirit* conversations with God as a Testament or Testimony for the Kingdom. In my opinion, a book can be written if we proactively compile all of the comments we post on someone else's feed or channel for recognition. At the same time, they do not realize that the book they are seeking to write is already within, in seed form.

Listen, every Divine Blueprint has a prewritten script (book), and if we do not take the time to document our experiences, lessons, Blessings, and testings, we can indeed bury the book we are inspired to write. What if we do not have the resources to write our Testimony or Testament? As long as we have breath in our bodies, the provisions are available, but we must Spiritually Till our own grounds to stir up the GIFT or develop a *Plan of Action*. Listen, God is not asking us to be perfect; He is asking us to become Christlike and usable for Kingdom Purposes. Why is a Plan of *Action* important in the Eye of God?

- ☐ He BLESSES us to be a Blessing.
- ☐ He FEEDS us to feed others.
- ☐ He LOVES us so that we can share the love.
- ☐ He GIVES us peace to be at peace with others.
- ☐ He GRANTS us mercy so that we can become merciful.
- ☐ He OFFERS us the wisdom needed to share with others.
- ☐ He ALLOWS us to have trials in our lives so we can become the Teacher or Mentor.
- ☐ He PROVIDES us with provisions for us to provide for others.
- ☐ He PROTECTS us so we can become protectors.
- ☐ He OPENS doors for us so that we can open doors for others.
- ☐ He is KIND to us to ensure we understand how to be kind to others.
- ☐ He has GIVEN us life to understand the value of life.

I am not here to pull the wool over anyone's eyes; instead, I am here to remove it with *Proactive Management*. As Believers, we count on or depend on faith as we should; however, our faith incorporates proactiveness, which is commonly overlooked. Then, once something happens, we run to the church for help, when the real CHURCH is within us. I am not saying the church should not assist; we must exhaust our resources in preparing for our seasons of drought. In my opinion, this is similar to Joseph preparing Egypt for its drought by effectively storing and preparing, *As It Pleased God*.

We often use the story of Joseph as a story of triumph, but we must also use it as a Divine Blueprint of PROACTIVENESS and LEVERAGE. How do I get proactiveness and leverage from Joseph? While Joseph was in his father's house, he was learning, understanding, and preparing. When Joseph was sold into slavery, ending up in Potiphar's house; here again, he was again learning, understanding, and preparing. When Potiphar's wife lied about Joseph, landing him in prison, he was still learning, understanding, and preparing. He did not know what God was going to do or how, but he remained on the proactive learning curve, building the leverage needed to facilitate his Blueprinted Purpose.

Suppose we do not learn, understand, prepare, and grow. In this case, we can become God's Chosen Elect in a famine depending upon someone else's provisions, subjecting ourselves to all types of cruelty and abuse for not having what we should have prepared for.

For the record, I am not here to point the finger; through many experiences, I can bring forth such Divine Information for such a time as this. Rest assured that my famine seasons have prepared me with the Divine Wisdom to facilitate the process of getting us Mentally, Physically, Emotionally, Spiritually, and Financially ready for whatever, with whomever. And then, training the next in line, passing the Torch of Wisdom, allowing the next generation to become better, stronger, and wiser without tripping over themselves.

How do we know what to do, *As It Pleases God*? Each man's Spiritual Negev (Underground or Hidden Reserve) is different based upon their Predestined Blueprint; therefore, we must incorporate God into the equation, covering ourselves with the Blood of Jesus and allowing the Holy Spirit to guide us.

Nonetheless, to get the Spiritual Negev flowing, *As It Pleases God*, we must use the Fruits of the Spirit and Christlike Character, allowing Him to unkink our qualmish kinks. What does this mean? We all have something to work on; however, the psyche will hide things from us to stay in control. Frankly, this is why we cannot see our own issues as they are; yet, we are quick to point the finger at someone else, not realizing we are subjected to the same thing under a different label, blinded by our wants, needs, desires, conditioning, and biases. More importantly, this is why I write inclusively, excluding no one, because we are all subjected to Spiritual Error or Omission!

According to the Heavenly of Heavens, to glean this information, *As It Pleases God*, we cannot leave any WILLING man behind. Why? If we desire a Spiritual Seal on our Divine Promises, we cannot become selfish, but an EXAMPLE instead. When we live by example with our flaws, quirks, and limitations, we enhance our authenticity without being a know-it-all.

I try to stay in my lane with what I know. What I do not know, I am quick to let someone know it is NOT my field of expertise. What is the purpose of limiting myself in such a manner? It opens the floodgates of learning or teachability on a level, confounding the human psyche. When our ego is on full alert, we do not learn as we should, and people are less likely to share what they know. On the other hand, releasing the ego from its job gives the mind an opportunity to glean as it should, allowing us to grow.

    Although emergencies do arise, however, if we are not proactively prepared, it could cause a major setback. How can we proactively prepare? Listed below are a few examples, but not limited to such:

- ☐ Job loss. Losing a job is one of the biggest setbacks known to man. For most, we are only two paychecks from being homeless; therefore, we should take a portion (10% of our salary) and place it in an interest-bearing reserve fund with at least 12 months of backup. Using this Spiritual Principle gives God FOUR cycled seasons to work on our behalf or move in our favor.

- ☐ Medical Crisis. We should ensure we have the appropriate insurance to cover our medical needs, and we can easily make deductible payments. In my opinion, this is the second biggest downfall of being in a debt crisis.

- ☐ Accidents. Once again, do not take accidents for granted; they happen! Therefore, we should ensure we have adequate insurance to keep an unforeseen accident from wiping us out. It is said, 'It is better not to need it and have it than to need it and not have it.'

- ☐ Home repairs. We should make sure we have insurance to cover home repairs to avoid costly maintenance expenses exceeding our proposed budget.

- ☐ Car repairs.

- ☐ Weather repairs or evacuations.

- ☐ Holiday spending.

Whatever it is or is not, we must become cautious about what is going on so that we can proactively prepare for it. I suggest a *Proactive Management List*, but choose what is conducive for the family and make it work, getting everyone involved. No one is too young or old to chip in, especially when the Family Vision is set, *As It Pleases God*. Although some family members may not get it, it will not be because they were not taught.

Just like Jacob taught *Proactive Management* to all of his children based on their capacity to receive, deceive, or rebel. Still, Joseph applied it more accurately than them all for our sake. Why did he apply it more? Joseph had the most pressure applied, squeezing out the Greatness from his Spiritual Negev. Is this fair? Absolutely. If we collapse under pressure, we invoke Kingdom Limitations by default; therefore, God will test us to see what we are working with or if we are ready. If not, it is back to the drawing board or Spiritual Classroom until we are Spiritually Seasoned, *As It Pleases Him*.

Does a life of hard knocks make us hard and cruel? No, it should not; it develops compassion, understanding, and mercy. Suppose we are hateful, cruel, or hard about our past experiences, and unwilling to serve another. In this case, we have underlying issues in need of reckoning, especially in the area of forgiveness and repentance.

Although everyone's issues are different, we all have a story to tell. Thus, I am not at liberty to judge another man's journey or what God uses to train them. But I will say this: We must pay attention to our fruits and character. If we negatively treat others as we have been treated, we are just as guilty as the perpetrator. So, be careful because a negative character trait or fruit as such will manifest into our *Something Else*, a seed after its own kind.

Why must we pay attention to our fruits and character? According to the Heavenly of Heavens, this is how we decipher the wolves in sheep's clothing, among the multi-faceted ways of pretense, without having to say one word. Really? Yes, really! With deep pockets or not, I make it my business to read the room, Mentally, Physically, Emotionally, Spiritually, and Financially. Not as a form of judgment, but AWARENESS of what or who I am dealing with, preventing my proactiveness from becoming negatively reactive.

When being about our Father's Business, we must know what to do and why, especially when presented with what is designed to build, motivate, teach, or distract us. In knowing the difference, we must master our ability to PROACTIVELY read the fruits and character of an individual with kindness, love, compassion, and steadfastness.

Why must we be kind, loving, compassionate, and merciful to those attempting to assassinate us, Mentally, Physically, Emotionally, Spiritually, or Financially? As a part of the Divine Strategy from the Heavenly of Heavens, it prevents foolery in the above areas from wiping us out! Plus, it proves we are the bigger person in the Eye of God, being able to forgive, repent, and keep it moving in the Spirit of Excellence. Once again, if God dealt us what we really deserved, we would not be here. Yet, through His Divine Grace and Mercy, we have the Blood of Jesus to give us a second chance or however much is needed, and we have the Holy Spirit to guide us.

Although my iniquities were many, and my disobedience was evident, God never gave up on me. And now, here we are, packing a POWERFUL punch for the Kingdom of God!

I do not care how it seems to the naked eye, what is coming out of your mouth, how you think, how much money you have, your credit score, or what people are saying about you. Dust yourself off, get up, and get back in the game, running your own race. In doing so, work on your fruits and character daily, redirecting them from negative to positive, bad to good, wrong to right, unjust to just, and so on.

In doing so and gaining your bearings, here is the Spiritual Seal: *"For all things are for your sakes, that grace, having spread through the many, may cause thanksgiving to abound to the glory of God. Therefore we do not lose heart. Even though our outward man is perishing, yet the inward man is being renewed day by day. For our light affliction, which is but for a moment, is working for us a far more exceeding and eternal weight of glory, while we do not look at the things which are seen, but at the things which are not seen. For the things which are seen are temporary, but the things which are not seen are eternal."* 2 Corinthians 4:15-18.

Listen, the only person who can count you out is YOU! You are renewed every morning, so give thanks for it and be about your Father's Business. If you do not know what it is, then ASK!

Once again, your Spiritual Negev is underneath your layers of *Something Else*, and it is your responsibility to Spiritually Till your own ground to break open what is already yours. However, if you allow what people say to cause you to revert or detour from your progressive efforts, *As It Pleases God*, then you have no reason to point the finger at anyone, and I mean NO ONE.

Now, if you are reading this book, then it is pretty apparent that you have what it takes. Your Spiritual Tools and Gifts are available; use them, use them, use them!

In *Business is Business*, make sure you use this information positively, and it will change the trajectory of your life GUARANTEED! Now, as we move on to the last chapter, *The Spiritual Negev*, it is designed to spark the FLOW to help bring your Spiritual Blueprint to life in a Business Format or Platform. As the *Deep Calleth Unto the Deep*, let us deep dive into the CORE of your being, extracting what is already.

Chapter Twelve

The Spiritual Negev

Our *Spiritual Negev* is comprised of healing waters, providing Divine Provisions for our Temples. When we become money-hungry, power-driven, or sexually thirsty, we can become blocked from our Spiritual Access to Supernatural Wisdom, Treasures, and Secrets of the Kingdom. Why? It causes the Spirit of Desperation to rise up within the human psyche, triggering us to stray away from our Predestined Blueprint. Or, it may cause us to pursue something or someone that is not a part of our Divine Destiny. Listen, there is nothing wrong with having power, money, and sex; the problem comes into play when they have us!

Circumventing the Plan of God, compromising our integrity, or when consumed by the lust of the eyes, the lust of the flesh, and the pride of life, they can have us operating as underprivileged individuals with all types of hidden and open blockages. To add insult to injury, it will have us walking around thinking we are right in our own eyes, when we are all so wrong in the Eye of God. So, it behooves us to add Him into our equational efforts of all things, even if we have it going on.

Why do we need to include God, especially when He has given us the strength to do whatever, with whomever? He does not violate anyone's free will. According to the Heavenly of Heavens, we must come into a free-will AGREEMENT with Him. In all simplicity, we either include or exclude Him, and He is okay with whatever decision we make. Please keep in mind that we cannot expect Him to clean up the mess He did not create, especially when walking around blind as a bat, plugging and playing, or dropping it like it is hot. Then again, He still will not violate our free will when we are walking like a tree with the 'wherever the wind blows, it is cool with me' mentality.

With *The Spiritual Negev*, whether we see ourselves or others as trees, we must eventually learn how to see correctly, truthfully, and clearly for Spiritual Growth and Enlightenment. How do we make walking as trees make sense, especially if we are not trees? Before we are fully healed and enlightened, *As It Pleases God*, we may see people in a distorted way, judging them based on outward appearances or other superficial factors. But as we grow in our Spiritual Understanding and Maturity, we are able to see people as they truly are, with all their strengths, weaknesses, and inner exquisiteness, creating a win-win regardless. How is it attainable in the Eye of God? By using the Fruits of the Spirit, behaving Christlike, becoming a Tree of Life, and being about our Father's Business without meddling in other folks' business.

With Spiritual Understanding and Maturity, *As it Pleases God*, we must speak adequately, allowing our tongues to become the pen of a ready writer. We must profoundly hear what the Spirit of the Lord is saying to the Church, as the Voice of God speaks, the Blood of Jesus covers, and the Holy Spirit guides.

According to the Heavenly of Heavens, our *Spiritual Negev* operates through authenticity, not through mass manipulative efforts. Whether we have or do not, everything we do, say, or become is a seed, and we should never allow anyone to make us feel less than others for not having what they have or envy the power or money they possess. If we do, we will open ourselves up to being manipulated to do things violating our conscience, only to pad their pockets, boosting their trend. At the same time, we sit back, holding the bag of debt or operating in Spiritual Error. So, it behooves us to get rid of the hype and grab hold of the Divine Blueprint, possessing *The Spiritual Negev*, containing everything we need to do what we are Predestined to do.

How do we know if we are operating in Spiritual Error? It varies from person to person, situation to situation, and so on. Nevertheless, here are a few personal cues, but not limited to such:

- ☐ When our flow is broken, blocked, or damned.
- ☐ When our conscience is violated.
- ☐ When serving rotten or negative fruits.
- ☐ When operating in folly.
- ☐ When spreading debauchery, lies, or chaos.
- ☐ When operating with malicious intentions.
- ☐ When becoming jealous, envious, prideful, greedy, competitive, or outright coveting.

Listen, the front or back door of our Blessings from God are also hidden within our *Spiritual Negev*, creating a natural flow. If our flow ceases, it may not be our *Spiritual Negev*; therefore, we must involve God in the equation. Please allow me to align accordingly: "*Then he brought me back to the door of the temple; and there was water, flowing from under the threshold of the temple toward the east, for the front of the temple faced east; the water was flowing from under the right side of the temple, south of the altar. He brought me out by way of the north gate, and led me around on the outside to the outer gateway that faces east; and there was water, running out on the right side.*" Ezekiel 47:1-2. What is the purpose of knowing this? Where God guides, *As It Pleases Him*, He will provide, period!

Our life will contain twists and turns like an hourglass as we pour out and allow ourselves to be poured into. The moment we find ourselves giving without receiving, an imbalance occurs; so, in our *Spiritual Negev*, we must know God is with us. He wants to provide water in our desert experiences, giving us a cloud by day and a pillar of fire by night. He also wants to quench the inner thirsts we often hide under *Something Else* to avoid unveiling our Spiritual Gifts, opting for the quick fixes without healing, learning, growing, or becoming better, stronger, and wiser. All these are needed to fulfill the Well of Promise, which connects us to our Spiritual Journey into Greatness, *As It Pleases God*, and our daily provision and protection.

When dealing with our Spiritual Gifts, we often think that a Plan of Action or Business Plan is not applicable. But, for where we are going, *As It Pleases God*, we will use both. Why do we need both? They are designed to get our mental wheels turning in the right direction, extracting the extractable, converting the convertible, and listening to the Voice of God.

Why do we need to extract, convert, and listen? Frankly, this prevents us from striking rocks of water or provisions when He says to speak to it. More importantly, similar to Numbers 20:10-13, we want to avoid becoming banned from the Promise as Moses did, especially when having a temper tantrum and unresolved emotional issues.

In the Eye of God, we must follow Divine Instructions, period. Disobedience is a quick way to turn on ourselves through self-righteous acts. What makes this so important in our *Spiritual Negev*? God's instructions may change at the drop of a dime, and we must be willing to obey; if not, we can miss the mark or cue. How can this happen? Most often, it is due to a temporary meltdown of unbelief caused by stress, fear, pressure, or panic.

Now, for the record, no one is exempt from feeling stressed, fearful, pressured, or panicky; however, we must know what to do and why. How should we handle ourselves when feeling this way? We must be quick to repent, forgive if necessary, plead the Blood of Jesus, and usher in the Holy Spirit, shifting the Spiritual Leverage in our favor.

When feeling any negative emotion, we can plead the Blood against it and then replace it with a positive emotion or scripture. For example, we can say, 'For the Spirit of Fear, the Blood of Jesus is against you; I cast down the Spirit of Fear, and I usher in the Spirit of Faith. God has not given me the Spirit of Fear, but of power, love, and a sound mind.' Can we really do this? Absolutely. Knowing the positive side of a negative emotion or thought is imperative to counteract it. Use Google if you need to; while you are at it, find the applicable scripture. More importantly, to place a Spiritual Seal, it is always in our best interest to say: THANK YOU and AMEN.

Amid all this, we must adequately align ourselves in all areas of our lives. Why? We must be *In The Know*, documenting, measuring ourselves, and doing our due diligence, *As It Pleases God*. What proof do we have regarding measuring ourselves? *"And when the man went out to the east with the line in his hand, he measured one thousand cubits, and he brought me through the waters; the water came up to my ankles. Again he measured one thousand and brought me through the waters; the water came up to my knees. Again he measured one thousand and brought me through; the water came up to my waist. Again he measured one thousand, and it was a river that I could not cross; for the water was too deep, water in which one must swim, a river that could not be crossed."* Ezekiel 47:3-7.

In properly governing where we are, where we are going, what to do, and why, we must measure the situation, circumstance, or event, *As It Pleases God*. Doing so lets us know what to do at the right time and what not to do. Here are a few items we must consider when establishing a Plan of Action or Business Plan. All of these will help us get back on track or stay on track, but not limited to such:

- ☐ We must recognize or pinpoint the issue, problem, or dilemma.
- ☐ We must define the issue, problem, or dilemma.
- ☐ We must figure out the solution to the issue, problem, or dilemma by doing our due diligence.
- ☐ We must determine if we need to give it to God without picking it up again.
- ☐ We must understand God's view and apply scripture.
- ☐ We must account for the internal and external costs of the issue, problem, or dilemma.
- ☐ We must create a system of implementation for the issue, problem, or dilemma.

- ☐ We must establish the win-win hidden in the issue, problem, or dilemma.

Sometimes, we have to redo or take remedial courses to get certain things right. I lost count of how many times I had to redo so many things in my life, but here we are!

Returning to the Plan of Action to update some things or receive instructions from our Heavenly Father is Wisdom in Progress. Here is what we need to know: *"He said to me, 'Son of man, have you seen this?' Then he brought me and returned me to the bank of the river. When I returned, there, along the bank of the river, were very many trees on one side and the other."* Ezekiel 47:6-7.

How do we know God is instructing us? The information begins to flow to and through us, primarily when documenting during our *Spirit to Spirit* Relational time, but not limited to such. More importantly, when the words, thoughts, and feelings of healing and restoration begin to flow, they will be one of our signs. *"Then he said to me: 'This water flows toward the eastern region, goes down into the valley, and enters the sea. When it reaches the sea, its waters are healed."* Ezekiel 47:8.

Listen, the Mind, Body, and Soul do not necessarily need to be healed for the Spirit of the Lord to provide feelings of being healed. When the inner knowing or peace resides within the human psyche, it is our Spiritual Cue. Please do not miss it by canceling it with negative thoughts, beliefs, words, biases, or doubts. Accept it, and keep it moving in the Spirit of Excellence, regardless of how it appears to the naked eye.

We are designed to grow, sow, and flow, giving back to the Divine Cistern in Earthen Vessel. *"And it shall be that every living thing that moves, wherever the rivers go, will live. There will be a very great multitude of fish, because these waters go there; for they will be healed, and everything will live wherever the river goes. It shall be that fishermen will stand by it from En Gedi to En Eglaim; they will be places for spreading their nets. Their fish will be of the same kinds as the fish of the Great Sea, exceedingly many."* Ezekiel 47:9-10.

What if we choose NOT to flow in positivity, exhibit the Fruits of the Spirit, or engage in debauchery? We place ourselves Mentally, Physically, Emotionally, and Financially in a position to become a swamp or marsh. Really? Yes, really. Please allow me to align: *"But its swamps and marshes will not be healed; they will be given over to salt."* Ezekiel 47:11.

Should we not become the salt of the earth? Absolutely! But if we are a swamp overtaken by a treacherous marsh, who in their right mind would take the risk of seeking our savory flavors in dangerous conditions, especially with the potential of being swallowed up by quicksand or creatures that we cannot see coming? Come on...we have to clean it up!

How do we know if we are on the right track? It varies from person to person, situation to situation, trauma to trauma, bias to bias, and so on. Nevertheless, here are a few things to look for, but not limited to such:

- ☐ We must look for growth instead of stagnation or resistance.
- ☐ We must look for palatable character and fruits in our people skills.
- ☐ We must look for indications of becoming stronger and wiser with sustainable listening, understanding, and teachability skills or characteristics.
- ☐ We must pinpoint the ability to improve with time instead of getting worse, dull, lukewarm, or stiff-necked.
- ☐ We must have the desire to align with the Word of God, making our best attempts to do the right things.
- ☐ We must begin to exhibit the fruits of the Spirit, healing the hungry soul within ourselves and others with our words, thoughts, beliefs, and presence.

When dealing with *The Spiritual Negev*, approaching our flowing river underneath our *Something Else* with this mindset will change the trajectory of a sprig of water to an undeniable overflow. Is there a guarantee on this? It depends upon our mindsets. Here is what the Bible has to say about this: *"Along the bank of the river, on this side and that, will grow all kinds of trees used for food; their leaves will not wither, and their fruit will not fail. They will bear fruit every month, because their water flows from the sanctuary. Their fruit will be for food, and their leaves for medicine."* Ezekiel 47:12.

If one desires to possess their portion of their Divinely Blueprinted Promise, it behooves them to claim it. If not, they can indeed miss out. Why? Our Forefathers missed the mark, and we do not have to follow suit. Here is the Divine Oath: *"Thus says the Lord GOD: 'These are the borders by which you shall divide the land as an inheritance among the twelve tribes of Israel. Joseph shall have two portions. You shall inherit it equally with one another; for I raised My hand in an oath to give it to your fathers, and this land shall fall to you as your inheritance.'"* Ezekiel 47:13-14. If we do not think this applies to us, leave it for the next in line, but do not blame anyone for the forfeiture. Why should we not lay the blame elsewhere? Our underground provisions are already within, similar to a *Diamond in the Rough*.

Diamonds in the Rough

In our *As It Pleases God* Program, we are adamant about finding the *Diamonds in the Rough* because they are usually the hardest shells to crack. Why are they so hard to crack? First, according to the Heavenly of Heavens, they possess the most value. Secondly, they coat negative emotions, excuses, fears, and procrastination with *Something Else* to protect themselves from predators. Thirdly, to avoid taking the initiative to solve their problems, issues, or mishaps. All of which God uses as Spiritual Tools to train us, helping us to help ourselves, and to recognize the same attributes in another while extending compassion and mercy. What is the purpose of becoming trained by God? It keeps the Vicissitudes, Cycles, and Debts of life from consuming us Mentally, Physically, Emotionally, Spiritually, and Financially.

The more protection a Believer needs, the more HIDDEN VALUE they possess to keep the counterfeits from taking what belongs to the Kingdom of God. What does this mean? God hides the *Diamonds in the Rough* in plain sight, where it takes a Spiritual Eye to see, a Spiritual Ear to hear, Spiritual Discernment to understand, and a Spiritual Tongue to articulate what most cannot.

When my ear is to the ground, I look for the hidden Talents, Gifts, Calling, or Creativity that most cannot see or overlook. If I am watching or paying attention to someone or something, good, bad, or indifferent, they possess something they may not be able to see within themselves as of yet, even if most people write them off. Then again, if I avoid watching or paying attention, I also see or hear something most overlook, even if they have deep pockets, status, or fame—I see, hear, and think beyond it, *As It Pleases God*. How do I know the difference? I know Spiritual Principles, and so should you! If you do not know, the Book of Proverbs is a great place to start. Why Proverbs? By the Grace of God, this is where I started, and now here we are. You cannot go wrong with Divine Wisdom speaking on your behalf, speaking to you, and speaking through you without having to say one word.

Since I operate in Divine Wisdom, *As It Pleases God*, most would get nervous about which category they fall under. Why? I may or may not give the lead in of what I already know or do not know; nor do I break my Spiritual Cover. However, I will say this: Some gravitate toward me or away, and my *Spiritual Negev* does not miss a beat; either you want it, or you do not. So, now you know! I paid the price to evolve into the person I am today. I do not force anything on anyone. Nor do I hit people over the head, allowing the Fruits of the Spirit and my Christlike Character to speak.

More importantly, I do not take the Will of God for granted, learning from everything and everyone to FEED God's sheep with outright humility and gratefulness. While at the same time, holding my own when needed, staying calm, cool, and collected, as the onlookers think I am a wuss! Remember, the smallest dogs have the loudest bark, and the biggest ones wait for the right moment to gain LEVERAGE!

For example, a diamond will remain a diamond regardless of the debris covering its shine, increasing its value until it is discovered, unearthed, or unveiled. A manufactured diamond cannot contend with a God-Made or Ordained one. Why can it not contend? First, God made man; without Him, nothing happens. Secondly, the age-appropriate substances connecting diamonds to the Source were created under layers of *Something Else* for the right time of exposure. If God does not want it unveiled, it will NOT be unveiled until the time is right, period.

In dealing with the *Diamonds in the Rough*, we are no different. In the extracting and converting phases, it is not that I place one person over another; it is simply that the developmental or willingness process must be expounded. What does this mean in layman's terms? First and foremost, the INTENTS of the heart can become a deterrent, which most are unaware of. WILLINGNESS is the second factor. The EGO is the third. Fourthly, is the level of DISOBEDIENCE. If one possesses debaucherous intents, rebelling unwillingness, continual disobedience, or a superfluous ego, they must sit the Spiritual Bench out until they come to themselves or awaken from their slumber. Why? In the Kingdom, they are a Spiritual Hotwire, zapping the intended helping hand while becoming dull, lukewarm, or stiff-necked.

Regardless of where we are, what we are going through, our level of dullness, or our stiff-necked demeanor, people must want to Spiritually Till their own ground for themselves, exposing their Gifts, Calling, Talents, Creativity, or Divine Blueprint to shine brightly. No one, and I mean no one, can do this for them; they must want it for themselves, and God will allow the Spiritual Teacher to appear to polish them up. What is the purpose of having a Spiritual Teacher? To develop the Spiritual Poshness, Courage, and Confidence needed to pursue or retreat when necessary, and know when to hold, fold, or walk away.

Now, some people may use power, money, and sex as a means of a temporary illusion of poshness, courage, or confidence. Still, it will reflect in their foolery efforts (such as unwise thoughts, carelessness, or bad decisions), negatively impacting the innocent. Of course, we all make mistakes as a part of our cleaving process (the cutting phase of a diamond). But having a déjà vu history of the same mistakes or behaviors should give us a reason to make changes, *As It Pleases God*, for the bruiting process (shaping into a specific cut). Then, allow the Fruits of the Spirit and Christlike Character to polish, cutting the dullness or cloudiness.

What is the purpose of cleaving, bruiting, and polishing? God will test and place us under His Spiritual Magnifying glass. If we do not pass the final inspection, *As It Pleases Him*, it is a do-over for us, even if we think we are ready. From many experiences, the lessons get harder, extremely challenging, and more pressurized when going back into the Spiritual Classroom.

Why does God take us through changes as if He is breaking us? He is not breaking us; He is MAKING us into what is already. For example, if we buy a box of cake mix, the cake is already in potential form. We simply must add the ingredients to get the rise and taste needed to bring forth the desired results of the cake. If we miss one ingredient, it will change the results and taste of the cake; even if it falls flat, has lumps, is overcooked, or undercooked, it remains a cake—just unappealing.

With our Predestined Blueprint, the cake principle is the same; however, God is going to get the shine out of us, even if it takes more time for the Vicissitudes and Cycles of Life to process, refine, or regraft us. Why does it take all of this? To get the Kingdom of God's stamp of Spiritual Approval or Commissionability, we must be processed, tested, and presented, *As It Pleases Him*.

The Divine Wisdom, Treasures, and Secrets of the Kingdom are not granted to anyone who wants them. Blasphemy, right? Wrong. *"But even if our gospel is veiled, it is veiled to those who are perishing, whose minds the god of this age has blinded, who do not believe, lest the light of the gospel of the glory of Christ, who is the image of God, should shine on them."* 2 Corinthians 4:3-4.

We must put in the work, Spiritually Tilling our own grounds to ensure we know our Blueprinted Path to keep us from becoming jealous, envious, prideful, greedy, or covetous of another man's Spiritual Journey. Why? We will bounce all over the place, attempting to do everything with anyone, promising power, money, and sex. For example, we will never find a diamond trying to become gold, and we will never find gold trying to become silver, and so on. They all possess value, but they all stay in their Blueprinted Lane.

What is the purpose of knowing about diamonds, gold, and silver? According to scripture, *"We have this treasure in earthen vessels, that the excellence of the power may be of God and not of us."* 2 Corinthians 4:7. When we think of treasures, the first things that come to mind would be diamonds, gold, and silver; therefore, there is a Divine Connection to us because some of the ingredients in them are also in us. So, the correlation is just. Really? Yes, really! Please allow me to align accordingly, *"We are hard-pressed on every side, yet not crushed; we are perplexed, but not in despair; persecuted, but not forsaken; struck down, but not destroyed—always carrying about in the body the dying of the Lord Jesus, that the life of Jesus also may be manifested in our body."* 2 Corinthians 4:8-10.

Just as diamonds, gold, and silver come with terms and conditions of the extracting and converting process, so does *The Spiritual Negev*. What does this mean, especially when having free will? We cannot glean from the Spiritual Well of God for selfish gain or reasons, not giving back to the Source. If we do, we can inadvertently turn on ourselves from the inside out, affecting or upsetting the balance of our lives and others.

As my GIVE BACK to the Kingdom of God, leveraging what money cannot buy, this book is designed to expand the Four Corners of the Divine Mindset one step at a time. All of which are designed to unleash the Spiritual Gold, Silver, Gems, Pearls, Diamonds, or whatever valuables are hidden within our *Something Else*.

FOUR CORNERS

In dealing with the Four Corners of the Divine Mindset, we must approach it strategically in the Spirit of Excellence, cleaning out the negative cobwebs. In excelling with the Eye of God hovering over *The Spiritual Negev*, we must begin to think positively and proactively with a SUPPORTIVE demeanor.

What does support have to do with our mindsets? Support has everything to do with the Four Corners of one's Divine Mindset, especially when dealing with their Predestined Blueprint. Listen, our lives have Divine Instructions; through the mind, we can Spiritually Download the specifics for the Spiritual Legs supporting it. What does this mean? Most items created by man contain four legs, points, or corners to hold them up. For example, a car has four wheels; a chair has four legs; a desk has four corners; a stove usually has four burners; our computer or television has four corners, a cross has four points, and so on. As humans, we can add more when extending a little creativity. Still, under normal circumstances, four usually get the job done unless excessive weight is carried, such as tractor-trailers moving big things.

Now, getting back to the Four Corners of the Divine Mindset, if it is overloaded with negativity or self-defying thoughts, we cannot download, *As It Pleases God*. The bottom line is that we need outside help, Spiritual Help, to be exact! If not, we will feel as if we have a ton of bricks weighing us down, especially when there is not one brick in sight.

When dealing with the mind, it does not calculate tangibly; it calculates INTANGIBLY first. Why? We are Spiritual Beings having a human experience. If we are unaware of this one fact, we can operate in Spiritual Error, building with worldly tools when God requires Spiritual Ones.

Here is what we need to know: "*The workmanship of the wheels was like the workmanship of a chariot wheel; their axle pins, their rims, their spokes, and their hubs were all of cast bronze. And there were four supports at the four corners of each cart; its supports were part of the cart itself.*" 1st Kings 7:33-34. When we put the 'Cart before the horse,' we will find ourselves operating without instructions, feeling our way through life with Spiritual Blindness without realizing we are blind in the Eye of God. Now, to get our mental wheels turning in the right direction, *As It Pleases Him*, we must develop ourselves from the inside out, beginning with the thoughts we think, building quality and credibility.

For this Spiritual Journey, we need to MASTER putting our positive thoughts in ACTION form. We can speak about positivity all day long, but if we do not put actions behind our thoughts, we will fall short without realizing it.

How do we operate with a Four Corner Mindset when dealing with others? Everyone is different; we must add the Holy Trinity into the equation when dealing with people. When someone has low self-esteem or is emotionally bankrupt, they can misread the Fruits of the Spirit based on their perceptional expectations.

For example, I am strategic, analytical, and forthcoming, so if someone is wishy-washy, problematic, or has a problem with someone questioning their behavior, thoughts, or beliefs, they would be offended by my method of operation. Meanwhile, for someone possessing a business mindset like myself, I am perceived differently and aligned with integral values, standards, and excellence.

From the *Four Corners*, when transitioning from our people skills, how do we develop a Business Plan, Plan of Action, or Mind Map, PINPOINTING our Spiritual Gifts, Callings, or Divine Purpose? We must understand that a Spiritual Journey is involved in unveiling them.

According to the Heavenly of Heavens, to obtain the full portion of our Predestined Blueprint, we must dig deep, Mentally, Physically, Emotionally, Spiritually, and Financially, aligning each area *As It Pleases God*.

Why are our Gifts, Callings, Talents, Creativity, Passion, or Purpose hidden deep within our life's journey? It is often said, 'Nothing ventured, nothing gained.' In the Eye of God, this cliché is applicable and relevant; without a commitment to the outcome, we tend to give up, become ungrateful, or be disrespectful at the slightest notion of defeat or resistance. For this reason, they are often hidden under our *Something Else* or weaknesses that need development before attaining them. Here are a few questions to answer when attempting to unveil in such a manner, but not limited to such:

- ☐ What are your strengths, interests, and weaknesses?
- ☐ Why do you enjoy your strengths?
- ☐ How do your interests benefit you and others?
- ☐ What are people saying about your weaknesses?
- ☐ How do you feel about your weaknesses?
- ☐ Are your weaknesses making you feel insecure, doubtful, or angry? Why?
- ☐ Why are your weaknesses a weakness?
- ☐ Where do you exhibit your weaknesses?
- ☐ When is the best time to work on your weaknesses?
- ☐ With whom do you exhibit weaknesses?
- ☐ How can you make your weakness a strength?
- ☐ What type of training is needed to become better at a weakness?
- ☐ What can your weaknesses teach you?
- ☐ What can you do to create a win-win out of your weaknesses?
- ☐ How can your weakness bring joy and satisfaction to you or another?
- ☐ What can you do to feel more confident about your weaknesses?
- ☐ How can you intertwine your weakness with your Gifts, Calling, Talents, Purpose, Passion, or Creativity?
- ☐ How can you make an old weakness a newfound strength?
- ☐ Are you willing to practice on your weaknesses daily?
- ☐ Are you ready to turn your weaknesses into Greatness?
- ☐ What are the applicable scriptures regarding your weaknesses?
- ☐ What does the Bible say about this weakness?

- ☐ What is God revealing to you in your *Spirit to Spirit* private time with Him?
- ☐ What are some positive words you can speak over your weaknesses?
- ☐ Are you willing to read through the answers to these questions daily and update them often?

What is the purpose of answering these questions thoroughly? Most of our issues lie in the questions we DO NOT ask and the answers we DO NOT receive. If we desire to overcome, *As It Pleases God*, we must MASTER how He thinks. Really? Yes, really! The Bible is riddled with questions and answers we often overlook. We are not formally trained to query and answer, giving the Vicissitudes and Cycles of Life permission to share the information needed for the Spiritual Classroom without us abusing it or indulging in idolatry.

I am Dr. Y. for a reason...I have tapped into my *Spiritual Negev* by asking the right questions and documenting the answers I now share with those daring to DIG DEEP. Once we have answered the questions above honestly, we will easily find the information for our Plan of Action, Business Plan, or Mind Maps, applying them accordingly. Remember, the answers are already hidden within, like a *Diamond in the Rough*.

Our layers of debris are only weaknesses covering the diamonds within, blocking the value we hold. How do I know? Every weakness I had was intertwined with my Gifts, Calling, Talents, Creativity, and Purpose for a time such as this. However, I had to know this for myself. More importantly, I had to Spiritually Till my own ground, challenging my weaknesses to PUT UP or SHUT UP! How did I do this? I had to learn the difference between positive and negative words, thoughts, beliefs, reactions, and behaviors.

Here is the deal: I trained my mind to accept the positive as food for the brain while challenging or rejecting the negative. Thus, if the negative could not justify its reason, prove its case, or give me a lesson for others to glean, it had to SHUT UP, period! Can we really train the mind to do this? Absolutely! We simply must know the DIFFERENCE in actionable form, determining how we will internally shut it down within the human psyche to prevent its penetration.

Most people become externally reactive when combating negativity. Whereas, unbeknown to most, the POWER lies in the ability to become INTERNALLY PROACTIVE without becoming jealous, envious, prideful, greedy, covetous, competitive, or comparing ourselves. By far, it helps to release the genuine DIAMOND of AUTHENTICITY.

How do we become Internally Proactive, releasing our Divine Shine? In our documenting efforts when dealing with the *Spiritual Negev*, here is an Internally Proactive Checklist, *As It Pleases God*, but not limited to such:

- ☐ We must IDENTIFY the problem.
- ☐ We must INVOLVE the Holy Trinity in the equation.
- ☐ We must REMAIN positive, productive, and fruitful.
- ☐ We must ACCOUNT for our role.
- ☐ We must PLAN for whatever, with whomever.
- ☐ We must REFUSE to allow doubt, fear, anger, or regret to yoke us.
- ☐ We must SET goals, reviewing and updating often.
- ☐ We must DETERMINE the next step.
- ☐ We must PRIORITIZE what is important and what is not.
- ☐ We must BECOME consistent and persistent.
- ☐ We must become WILLING to ask for help, receive help, or take risks.
- ☐ We must FOCUS on the solution.
- ☐ We must LEARN from whatever, with whomever.
- ☐ We must PRACTICE on whatever, with whomever.
- ☐ We must VISUALIZE the win-win or positive outcome.
- ☐ We must SHARE our findings to build another.
- ☐ We must SURROUND ourselves with positive people, places, and things.
- ☐ We must REWARD ourselves amid all, gearing up for what is next.

In transitioning from a Spiritual Mindset, I will put on my business hat for the remainder of this chapter. I will also close it with specific instructions to maximize our Heaven on Earth expenditures, *As It Pleases God*, especially since we have established the foundational WHY of this chapter with our *Spiritual Negev*, the *Diamonds in the Rough*, and the *Four Corners*. What makes this so important to our Heavenly Father? Knowing how to put our Spiritual Tilling efforts to work for us is imperative, opening the Promised Greatness from the Ancient of Days, and releasing it into our NOW. With this in mind, let us move on to put our Spiritual Gifts, Talents, and Creativity into workable ACTION form through an occupational or entrepreneurial format. While simultaneously developing the mindset to establish *Business Credit*, As It Pleases God, building *Supernatural Leverage* to be about our Father's Business.

Business Credit

When building credit in our *Spiritual Negev* from a proficient perspective, we must build business and personal credit as indispensable tools. Why? When operating in Purpose on purpose, we need to leverage personal credit to build our *Business Credit* from the infant to the mature stages to finance our business adequately. What if we do not have personal credit? If we do not have personal credit, we need to work on it and build business credit, one step at a time.

Once again, when doing business, *As It Pleases God*, it is designed as a TOOL! Regardless of where we are on our journey, we need to establish a credit history. The sooner we start, the better off we are, even if we have not mastered what we are doing or where we are going. Waiting until we have all of our duckies in a row may not be the best option. Why? We must learn, grow, and sow back into the Kingdom when called upon while developing our faith. Here is the deal: if we do not learn, we cannot grow. If we do not grow, we cannot sow or expand our mindsets beyond where we are, causing wavering faith.

For example, we have an employee working for a company for over 20 years, and the company goes up for sale 1 year before being publicly posted. This employee wanted to buy the company but complained that they did not have the money to do so; therefore, they tried to recruit buyers from their circle of friends. I advised this individual to purchase the company because they knew the company inside out, and I would help them with the process. Here is what I recommended for their 1-year plan:

- ☐ Make their interest in purchasing the business known.
- ☐ Work on their credit while developing a strategy.
- ☐ Save as much money as possible from the employee status to finance the transition to the employer status.
- ☐ Get a *Business Plan* to envision their vision.
- ☐ Work on a *Plan of Action* to obtain funding for a business already making money.

They declined because of fear, a limited mindset, and the conditioning of being an employee, not an employer. As a result, this employee had to train the individuals who eventually purchased the business. A few months later, once trained and having received the information needed to function, they fired this employee. Why would they do such a thing? The employee was hung up on the old system of doing business, trying to boss them around. Therefore, the new owners got tired and decided to bring in a new crew to make their vision work.

Work experience means very little if it is misappropriated, underdeveloped, misused, or used to bully. Our experience on a job, in a business, or in our personal lives must be appropriately leveraged. If not, it can become kryptonite, halting our *Spiritual Negev*. Why would we become blocked? By not combining our work, home, business, or personal experiences with our Spiritual Gifts or Divine Blueprint, we may think we have it going on. When in reality, we cannot hit a lick at a crooked stick. Who am I to judge, right? Absolutely. No judgment is intended; nevertheless, while becoming an expert on someone else's vision, we must also work on our Predestined Blueprint, developing the God-Given Expert from within ourselves.

Let me put this in perspective: Everyone wants to be successful, whether as a business owner or a millionaire, without understanding what it takes or accounting for the price, stressors, pressures, injustices, and responsibilities of being one. Nevertheless, throughout my journey, there is a preconceived notion that millionaires know everything. Truthfully speaking, this is not true at all; as a matter of fact, no one knows everything!

If we take this a little further, 80% of millionaires do not have degrees! But here is the kicker: 90% of their employees do! So, what does this tell you? Being a millionaire is a MINDSET comprised of systems, strategies, concepts, obedience, perseverance, the quest for know-how, delegation, and what is written or documented in black and white.

Here is the deal: The millionaires without degrees are not stupid by a long shot. When they have an idea, project, or concept, they are Genius enough to get someone with a degree or specialization who knows what they are doing to implement, guide, or tell them what to do with what they envision.

Now, the keyword is **ENVISION** (In Your Vision). How do we make this make sense? Okay, let me break this down for you: An already millionaire pays someone to take the ideas of what they have in their mind, put it on paper, develop a system or strategy, and get their approval when it is done. If it looks right, sounds right, and makes money, it is a go, and everyone gets paid. Simple enough, right? On the other hand, if it does **NOT** look right, if it does **NOT** make money, then it is back to the drawing board, and nobody gets paid until it is correct.

If you want to tell people what to do or boss them around, this is not a millionaire or business mentality! From a business perspective, most often, this is why we miss the mark with our people skills, or we become hated by those we work for or work with. Listen, we do not need to be pocketable millionaires to obtain a millionaire mindset. Once we establish this mindset, *As It Pleases God*, the Divine Provisions Mentally, Physically, Emotionally, Spiritually, and Financially will come in due season with no shame attached.

From the Ancient of Days until now, here is the FIRST SECRET most overlooked: The goal is to acquire a team of individuals to TELL us and DOCUMENT what to do about what we Envision. Why? For the simple fact, we DO NOT have all the answers, and we may need a third party involved to trigger our Inner Genius or uncover our buried Wisdom. While simultaneously documenting it in black and white, capturing this actionable Biblical Principle: *"Write the vision and make it plain on tablets, that he may run who reads it."* Habakkuk 2:2.

The second secret is that while making provisions on a job, setting aside time to develop what is already within is imperative. What if we do not have time? If we have time to talk on the phone, watch television, use social media, and so on, we have time! We simply need to rethink how we spend it and why, helping us to fill in the blanks of whatever, with whomever. Here is the Spiritual Seal and actionable Biblical Principle needed: *"For the vision is yet for an appointed time; but at the end it will speak, and it will not lie. Though it tarries, wait for it; because it will surely come, it will not tarry."* Habakkuk 2:3.

The goal of this Divine Principle regarding your *Spiritual Negev* is designed to teach you how to take the ideas, thoughts, or vision out of your mind, get them on paper, build a roadmap, and give you an idea of what it is going to take to achieve it. How can this help? Here is how, but not limited to such:

- ☐ To help you find your Niche.
- ☐ To give you the Godly Principles of BLESSING your business.
- ☐ To help you decide the type of business to set up.
- ☐ To help you get a Spiritual Marketing System.
- ☐ To give you Wisdom on how to Work, Present, and Sell It.

In establishing a business, at some point, we must take the time to think, rethink, and become succinct. If not, we cannot develop the vision, establish longevity, build our business credit to finance it, or create the leverage needed to become one of the Business Elites. If we have someone else to do all the work without our involvement, we will not know what is going on, leaving us open to deceptive measures or having the wool pulled over our eyes.

In *Business is Business: As It Pleases God*, the ultimate goal is to place ourselves on the Leading Edge, where our competitors try to emulate but cannot duplicate. How is it possible for our competitors not to duplicate? We must tap into our *Spiritual Negev*, releasing our Spiritual Gifts according to our Divine Blueprint, Spiritual Fruits, and Christlike Character while being about our Father's Business.

On the other hand, we can become duplicated if we miss a part of this Spiritual Equation. Why can we become duplicated as Believers? We do not have a Spiritual Seal, which leaves us or our business open to counterfeit fingerprints.

Once we place a Spiritual Seal, *As It Pleases God*, it grants our business endeavors a unique fingerprint called the Real Deal. Unbeknownst to most, when one is the Real Deal, people will come in droves, trying to discredit or assassinate our character, fruits, or mission without realizing what they are doing. How can they not know? The enemy will use anything or anyone, especially the ones we love, to cause the mind or psyche to jump the track. So, we must stay on ready, knowing and understanding our Divine Passion or Blueprint, leaving NO STONE UNTURNED.

Once again, we cannot put the cart before the horse, especially when starting a new business. If we do not know or understand our Divine Passion or Blueprinted Purpose, we can become easily manipulated or traumatizedly shaken to the core.

When engaging in business, the questions on your paperwork will ask you for some of the same information from your Business Plan or Plan of Action. The goal is to prepare you for those questions in advance to ensure you are not overwhelmed with the process. This is my reason for putting this section in the last chapter; I wanted you to read the whole book because I will not put all of the Nuggets of Wisdom in one place! I need you to soak up the information and then apply it accordingly.

In our Spiritual Negev, God is adamant about having our Spiritual Fruits, Character, and Predestined Blueprint documented and checked consistently. Why? People may not buy us, our brand, or our product because:

- ☐ We may not be buying ourselves.
- ☐ It may not be adequately packaged.
- ☐ We may lack the ability to connect with them.
- ☐ We are not presenting what they need.
- ☐ We may not be showing the benefits associated.
- ☐ They may not like our approach.
- ☐ Our vibe may be off.
- ☐ We may lack sincerity.

Most people dislike selling as much as they avoid salespeople, without realizing that we sell and promote ourselves whenever we open our mouths, with every move we make, etc. Regardless of how we try to rationalize and justify, we all sell ourselves in some way, shape, or form, making everyone a salesperson whether we like it or not.

So, if you are not getting what you want, simply check or adjust what you are doing and why you are doing it. The quality of your product is revealed by your attitude, actions, reactions, and how you make people feel. Today, take the time to choose your words carefully; you never want to sell yourself short when you are quality at its best. Plus, there is no reason why you should not be able to succeed at what you do best. If you follow the process that I am laying out for you...you will thank me later because business professionals capitalize on newcomers for their lack of knowledge. So, I am here to walk you through, especially with the domain names.

If you are starting a new venture, do not, and I repeat, do not submit paperwork on that business before you purchase the domain name. Make sure you buy the domain name first. Suppose you file the paperwork for a business on a city, county, or state level without purchasing your desired domain name first. In this case, it will most likely no longer be available to you at a reasonable price. A company will purchase the domain name at $21.99 or less, and sell it back to you for $500.00 or more. For example, I filed for a county license for my company called xye3, and then a week later, tried to purchase the domain www.xye3.com; it said the domain name had already been taken, but it is for sale for $500.00. Yet, last week the domain was available for $21.99. Nevertheless, you must decide on your process or way of doing things relating to your business.

In *Business is Business: As It Pleases God*, I can only lead you and reduce the headache or heartache associated with the cost of doing business in the real world. In tapping into our underground *Spiritual Negev* from a business perspective or to establish a measure of credibility, here is what we need, but not limited to such:

- We must understand or have an idea of our Gifts, Callings, Talents, Creativity, Passion, or Purpose.
- Decide on the type of business endeavor.
- Determine the products we intend to sell.
- We must establish a business name. Decide on the name of your business. Write out 20 different names and then narrow it down to one based on the domain search process or company name availability. Make sure you do a Division of Corporations free online search to ensure your new business name is not already being used in the state where you will be doing business. Try to keep your web address as a dot.com, if possible.
- Purchase your Domain Name. I personally prefer using GoDaddy to purchase my domains. In my opinion, they have so much to offer your business and the best customer service.
- Set up your email address. You will need all of this information when filling out your business paperwork. Gmail accounts work great because they have many features that help promote your business and connect to your Social Media accounts.
- We must develop a professional logo.
- We must get a website with Wix or GoDaddy. It is best to choose a plan that accepts credit card payments.
- We must have our Business Plan and Plan of Action documented. SBA and SCORE have a lot to offer you regarding help with your small business. It is the U.S. Small Business Administration; they assist with startup costs and help with your Business Plan.
- Determine where you are going to set up your business. Please check the zoning laws before committing to a specific location. You must do your homework on a location before investing in one that cannot pass zoning restrictions predicated on the type of business. Depending on the type of business, you can always use the Post Office as a great alternative; their P.O. Boxes are not expensive, but bank and state agencies will require brick-and-mortar addresses. In addition, you can always use a virtual office if

you cannot find an office. Check your local listings for the Virtual Office Spaces in your area, which give you options to cut costs or offer space sharing! If you are just beginning, you can set up a temporary business mailing address and phone number to get the ball rolling before establishing a permanent one.

- We must make sure our personal credit is separate from our business credit.
- We must decide on a business structure by setting up a Corporation (for-profit or non-profit), LLC (Limited Liability Company), or Sole Proprietorship.
- We must get an EIN number from IRS.gov.
- We must open a business checking account with the suggested banks, Wells Fargo, Chase, or Regions. Make sure there are no insufficient funds linked to this account.
- We must establish a business phone line.
- We must register our business with Dun & Bradstreet to get a DUN's number.
- We must master the ability to track our expenses using our credit card statements.
- We must complete our business budget forms.
- Set up Facebook, YouTube, Instagram, Snapchat, Reddit, Pinterest, LinkedIn, Google+, and Twitter accounts. In my opinion, this is the best time to set up your social media accounts.
- Establish a good marketing plan.
- Get professional-looking promotional material such as business cards, company letterhead, invoices, and brochures.

What is the purpose of adhering to this list? Before establishing any form of Business Credit, we must establish a credible business. Although some people are in business making money, it does not mean they are credible or legal. They do not have the proper paperwork in place, especially a business plan, website, EIN number, Dun's number, business checking account, business phone, or the proper filings with the state where they live.

Defining the requirements for a new business startup from state to state can be perplexing and time-consuming. Many agencies have different regulations and various aspects of business operations; however, each state will also have its own guides. These are the basic requirements that apply to all businesses, such as:

- ☐ Sole Proprietorship
- ☐ Partnership
- ☐ General Partnership
- ☐ Limited Partnership
- ☐ Limited Liability Company (LLC)
- ☐ Corporation

Sole Proprietorship is an unincorporated business consisting of one owner who pays taxes on the profits from the business. This type of business is very simple, with few government regulations; however, it has the greatest risk and liability. Although it may be less paperwork and easier to set up, it is also the easiest to take down. Most new businesses that do not understand the liabilities involved opt for this initially, but later change their minds to form an LLC.

Partnership is when two or more people are involved in the ownership of an unincorporated business. This setup is similar to the Sole Proprietorship but with two or more people contributing to all aspects of the business, sharing in the profits, losses, and the same liabilities of the company. Unfortunately, it exposes the owners to personal liabilities as well.

General Partnership is when two or more individuals own a business, intending to earn profits. Profits are presumed equally distributed among the partners unless otherwise stated in a written contract. This partnership exposes the owners to personal liabilities as well.

Limited Partnership is when two or more individuals own a business, and are separate partners. One is a general partner, and the other is a limited partner for specific responsibilities based on the agreement outlined in the file elections. Example: The General Partners are involved in the day-to-day management of the business, and the Limited Partners are usually the investors with limited personal liability.

Limited Liability Company (LLC) is where the owners are called members and have limited liability. What this means is they are not totally liable for all debts and liabilities of the LLC. They are not bound by the same strict rules set forth when having a corporation. Most states do not restrict members; it can be an individual, corporation, another LLC, or a foreign company. It can be as simple as a single or husband/wife-owned LLC. It is a popular choice for smaller businesses because it is a little easier, and it protects your personal assets from your business assets. When doing business, it is always good to separate the two. The only companies NOT allowed to form an LLC are Banks, Non-Profit Organizations, Certain Financial Institutions, and Insurance Companies.

Corporation is the most complex organization to form due to the amount of paperwork required and the fact that the corporation has shareholders. There are four types of corporations: C corporations, S corporations, Non-Profit Corporations, and Professional Corporations, which are structured and taxed differently. They all have their advantages and disadvantages. Shareholders play a vital role in the company and contribute to the capital, taking on the roles and responsibilities of a person. However, an individual can contribute to, perform on behalf of, or speak for the corporation. Yet, the bottom line is that the shareholders are indeed the entity with the power, duty, and rights of the corporation.

Sadly, this is how the local Mom and Pop, without any prior business knowledge, get sucker punched into signing a contract to go public with a chain of stores. Although they may have more leverage, a more comprehensive platform, and big money, they now have no say-so in their business or are outright benched! So, exercise extreme caution when deciding what type of company you would like to set up.

Each state has laws regarding the sections, and tax purposes vary from state to state for corporations. Each structure has advantages and disadvantages; please seek legal counsel to ensure you select the best choice for your business. Once again, SBA and SCORE are great alternatives for you as well. They have great counselors/mentors who will assist you with little or no cost. As you can see, it can get pretty lengthy; however, you have to decide what is best for you and your business. Nevertheless, we must invest in a Business Plan, allowing others to visually see our vision documented. Listen, it does not need to be perfect; it just needs to be documented with a work-in-progress mentality.

WRITING A BUSINESS PLAN

When writing a Business Plan, the goal is to document, document, document. According to the Heavenly of Heavens, it helps to build our FAITH, CONFIDENCE, and COURAGE in all areas. Writing a plan may not be an overnight process, but we can invest in documenting one word at a time to build a sentence. A few sentences will make a paragraph. A few paragraphs will complete a section. With each section completed, we will eventually have a Business Plan, one step at a time.

To view a Business Plan as a whole can become overwhelming at times, but if we break it down into words, paragraphs, and sections, in the end, we will have what we need. When embarking upon each section, we need to know the *What, When, Where, How, Why*, and with *Whom*. Some may apply, and some may not, but it does get our mental wheels turning in the right direction, breaking the stagnation to bring forth a FLOW of our *Spiritual Negev*.

According to the Heavenly of Heavens, our Divine Vision has a voice, and if we place a Spiritual Demand on it, *As It Pleases God*, it must speak! When it does, we must capture it on paper; if not, it will become silent again. Once again, here is the Spiritual Seal to leverage when doing so: *"For the vision is yet for an appointed time; But at the end it will speak, and it will not lie. Though it tarries, wait for it; Because it will surely come, It will not tarry."* Habakkuk 2:3. Amid all, our Predestined Blueprint belongs to us for others. It is our responsibility to extract and convert it and then present it to the Kingdom in Earthen Vessel based upon the Law of Reciprocity or Seedtime and Harvest.

Your Business Plan will have different topics, along with supporting material. The topics are:

- ☐ Executive Summary
- ☐ Profile of Business
- ☐ The Company
- ☐ Mission Statement
- ☐ Company's Vision
- ☐ Objectives
- ☐ Management
- ☐ Organizational Structure
- ☐ Organizational Management
- ☐ Business Credentials
- ☐ Company licenses
- ☐ Company Accreditations
- ☐ Market Analysis
- ☐ Market Location
- ☐ Market Description
- ☐ Market Qualifier
- ☐ Competition
- ☐ Marketing Strategy

- ☐ Pricing and Profitability
- ☐ Product or Service Distribution
- ☐ Sales Strategy
- ☐ Operations
- ☐ Financial Statements
- ☐ Startup Requirements
- ☐ Budget
- ☐ Cash Flow Statement
- ☐ Conclusion

What is the purpose of leveraging our business in such a manner? Most businesses fail due to improper financial management, not having access to capital, the lack of business credit, the fear of pursuing business leverage, or cluelessness about the company's objectives. Most businesses do not have a Business Plan to guide or remind them of their vision; as a result, they find themselves all over the place, doing this or that for the dollar.

When dealing with our *Spiritual Negev*, we have a reason for doing what we do, *As It Pleases God*. Doing anything with anyone for the dollar is not wise, especially when tapping into what is Divine, according to our Predestined Blueprint. Really? Yes, really. The Streams of God are not for those easily strayed by the dollar sign. Nor is it for those who jump into anything without a sense of Spiritual Discernment. For this reason, we must manage our finances accordingly.

When exhausting our personal credit for business purposes, we overload ourselves with too much debt. Therefore, funding for the business needs to be on a business line of credit or credit card, and our personal needs must go on our personal credit, creating a balance between the two. In addition, it helps us to leave a paper trail of our expenditures for tax purposes with itemized statements accepted by the IRS, even if we have lost the receipt or it has faded. So, it behooves us to keep our personal and business credit separate.

To develop and maintain financial power and freedom, we must build our business portfolio, even if we are not fully ready to embark upon it. What does this mean? We should not wait to begin the process; we must take baby steps, building our strength and endurance while gainfully employed. In so many words, while working on a job, we should also carve out time to build a business or work on a roadmap.

To get started, follow the steps from the above checklist. Once a business is registered with state and federal agencies, it can begin building its credit line. Here are the goals:

- ☐ 1 Bank loan or line of credit. Secured or Unsecured.
- ☐ 3 Business credit cards with <u>American Express</u>, <u>Chase</u>, <u>Capital One</u>, <u>Sam's Club</u>, or <u>Wells Fargo</u> for unsecured.
- ☐ 5 Vendor trade lines for a net 30, 60, or 90-day with Amazon Business, Quill, Uline, Crown Office Supplies, Office Depot, Staples, Home Depot, Lowes, or Nav.

When committing to operate in the Spirit of Excellence, it gives us more of a reason to get our resources together without shortchanging ourselves and others by taking shortcuts or the easy way out. Venturing out into business does take a commitment, a building commitment, to be exact. In doing so, here is what we need, but not limited to such:

Acceptance	Generosity	Persistence
Adaptability	Goal-Setting	Planning
Adaptability	Good Judgment	Positive attitude
Ambition	Gratitude	Problem-solving
Assertiveness	Honesty	Productivity
Attention to Detail	Hope	Professionalism
Calmness	Humility	Repentance
Communication	Humor	Resourcefulness
Confidence	Imagination	Respect
Consistency	Independence	Self-Awareness
Courage	Innovativeness	Self-Confidence
Creativity	Integrity	Self-Discipline
Decision-Making	Interdependence	Self-Reliance
Dedication	Leadership	Strategic Planning
Determination	Listening	Strategic Thinking
Discipline	Love	Stress Management
Efficiency	Loyalty	Teamwork
Empathy	Motivation	Time Management
Enthusiasm	Open-Mindedness	Trustworthiness
Fairness	Optimism	Understanding
Flexibility	Organization	Versatility
Focus	Passion	Vision
Forgiveness	Patience	Willingness
Favor	People Skills	Willpower

Building a business with our Gifts, Calling, Talents, and Creativity takes a lot of nurturing; therefore, we must enhance our patience and understanding skills. Why? To develop a ROAR, *As It Pleases God*, we must **R**espect ourselves and others, **O**vercome our setbacks and challenges, **A**chieve our desires, and **R**each back to help someone else.

In conclusion, when being about your Father's Business, *As It Pleases Him*, you cannot give up on yourself, no matter what. Simply learn the lessons, document, and keep it moving in the Spirit of Excellence with a Win-Win MINDSET. If you do, I promise your *Spiritual Negev* will begin to flow, drenching you with Divine Greatness. Many Blessings to all.

Dr. Y. Bur

www.DrYBur.com

www.ingramcontent.com/pod-product-compliance
Lightning Source LLC
Chambersburg PA
CBHW071709160426
43195CB00012B/1628